Shaping Urban Infrastructures

Shaping Urban Infrastructures

Intermediaries and the Governance of Socio-technical Networks

Edited by

Simon Guy, Simon Marvin,
Will Medd and Timothy Moss

publishing for a sustainable future

London • Washington, DC

First published in 2011 by Earthscan

Earthscan Ltd, Dunstan House, 14a St Cross Street, London EC1N 8XA, UK
Earthscan LLC, 1616 P Street, NW, Washington, DC 20036, USA

Earthscan publishes in association with the International Institute for Environment and Development

For more information on Earthscan publications, see www.earthscan.co.uk or write to earthinfo@earthscan.co.uk

ISBN: 978-1-84971-068-8

Typeset by 4word Ltd, Bristol
Cover design by Yvonne Booth

A catalogue record for this book is available from the British Library

Library of Congress Cataloging-in-Publication Data

Shaping urban infrastructures : intermediaries and the governance of socio-technical networks / edited by Simon Guy ... [et al].
    p. cm.
  Includes bibliographical references and index.
  ISBN 978-1-84971-068-8 (hardback)
  1. Municipal services. 2. Municipal services--Technological innovations. 3. Municipal services--Environmental aspects. 4. Brokers in public contracts, etc. 5. Infrastructure (Economics) I. Guy, Simon.
  HD4431.S525 2010
  363.6--dc22
                        2010018629

At Earthscan we strive to minimize our environmental impacts and carbon footprint through reducing waste, recycling and offsetting our CO_2 emissions, including those created through publication of this book. For more details of our environmental policy, see www.earthscan.co.uk.

This book was printed in the UK by TJ International, an ISO 14001 accredited company. The paper used is FSC certified and the inks are vegetable based.

Contents

List of Figures, Tables and Boxes

Figures

Tables

Box

List of Acronyms and Abbreviations

AMF	French Mayors Association
ANT	actor network theory
BEA	Business Environment Association
BWB	Berliner Wasserbetriebe
CAB	Citizens Advice Bureau
CaFCP	California Fuel Cell Partnership
CARB	Californian Air Resources Board
CELECT	Control Electric
CHP	combined heat and power
CLEAN-E	Clean Energy Network for Europe
CNW	Chemicals Northwest
COD	chemical oxygen demand
CUTE	Clean Urban Transport Europe
DCLG	Department for Communities and Local Government
DGTREN	Directorate-General for Energy and Transport
EA	Environment Agency
EAWAG	Swiss Federal Institute for Aquatic Science and Technology
EC	European Commission
EEG	Renewable Energy Act [Germany]
Eugene	European Network for Green Electricity
EV	electric vehicles
FAS	Flood Advice Service
FCV	fuel-cell vehicles
FMD	foot and mouth disease
FNCCR	National Federation for the Management of Local Public Utilities
GDP	gross domestic product
gGmbH	non-profit limited company

GLA	Greater London Authority
HEV	hybrid vehicles
ICEV	internal combustion engine vehicle
IRBM	integrated river basin management
IS	industrial symbiosis
KWB	Berlin Centre of Competence for Water
KWB	Kompetenzzentrum Wasser Berlin [Berlin Centre of Competence for Water]
LEV	low emission vehicle
LHP	London Hydrogen Partnership
M&E	mechanical and electrical engineering
MBC	Mersey Basin Campaign
MNC	Multinational Corporation
NASR	Natural and Artificial Systems for Recharge and Infiltration
POS	point of sale
R&D	research and development
RMS	Remote Metering Systems [company name]
ROCs	Renewables Obligation Certificates
RVIs	river valley initiatives
SenFin	Senate Department for Finance
SenWirt	Senate Department for Economics and Public Utilities
SenWiss	Senate Department for Science and Research
SMEs	small and medium-sized enterprises
SWEL	Sustainable Water Environment in Lancashire
TDPs	technology development pathways
TM	transition management
TSB	Technology Foundation of Berlin
TT	technological transitions
TWh	Terawatt-hour
UWW	Urban Wastewater directive
VUE	Verein für umweltfreundliche Energie [Association for Environmentally Friendly Energy]
WFD	European Union Water Framework Directive
ZEV	zero emission vehicle

About the Contributors

Ross Beveridge is a Research Assistant at the Leibniz Institute for Regional Development and Structural Planning, Erkner, Germany.

Heather Chappells is an Honorary Research Fellow in the Lancaster Environment Centre at Lancaster University, United Kingdom.

Jan Fischer is an Early Career Fellow at Oxford Brookes University, United Kingdom.

Simon Guy is Professor of Architecture, Head of the School of Environment and Development, and Director of the Manchester Architecture Research Centre (MARC) at the University of Manchester, United Kingdom.

Marko Hekkert is Professor of Dynamics of Innovation Systems in the Copernicus Institute of Sustainable Development at Utrecht University, the Netherlands.

Mike Hodson is a Research Fellow at the Centre for Sustainable Urban and Regional Futures (SURF), University of Salford, United Kingdom.

Sarah Mander is a Research Fellow at the Tyndall Centre for Climate Change Research at the University of Manchester, United Kingdom.

Simon Marvin is Professor and Co-director at the Centre for Sustainable Urban and Regional Futures (SURF), University of Salford, United Kingdom.

Will Medd is a Lecturer in Human Geography in the Lancaster Environment Centre at Lancaster University, United Kingdom.

Timothy Moss is Deputy Director of the Leibniz Institute for Regional Development and Structural Planning, Erkner, Germany.

Sally Randles is a Research Fellow in the Centre for Research on Innovation and Competition (CRIC) at the University of Manchester, United Kingdom.

Harald Rohracher is Associate Professor in the Department of Science and Technology Studies at Alpen-Adria University of Klagenfurt, Austria.

Ruud Smits is Professor of Technology and Innovation in the Copernicus Institute for Sustainable Development at Utrecht University, the Netherlands.

Harro van Lente is Associate Professor in the Copernicus Institute for Sustainable Development at Utrecht University, and Professor of Philosophy of Sustainable Development at Maastricht University, the Netherlands.

Bas van Waveren was until recently a Research Associate in the Copernicus Institute for Sustainable Development, Utrecht University, the Netherlands.

Ulrike von Schlippenbach is a Research Assistant at the German Academy of Science and Engineering (ACATECH), Berlin, Germany.

Rebecca Whittle is a Research Assistant in the Lancaster Environment Centre at Lancaster University, United Kingdom.

Preface

This book has been a long time in the making. It draws together research undertaken over an extended period, and reflects conversations between a wide range of participants both inside and beyond two key European Union (EU) research projects. The background to the book is contained in an earlier volume, *Urban Infrastructure in Transition: Networks, Buildings, Plans*, edited by Simon Guy, Simon Marvin and Timothy Moss, published by Earthscan in 2001 and widely referenced in urban and technology studies. The book focused on dramatic shifts in the management, governance and use of technical networks due to processes of privatization, liberalization, technological innovation and environmental regulation, and explored how these reconfigurations were opening up opportunities for wider environmental innovation across Europe. It was largely based upon comparative research undertaken by a team of researchers based at the Leibniz Institute for Regional and Structural Planning (IRS; Germany), the University of Newcastle (UK) and the Danish Technical University (DTU) under an EU research programme, 'Environment and Climate' (1994–98), within a project titled 'Technical networks as instruments of sustainable flow management: A comparative analysis of infrastructure policy and planning in European urban regions' (contract ENV4-CT96-0249), 1996–98.

In the conclusions to that book, we observed that the debate over sustainable infrastructure and cities was highly contested, and how, within these changing contexts of network management, 'new and sometimes unlikely partnerships may be formed in the pursuit of alternative urban futures' (p205). Thus we suggested:

> *The research challenge is to map the multiple constructions of the sustainable city, to understand the changing social contexts that produce them and to build an understanding of the multiple*

logics emerging to reorder social relations, resource flows and urban form (Guy et al, 2001, p205).

In particular, we noted the challenge of developing a new 'way of seeing' networks that avoided disconnecting production and consumption, policy and practice, the local and the global. In order to advance this agenda, we proposed a new research project that focused on the institutional spaces 'in-between' these often polarized realms to explore the processes of reordering social relations, and the new 'intermediary' identities, collaborations and forms of intermediation that resulted. In doing so, we expanded our network to include researchers from SURF at the University of Salford (UK), the Institute of Urban Environment & Human Resources at the Panteion University of Political and Social Sciences (UEHR; Greece), the Metropolitan Research Institute (Hungary), and the Urban Alternatives Association (GRAAL; Bulgaria). This international research project was funded by the European Commission under the Framework 5 Programme, Key Action 'Sustainable Management and Quality of Water', and was titled 'New intermediary services and the transformation of urban water supply and wastewater disposal systems in Europe' (contract EVK1-CT-2002-00115); it ran from November 2002 to October 2005. The aim was to look across sectors in six European countries to explore new contexts of infrastructure governance, in order to identify the emergence of new intermediary actors and new forms of intermediation that might promote and even accelerate innovatory practice. The results from this project form the platform from which this collection emerged. This collection reports on our conceptual framework and theoretical thinking, our methodological approach, three of our case study findings, and finally our tentative conclusions on the potential role of intermediaries in transforming infrastructure networks along a more sustainable trajectory.

In conducting the research we discovered other research teams working to similar ends. We have invited some of the key researchers to contribute to this collection so that the book contains the latest theoretical and empirical work, and offers a better overall coverage of the field as it exists today. We want to thank these authors for working with us on the collection. We would also like to acknowledge and thank all our research collaborators on our most recent EU project, who have all contributed directly or indirectly to the book: Ross Beveridge, Morten Elle, Cordula Fay, Panagiotis Getimis, Jozsef Hegedüs, Birgitte Hoffmann, Vasilis Markantonis, Jochen Monstadt, Matthias Naumann, Susanne Balslev Nielsen, Vesselina Penevska, Eszter Somogyi, Markus Wissen and Dimitrios Zikos. Our thanks are also due to the European Commission for funding the research project on which this book is based. We hope the book offers a useful contribution to the ongoing debate about the shaping of urban infrastructures.

Simon Guy, Manchester
Simon Marvin, Salford
Will Medd, Lancaster
Timothy Moss, Erkner

1
Intermediaries and the Reconfiguration of Urban Infrastructures: An Introduction

Timothy Moss, Simon Guy, Simon Marvin and Will Medd

Introduction

Modern cities exist and function because of the highly developed systems which underlie them, ensuring that electricity, gas, heating, clean water and so on are moved efficiently from provider to user, and that waste is removed. Technical networks are the bedrock of urban development, physically and metaphorically. The services they provide are a precondition for basic standards of living, economic growth and environmental protection in and beyond the city. Comprising not just physical artefacts, such as power plants or sewers, but also organizational structures, institutional arrangements and socio-cultural meanings, these urban infrastructures represent complex socio-technical systems serving multiple purposes. Once established, they generally possess a high degree of path dependency; that is, by virtue of their physical embeddedness in urban (sub-)structures and their reliance on powerful regulatory and economic interests, they tend to be resistant to change. Since the 1980s, however, urban infrastructures have come under increasing pressures to adapt. Firstly, the political economy of socio-technical systems has diversified hugely following trends towards the liberalization, privatization and commercialization of utility services. Secondly, the socio-technical configuration of urban infrastructures is altering subtly but distinctly with the emergence of new, smart technologies, capable of providing more efficient services tailored to specific locations or user-groups. Thirdly, stricter and more ambitious environmental regulation in industrialized countries is providing a powerful driver for more resource-efficient and low-pollution forms of service provision and use. Overall, these forces for change are challenging the conventional logic of 'build and supply', and generating new ways of making utility services more environmentally, socially and economically sustainable.

Who, though, is instrumental behind the current transition of these socio-technical systems? Who is shaping the urban infrastructures of the future? The issue of agency behind the reconfiguration of urban infrastructures is central to this book. Ongoing and past transitions to socio-technical systems are widely studied in terms of the influence of service providers, users and regulators. The focus of attention is generally on the utilities, adapting to privatization or liberalization, on the economic and environmental regulators, setting new institutional frameworks, or (to a lesser extent) on the consumers and changing patterns of resource use. By contrast, very little attention has yet been paid to those actors working in-between this triad of provider, regulator and user. As any case study of urban infrastructures in transition will reveal, such processes are rarely populated exclusively by utilities, consumers and regulators; they are socially, organizationally and politically much more complex. The recent shifts in the way urban infrastructures are organized, by making utility markets more differentiated and utility services increasingly diverse, are creating openings for the emergence of new actors and the reordering of existing relations. Of particular interest are those actors who characteristically work in-between the other actors and across different realms of action, in particular between production and consumption. These 'intermediaries' are the focus of this book. Examples include non-governmental organizations (NGOs) who develop green energy labelling schemes in collaboration with producers and regulators to guide the user, consultants who advise businesses on how to save resources, and travel agents who match users with providers. It is postulated that such intermediaries play an important, but hitherto neglected, role in reshaping the relations between production and consumption relating to urban infrastructures. Potentially, it is argued, they can influence the direction that technological transitions take, the sustainability of urban technical networks and the governance of these systems.

This book presents the first authoritative collection of empirical and conceptual research on intermediaries and processes of intermediation relating to urban infrastructures. The book's purpose is to investigate how far and in what ways intermediaries have a transformative influence on socio-technical networks. The key policy and research interest lies in ascertaining whether intermediaries can effect systemic change to urban infrastructures, in particular in the interest of advancing more sustainable modes of production and consumption. At the same time, the transformative capacity of intermediaries cannot be taken for granted. The flip side of the book's purpose is to reveal also how intermediaries can stall change, in their own interest, thereby contributing to system obduracy. In this way, the focus on intermediaries provides a critical context for wider societal learning about forms of agency behind socio-technical change. The importance of place is central to this endeavour: our particular interest lies in exploring how intermediaries are altering the relationship between socio-technical networks and the localities they serve.

This introductory chapter sets out the rationale for studying intermediaries as a window on the shifting governance of urban infrastructures. It first elaborates the nature of transition to socio-technical networks today, focusing on the relationship between production and consumption in urban contexts. It then introduces and explains the concept of intermediaries as used throughout the book. From this it derives the principal research objectives and questions guiding all the chapters. The chapter concludes by outlining the structure of the book and the role of each section in contributing to the book's objectives.

Urban infrastructures in transition

Since the mid-1990s there has been a surge of academic and policy interest in the reconfiguration of urban infrastructure systems (Coutard, 1999; Graham and Marvin 2001; Guy et al, 2001; Coutard, 2005). Studies of liberalization and privatization have plotted shifts in the balance of power, and the relationships between utility companies, state regulators and consumers (Newbery, 1999; Finger and Allouche, 2002; Page and Bakker, 2005). Research on technological innovation has explained the influence of state-led regulatory or financial incentives on technology uptake (Jamison and Rohracher, 2002). Work on changing consumption patterns has directed attention to shifts in actor roles and relations (Southerton et al, 2004; Summerton, 2004). Transition research, in particular, has emerged as a dominant frame of reference for much work in this field. Building on insight from innovation studies, social studies of science and technology, and policy analysis, research on technological transitions and transition management analyses long-term systemic transformations to socio-technical systems (Geels, 2004; Kemp and Loorbach, 2005). Transitions research investigates not only the dynamics of socio-technical change, such as emerging new technological innovation systems (Johnson and Jacobsson, 2001; Bergek et al, 2008; Markard and Truffer, 2008), but also, significantly, opportunities for shaping socio-technical change, in particular deliberate interventions designed to direct socio-technical systems along more sustainable pathways (Rip and Kemp, 1998; Elzen et al, 2004; Geels, 2005; Smith et al, 2005; Grin, 2008).

Where transition research falls short is in considering the importance of place in this analytical framework. How socio-technical change is shaped by – and itself shapes – the city or region where it occurs is a crucial aspect absent from much transition research. Exploring how technological transitions and urban transitions shape each other is a core issue of ongoing research in this field.

Our book contributes to this debate by highlighting the role of the city and the region in technological transitions, as mediated by intermediary organizations. It builds on conclusions drawn from earlier collaborative research by the editors on the nature of ongoing transitions to urban infrastructures in Europe (Guy et al, 2001), several of which emphasized the importance of place. There we argued the need to understand better, firstly, how social and technical systems interact in a specific local context; secondly, how resource provision and use involves interaction across multiple, overlapping spatial scales; and, thirdly, how sustainable urban and regional futures are highly contested. From this we concluded:

> *The research challenge is to map the multiple constructions of the sustainable city, to understand the changing social contexts that produce them and to build an understanding of the multiple*

*logics emerging to reorder social relations, resource flows and
urban form (Guy et al, 2001, p205).*

If transition research has tended to overlook the constitutive functions of place
to socio-technical transitions, studies of resource use by infrastructure systems
has in the past tended to distinguish too sharply between processes of production and consumption. Much existing work has focused on either the
production side (e.g. the impact of liberalization on service providers) or the
consumption side (e.g. the roles of users as active agents in the management
of networks) following quite distinct logics. However, as historical and comparative research demonstrates, attempts to constitute different organizational
arrangements (e.g. privatization, liberalization) and technical solutions (e.g.
metering) on the supply side are closely entwined with the identities and practices of users (Guy and Marvin, 1996; Rohracher, 2003; Southerton et al,
2004; Trentmann, 2006). The focus of attention in research and policy is typically around important tensions in the relationship between utility companies,
consumer needs and regulation processes (see Summerton, 1994; Bakker,
2003; Mohajeri et al, 2004; Swyngedouw, 2004).

Our earlier work also highlighted the existence and interaction of different logics of utility services, sustained by an increasingly rich proliferation of
actors engaging in water and energy governance (Guy et al, 2001). It provided
three important reasons for the need to look across and beyond the classic
triad of provider/user/regulator when exploring ways of making utility services more sustainable. Firstly, we need to develop a better understanding of
the relationship *between* these three actor groups. This applies in particular to
the structures, modes and politics of their interaction and critical areas of contestation. Secondly, we need to consider the emergence of new actors and new
functions in the wake of ongoing change to socio-technical systems. Processes
of commercialization, ecological modernization and the reconfiguration of the
state, inter alia, are opening up the governance of urban infrastructures to different types of organizations operating in a variety of arenas. Thirdly, the
interfaces between actors of urban infrastructure and the physical, social and
cultural contexts within which they work are proving a promising line of
investigation for revealing important, new features of how these systems are
organized today (see Swyngedouw, 2004; Kaika, 2005). The current book
addresses one type of emergent actor commonly found at the nexus between
production and consumption: the intermediary. How these intermediaries are
reshaping urban infrastructures and what consequences they can have for
practices of production and consumption are central issues addressed in the
forthcoming chapters. First, though, we need to explain what we mean by the
term 'intermediary'.

Intermediaries, intermediation and the relational nature of socio-technical change

One basic definition defines an intermediary as 'an intermediate agent or
agency; a go-between or mediator' (Dictionary.com, accessed on 20 April

2010). What intermediaries do, then, is work in-between, make connections, and enable a relationship between different persons or things. The term 'intermediaries' is used increasingly to describe organizations operating in-between other actor groups, but there exists no common conceptual understanding or even an agreed definition of what intermediaries are. For example, reviewing how the concept of intermediaries is applied by different disciplines, we find the term used in relation to the following: 'social intermediaries' blurring the distinction between economy and society (Piore, 2001); 'cultural intermediaries' changing relations of mediation between culture and economy (Cronin, 2004); 'market intermediaries' within the context of shifting relations between production and consumption (Randles et al, 2003); 'systemic intermediaries' enabling the emergence of new modes of systems innovation (van Lente et al, 2003); 'labour intermediaries' addressing labour market restructuring (Kazis, 1998); 'knowledge intermediaries' within the new knowledge economy (Iles and Yolles, 2002); 'welfare intermediaries' enabling joined-up working in social welfare (Allen, 2003); 'planning intermediaries' facilitating the coordination of public–private initiatives in town centre management (Paddison, 2003); and debates on intermediation, re-intermediation and disintermediation in relation to 'financial intermediaries' (Allen and Santomero, 1998), 'commercial intermediaries' (Brousseau, 2002) and 'information intermediaries' (Ehrlich and Cash, 1999).

Looking across this literature, we find the concept of the intermediary is used to describe quite different sets of actors. Such actors can be individuals, organizations, networks, institutions, processes or even technologies. Their distinguishing feature as an intermediary is not their organizational structure. It is the work that an actor, of whatever form, performs that constitutes it as an intermediary. What makes it an intermediary is where it 'sits': for example, between welfare services, professionals and clients (Allen, 2003); between production and consumption (Randles et al, 2003), culture and economy (Cronin, 2004), or the economy and society at large (Piore, 2001); or between private, public and third sectors (Paddison, 2003; van Lente et al, 2003). This literature reveals, therefore, a common interest in a particular set of actors who are positioned in-between other actors, institutions, processes or interests. There is, however, rarely any conceptual interrogation of the concept of 'intermediary', or of the implications that different understandings of intermediary organization and intermediary work might have for transforming the relationship between different actors (see Lawless, 2001; Kohl, 2003; Phillipson et al, 2004; Atherton, 2006). Where reviews of intermediaries do take place, they tend to be situated within a particular domain of research (e.g. Howells, 2006, on innovation) without wider critical reflection.

The book builds on this relational understanding of intermediaries. Accordingly, intermediaries are defined by the relations within which they are situated, rather than by a particular organizational characteristic or form. This basic conceptualization serves the purposes of the book in several ways. Firstly, it resonates powerfully with our interest in the relational nature of urban infrastructures in transition. How actors work across boundaries of socio-technical systems – whether geographical, organizational, sectoral or cultural – is central to our interest in intermediaries. Examples covered in this book include working in-between different sets of social interests, in-between different natural, institutional and economic geographies, and in-between technological and social contexts. Secondly, defining intermediaries by their function rather than their structure enables us to include in the analysis actors of highly different organizational status. The chapters of this book address actors such as NGOs, small and medium-sized enterprises (SMEs) or consultants, as well as the social networks more commonly associated with intermediation. Thirdly, we can thereby include in our analysis the work of actors that are not deliberately created as an intermediary, but which perform an intermediary function nevertheless. Rather than restricting the analysis to bridge-builders, mediators and facilitators, we also include brokers, educators, lobbyists, gatekeepers and image-makers in our understanding of intermediaries. Fourthly, as these examples indicate; intermediaries do not occupy a neutral position in dealing with other actors. They may well mediate or facilitate, but are by no means benign in the work they perform.

This general assumption of neutrality in the work of intermediaries is a key issue of contention picked up in the writing of the science and technology philosopher Bruno Latour (1993 and 2005). Latour's argument is established in relation to a specific problem, namely, the way in which the modern world attempts to produce separation. In this world, we treat nature and society as if they can be held apart and intermediaries 'merely transport, convey, transfer' between them (Latour, 1993, p80). Consequently, knowledge is situated on either side of the division and intermediaries are given no importance of their own. They are, in science and technology language, 'black boxed' as mere transporters of relationships between already existing entities. The concept of the intermediary, Latour argues, supposes something that 'transports meaning or force without transformation: defining its inputs is enough to define all outputs' (2005, p39). However, in Latour's view, we should acknowledge the process of hybridization, a process whereby the words of 'society' and 'nature' can never really be separated. Consequently, we should recognize the role all entities come to play in the production of 'nature(s)' and 'society(ies)'. We need to deal with 'the heterogeneous nature of the ingredients making up social ties' (Latour, 2005, p35).

If we approach the world in this way, as constituted through the relations between heterogeneous materials, then we have to be sensitive to the agency we ascribe to such materials. To express agency, Latour prefers the term 'mediator' to 'intermediary':

> *No matter how* complicated *an intermediary is, it may, for all practical purposes, count for just one – or even for nothing at all because it can be easily forgotten. No matter how apparently simple a mediator may look, it may become* complex; *it may lead in multiple directions which will modify all the contradictory accounts attributed to its role (Latour, 2005, p39).*

For Latour, it is mediators that 'transform, translate, distort, and modify the meaning of the elements they are supposed to carry' (2005, p39). In other words, following Latour, if we see actors as intermediaries, whether they be objects, people, organizations or institutions, we may not be giving them a status in defining the very dynamics we wish to understand; we may not recognize their role as mediators in Latour's sense.

Our approach is loyal to Latour, except that we prefer to retain the label 'intermediary'. In contrast to Latour, we do not assume neutrality; intermediaries do not merely facilitate. It is precisely the hidden work of this intermediation that we want to illuminate. We want to look beyond the formal roles and responsibilities of different actors involved in the governance of urban infrastructures to raise the visibility of a whole host of actors, activities and relations, including informal arrangements, hidden technologies and hidden work that are important, even if not visible, to the dynamics of such socio-technical systems (Star, 1999). Understanding this means exploring how a change in one set of actors, activities or processes will have implications elsewhere in the sector. We therefore follow Latour's intentions, but, for the purposes of our analysis, not his definition. We recognize the role of intermediaries as mediators in his sense, 'that is, actors endowed with the capacity to translate what they transport, to redefine it, redeploy it, and also to betray it' (Latour, 1993, p81).

In the field, urban infrastructures in transition, the very intermediary roles that Latour wants to attribute agency to, are, to date, rendered largely invisible in mainstream analysis, as we have argued. Our concern is to draw attention to a set of actors who indeed do the work of translation, redefinition, redeployment and so on in relation to, and in-between, sets of relationships around socio-technical systems. We will show that these intermediaries, once they are made visible and named, are not neutral players, nor simply arbitrators. Through the work they do in ordering and defining relationships, they are – in Latour's sense – 'mediators' of the governance of socio-technical networks.

Purpose of the book

The purpose of this book is, therefore, to critically appraise the way intermediaries work and the implications they have for the governance of urban socio-technical networks. Using original conceptual and empirical analyses of intermediary organizations and activities from a variety of infrastructure sectors and approached from multiple disciplinary perspectives, the book explores the significance of intermediaries as both product and medium of the shifting governance of urban infrastructures. We argue that these intermediaries and the often hidden work which they perform are highly significant for the following reasons:

- Firstly, they are, by virtue of their existence and action, indicative of a broadening and diversification of the social organization of these systems, thereby acting as windows on this transformation process.

- Secondly, they possess the ability to work across the often impermeable boundaries between different actor groups, arenas of action or geographical scales, which have characterized the governance of these infrastructure systems in the past.
- Thirdly, for this reason they are potentially valuable actors for advancing EU and national policy objectives for greater stakeholder participation, cross-sectoral coordination and service innovation in the fields of energy, water, wastewater and mobility management.

Whilst taking this transformative potential of intermediaries as our point of departure, we caution against overoptimistic assumptions of their capacity and their interests. Like any other actor, intermediaries pursue their own agendas and can work against systemic change if it suits their interests.

The book provides the first critical synthesis of work on cities and intermediation relating to urban infrastructures. It does three things: First, it provides a guide to wider conceptual and theoretical approaches to cities, transitions and intermediation within a governance framework. Second, it examines empirical examples of the work of intermediaries across the full range of urban infrastructures in Europe and the USA, including energy, waste, water and mobilities. Third, it provides an analysis of the work of intermediaries across different scales, ranging from the domestic setting and buildings to localities, cities and regions.

The overarching question guiding the book is: How far and in what ways are intermediaries transformative to urban infrastructure systems? This central issue is broken down into four subordinate questions, which are addressed – in varying degrees – by all the chapters:

1   In what contexts do intermediaries emerge?
2   What is the relational nature of their work?
3   In what ways are they effecting systemic change to urban infrastructures?
4   How are they influencing the governance of urban infrastructures?

The authors address these questions from diverse but complementary analytical perspectives of urban sociology, environmental policy, urban planning, regional development and innovation studies. The book sets the empirical studies in the context of three conceptual debates highly pertinent to intermediaries: on the governance of socio-technical systems; on technological transitions; and on urban transitions. The subsequent chapters explore empirically one key dimension of intermediary work and its relevance to the governance of socio-technical networks: for instance, how they position themselves between production supply and demand, and work across multiple scales; how they bring together and generate different types of expertise; how they can facilitate technological innovation; or how they seek to fill institutional gaps. Overall, the book provides not only an original and critical appraisal of intermediaries as agents of change, but also an empirically rich commentary of the challenges facing research and policy on socio-technical systems, with important lessons for environmental governance in general and policy delivery in particular.

Structure of the book

Part I – Conceptual Framework – introduces the conceptual approaches chosen to explore the potentially transformative role of intermediaries. These approaches address, firstly, the shifting governance of socio-technical systems; secondly, intermediaries and system transitions; and, thirdly, the role of cities as contexts for reshaping infrastructure. Each of these three chapters provides, through theoretical discussion and empirical case studies, a distinct but complementary perspective on the role of intermediaries in urban infrastructures. In the first chapter of the section – Intermediaries and the Governance of Urban Infrastructures in Transition – Timothy Moss brings the governance of networked services to the conceptual table and explores how the study of intermediary organizations provides a window on the shifting governance of network services. This chapter, using examples of water governance from across Europe, places particular emphasis on how collective goals can be pursued through intermediaries and processes of intermediation under shifting governance structures and processes. In the second chapter – Systemic Intermediaries and Transition Processes – Harro van Lente, Marko Hekkert, Ruud Smits and Bas van Waveren outline the emergence of 'systemic intermediaries' which function at a system or network level. Set within the literature on systems of innovation, and illustrated through the example of the California Fuel Cell partnership, the chapter contrasts the network orientation of systemic intermediaries with more traditional, bilateral intermediary organization. In Cities Mediating Technological Transitions, Mike Hodson and Simon Marvin also build on the literature on systemic transition, and, through a case study of the reconfiguration of London's energy infrastructure, highlight the importance of place in understanding transition. Through this the chapter analyses the ways in which different roles of strategic intermediary organizations, operating across different socio-technical networks, intervene in the domain between technological possibilities and territorial context.

Part II – Intermediaries in Network Transitions – provides rich illustrations of intermediaries in practice, covering a wide range of socio-technical networks, from electricity and water supply to wastewater treatment and air transportation. In each case, the chapter sets the emergence and activity of intermediaries in the context of different drivers of network transitions, whether market liberalization, environmental regulation or privatization. In Constructing Markets for Green Electricity, Harald Rohracher explores intermediation in the creation and coordination of consumer choice for green electricity labelling in Germany and Switzerland. This chapter places particular emphasis on the role that NGOs have played in translating between the different logics of demand, supply and regulation, and in creating new links between incumbent and new actors in the electricity sector. In contrast to Rohracher's NGOs as civil-society intermediaries, Ross Beveridge and Simon Guy draw heavily on early actor-network theory to 'follow' a commercial consultancy in North England that emerged in the context of the European Urban Waste Water Directive (UWW) in their chapter Innovation to Intermediaries: Translating the EU Urban Wastewater Directive. The chapter charts the translation work of this eco-preneur as part of the process of dispersing and circulating the UWW through a process of multiple translations. Timothy Moss and Ulrike von Schlippenbach, in The Intermediation of Water Expertise in a Post-privatization Context, shift the focus to the key bridging functions of a strategic intermediary, constituted as a formalized network of business, research and government communities. Set in the context of the partial privatization of the Berlin Water Utility in 1999, the chapter charts the intermediation between diverse actor groups, different policy fields and different spatial scales. The chapter Mobility, Markets and 'Hidden' Intermediation: Aviation and Frequent Flying, by Sally Randles and Sarah Mander, analyses a range of market intermediaries (media, internet, travel agents) operating in-between production and consumption. In particular, they focus on the role that these intermediaries play in driving up aviation consumption and thus undermining policy-makers' attempts to bring aviation emissions down. Part II, then, as well as bringing together studies of energy, water, wastewater and transport, illustrates the emergence of different forms of strategic intermediary and the different types of work that intermediaries can undertake.

Part III – Intermediaries and Scalar Transitions – shifts the focus to look more explicitly at the intermediation of transitions at different scales that sit within and around the urban level. Here, the empirical studies all address different action arenas created, or at least shaped, by intermediary organizations. They each focus on a particular type of boundary work characteristic of intermediaries: between regional strategies and local practice of water management; between environmental regulations and buildings; between electricity production and consumption; and between the crisis and recovery phases of flood management. Part III begins with a study of the processes of translating regional strategies for sustainable water management to the local level in Strategic Intermediation: Between Regional Strategy and Local Practice, by Will Medd and Simon Marvin. Through a case study of North West England, the chapter draws attention to the spatiality of socio-technical infrastructures, and invites an understanding of the fluid space of intermediation between regional and network space. Simon Guy and Jan Fischer's chapter – Re-interpreting Regulations – draws attention to the space of intermediation between the design and regulation of buildings. Within this space, architects are analysed as 'interpretive intermediaries', situated between the textual and representative challenges of performance-based regulation, and the challenges this entails identified. The following chapter – Smart Meters as Obligatory Intermediaries, by Simon Marvin, Heather Chappells and Simon Guy – focuses on the 'smart meter' as a technological intermediary, one that can transform the social relations between users and the suppliers of essential resources. It highlights how the application of a new technology can generate more intensive and visible forms of 'boundary crossing', in this case at the interface between the utility and the consumer. Finally in Part III, Bridging the Recovery Gap, by Rebecca Whittle and Will Medd, examines the role of intermediaries in disaster recovery, exploring the forms of intermediation that emerge during the extended processes of urban flood recovery. Drawing on a case study following the summer floods of 2007 in Hull, northern England, the chapter offers an account of the experience of intermediation 'on the front line', and a critical evaluation of the gap between the lived experience of flood recovery and the policy lessons learnt.

Finally, the concluding chapter by the editors summarizes the key themes and findings emerging from the book, focusing on the degree to which intermediaries are transformative in reshaping the socio-technical organization of urban infrastructures. From this, implications are drawn for future policy development and a research agenda for the future is mapped out.

References

Allen, C. (2003) 'On the logic of "new" welfare practice: An ethnographic case study of the "new welfare intermediaries"', *Sociological Research Online*, vol 8, no 1, www.socresonline.org.uk/8/1/allen.html (accessed on 7 August 2008)

Allen, F. and Santomero, A. (1998) 'The theory of financial intermediation', *Journal of Banking & Finance*, vol 21, nos 11/12, pp1461–1485

Atherton, A. (2006) 'Should government be stimulating start-ups? An assessment of the scope for public intervention in new venture formation', *Environment and Planning C: Government and Policy*, vol 24, no 1, pp21–36

Bakker, K. (2003) 'From public to private to ... mutual? Restructuring water supply governance in England and Wales', *Geoforum*, vol 34, no 3, pp359–374

Bergek, A., Jacobsson, S., Carlsson, B., Lindmark, S. and Rickne, A. (2008) 'Analyzing the functional dynamics of technological innovation systems: A scheme of analysis', *Research Policy*, vol 37, pp407–429

Brousseau, E. (2002) 'The governance of transactions by commercial intermediaries: An analysis of the re-engineering of intermediation by electronic commerce', *International Journal of the Economics of Business*, vol 9, no 3, pp353–374

Coutard, O. (1999) 'Introduction. The evolving forms of governance of large technical systems', in O. Coutard (ed) *The Governance of Large Technical Systems*, Routledge, London/New York, pp1–16

Coutard, O. (2005) 'Urban Space and the Development of Networks: A Discussion of the "Splintering Urbanism" Thesis', in O. Coutard, R.E. Hanley and R. Zimmermann (eds) *Sustaining Urban Networks. The Social Diffusion of Large Technical Systems*, Routledge, Abingdon, pp48–64

Cronin, A. (2004) 'Regimes of mediation: Advertising practitioners as cultural intermediaries', *Consumption, Markets and Culture*, vol 7, no 4, pp349–369

Ehrlich, K. and Cash, D. (1999) 'The invisible world of intermediaries: A cautionary tale', *Computer Supported Cooperative Work*, vol 8, nos 1/2, pp147–167

Elzen, B., Geels, F.W. and Green, K. (2004) *System Innovation and the Transition to Sustainability*, Edward Elgar, Cheltenham

Finger, M. and Allouche, J. (2002) *Water Privatisation. Trans-national Corporations and the Re-regulation of the Water Industry*, Spon Press, London/New York

Geels, F.W. (2004) 'From sectoral systems of innovation to socio-technical systems. Insights about dynamics and change from sociology and institutional theory', *Research Policy*, vol 33, nos 6–7, pp897–920

Geels, F.W. (2005) *Technological Transitions and System Innovations. A Co-Evolutionary and Socio-Technical Analysis*, Edward Elgar, Cheltenham

Graham, S. and Marvin S. (2001) *Splintering Urbanism: Networked Infrastructures, Technological Mobilities, and the Urban Condition*, Routledge, London

Grin, J. (2008) 'The multilevel perspective and design of system innovations', in J.C.J.M. van den Bergh and F.R. Bruinsma (eds) *Managing the Transition to*

Renewable Energy – Theory and Practice from Local, Regional and Macro Perspectives, Edward Elgar, Cheltenham, pp47–79

Guy, S. and Marvin S. (1996) 'Transforming Urban Infrastructure Provision: The Emerging Logic of Demand Side Management', *Policy Studies*, vol 17, no 2, pp137–147

Guy, S., Marvin S. and Moss, T. (eds) (2001) *Urban Infrastructure in Transition. Networks, Buildings, Plans*, Earthscan, London

Howells, J. (2006) 'Intermediation and the role of intermediaries in innovation', *Research Policy*, vol 35, no 5, pp715–728

Iles, P. and Yolles, M. (2002) 'Across the great divide: HRD, technology translation, and knowledge migration in bridging the knowledge gap between SME's and universities', *Human Resource Development International*, vol 5, no 1, pp23–53

Jamison, A. and Rohracher, H. (eds) (2002) *Technology Studies and Sustainable Development*, Profil Verlag, Munich/Vienna

Johnson, A. and Jacobsson, S. (2001) 'Inducement and blocking mechanisms in the development of a new industry: The case of renewable energy technology in Sweden', in R. Coombs, K. Green, A. Richards and V. Walsh (eds) *Technology and the Market. Demand, Users and Innovation*, Edward Elgar Publishing, Cheltenham/Northampton, pp89–111

Kaika, M. (2005) *City of Flows: Modernity, Nature, and the City*, Routledge, New York/London

Kazis, R. (1998) *New Labor Market Intermediaries: What's Driving Them? Where are They Headed? Taskforce on Reconstructing America's Labor Market Institutions*, MIT Press, Cambridge, MA

Kemp, R. and Loorbach, D. (2005) 'Transition management: A reflexive governance approach', in J.-P. Voss, D. Bauknecht and R. Kemp (eds) *Reflexive Governance for Sustainable Development*, Edward Elgar, Cheltenham

Kohl, B. (2003) 'Nongovernmental organizations as intermediaries for decentralization in Bolivia', *Environment and Planning C: Government and Policy*, vol 21, no 3, pp317–331

Latour, B. (1993) *We Have Never Been Modern*, Harvard University Press, Cambridge, MA

Latour, B. (2005) *Reassembling the Social: An Introduction to Actor-Network Theory*, Oxford University Press, Oxford

Lawless, P. (2001) 'Community economic development in urban and regional regeneration: Unfolding potential or justifiable scepticism?', *Environment and Planning C: Government and Policy*, vol 19, no 1, pp135–155

Lente, H. van, Hekkert, M., Smits, R. and Waveren, B. van (2003) 'Roles of systemic intermediaries in transition processes', *International Journal of Innovation Management*, vol 7, no 3, pp247–279

Markard, J. and Truffer, B. (2008) 'Technological innovation systems and the multi-level perspective: Towards an integrated framework', *Research Policy*, vol 37, pp596–615

Mohajeri, S., Knothe, B., Lamothe, D.-N. and Faby, J.-A. (eds) (2004) *Aqualibrium. European water management between regulation and competition*, European Commission, Brussels

Newbery, D.M. (1999) *Privatization, Restructuring, and the Regulation of Network Industries*, MIT Press, Cambridge, MA/London

Paddison, A. (2003) 'Town Centre Management (TCM): A case study of Achmore', *International Journal of Retail & Distribution Management*, vol 31, no 12, pp618–627

Page, B. and Bakker, K. (2005) 'Water governance and water users in a privatised water industry: Participation in policy-making and in water services provision: A case study of England and Wales', *International Journal of Water*, vol 3, no 1, pp38–60

Phillipson, J., Gorton, M., Raley, M. and Moxey. A (2004) 'Treating farms as firms? The evolution of farm business support from productionist to entrepreneurial models', *Environment and Planning C: Government and Policy*, vol 22, no 1, pp31–54

Piore, M.J. (2001) 'The emergent role of social intermediaries in the new economy', *Annals of Public and Cooperative Economics*, vol 72, no 3, pp339–350

Randles, S., McMeekin A. and Warde, A. (2003) 'Interdependence and markets: The organization of exchange, market regulation and interdependencies of markets', Paper presented at joint workshop of CRIC-CEPN, Manchester, UK, 5–6 June

Rip, A. and Kemp, R. (1998) 'Technological change', in S. Rayner and E.L. Malone (eds) *Human Choice and Climate Change: Resources and Technology*, Batelle Press, Columbus, OH, pp327–399

Rohracher, H. (2003) 'The role of users in the social shaping of environmental technologies', *Innovation – The European Journal of Social Science Research*, vol 16, no2, pp177–192

Smith, A., Stirling, A. and Berkhout, F. (2005) 'The governance of sustainable socio-technical transitions', *Research Policy*, vol 34, no 10, pp1491–1510

Southerton, D., Chappells, H. and Vliet, B. van (eds) (2004) *Sustainable Consumption: The Implications of Changing Infrastructures of Provision*, Edward Elgar, London

Star, S.L. (1999) 'The Ethnography of Infrastructure', *American Behavioral Scientist*, vol 43, no 3, pp377–391

Summerton, J. (1994) *Changing Large Technical Systems*, Westview Press, Boulder, CO

Summerton, J. (2004) 'The new "energy divide": Politics, social equity and sustainable consumption in reformed infrastructures', in D. Southerton, H. Chappells and B. van Vliet (eds) *Sustainable Consumption: The Implications of Changing Infrastructures of Provision*, Edward Elgar, London, pp49–64

Swyngedouw, E. (2004) *Social Power and the Urbanization of Water: Flows of Power*, Oxford University Press, Oxford

Trentmann, F. (2006) 'The modern genealogy of the consumer. Meanings, identities and political synapses', in J. Brewer and F. Trentmann (eds) *Consuming Cultures, Global Perspectives, Historical Trajectories, Transnational Exchanges*, Berg, Oxford/New York, pp19–69

PART I

CONCEPTUAL FRAMEWORK: GOVERNANCE, TRANSITIONS AND CITIES

Simon Marvin

Introduction

Part I of the book sets out a wider conceptual framework for understanding the work of intermediaries in both structuring infrastructure systems and restructuring systemic change in the social and technical organization of networks. The conceptual frameworks examined in this section focus on the relations between intermediaries and, firstly, the governance of socio-technical systems; secondly, the role of systemic intermediaries in efforts to restructure the organization of infrastructure networks; and thirdly, the critical role of cities as political contexts for reshaping infrastructure according to wider territorial politics and priorities.

The chapters in this section each address the following three questions. Firstly, how do mainstream conceptual and theoretical frameworks in governance, transitions and urban studies currently conceptualize the role of intermediaries and intermediation? Secondly, what different roles do intermediaries have in maintaining and/or reshaping network transitions – are they transformative or do they maintain the status quo? Thirdly, critically what are the consequences for understanding intermediaries in network transitions – in terms of the degree to which they delimit or extend network transformation?

Each of these chapters addresses a particular conceptual leg for understanding the potentially transformative role of intermediaries: governance of infrastructure (Moss); system transition and innovation (van Lente et al); and urban governance and politics (Hodson and Marvin).

The first chapter, by Timothy Moss, in Part I outlines the case for studying intermediary organizations as a window on the shifting governance of infrastructure network services. It explores the notion of intermediaries and intermediation in the governance literature, and examines how intermediaries can influence the pursuit of collective goals in the socio-technical organization of infrastructure networks. Against this conceptual backdrop, the chapter sets out the key governance challenges emerging from the ongoing transformation of infrastructure systems in terms of four sets of changing relations: between the state and the utility; between service provider and user; between infrastructure and urban systems; and between infrastructure and the environment. It then provides empirical illustration of the emergence of intermediaries in the water sector across Europe, the relational nature of their work, the interests they pursue and the implications they produce.

The second chapter, by Harro van Lente and colleagues, focuses on the emergence of a new type of intermediary organization, which functions at system or network level, in contrast to traditional intermediary organizations that operate mainly bilaterally. These 'systemic intermediaries' are important in long-term and complex changes such as transitions to sustainable development, which require the coordinated effort of industry, policy-makers, research institutes and others. They use the 'systems of innovation' approach to characterize the roles of traditional and systemic intermediary organizations. A review of recent changes in innovation systems points to the need of more systemic efforts, such as the articulation of needs and options, the alignment of relevant actors and the support of learning processes. In a phase model of transitions, additional roles of systemic intermediaries are identified. A case study of the Californian Fuel Cell Partnership shows how the efforts of systemic intermediaries in encompassing systemic innovations are useful and necessary, but not sufficient.

The final chapter in this section, by Mike Hodson and Simon Marvin, examines how new approaches to technological transitions and their management have generated considerable interest in urban research and policy circles in recent years. The development of this body of work may be seen as a response to the complexities, uncertainties and problems which confront many Western societies, in organizing 'sustainably' various aspects of energy, agriculture, water, transport and health systems of production and consumption; problems which are seen as systemic and entwined, or embedded in a series of social, economic, political, cultural and technological relationships. For all the light that transitions approaches shine on such processes, they say little explicitly about the role of places – localities, cities and regions. This chapter addresses this deficit by looking at the way in which London is currently beginning to shape a systemic transition in its energy infrastructure. It outlines and discusses key aspects of the roles of strategic intermediary organizations, which have been strategically set up to intervene between technological possibilities and the territorial context of London. The case study of London highlights an emblematic example of a city's attempt to systemically reshape its energy infrastructure and the lessons to be drawn from this.

2
Intermediaries and the Governance of Urban Infrastructures in Transition

Timothy Moss

Introduction

The social organization of water and energy provision and use has been undergoing radical change in Europe since the mid-1980s. Core components of this ongoing transformation process are the restructuring of utility markets, the reconfiguration of regulation, changes to consumption patterns and the advent of viable alternative technologies (Graham and Marvin, 2001; Guy et al, 2001; Coutard et al, 2005). All these dimensions of change to infrastructure systems have far-reaching implications for their governance. As the markets for utility services become more competitive, new actors emerge, services become more varied and consumers play an increasingly active role, the issue of how to govern these socio-technical networks so as to secure and maximize the multiple benefits they provide is proving highly challenging. This challenge is all the more pertinent given the key role which infrastructure systems, such as for water and energy, play in pursuing European Union (EU) and national policy goals to secure the supply of essential services at affordable prices, to minimize their impact on the environment, to protect the climate, and to act as a vehicle for technological innovation.

Where governance issues are explicitly referred to in the literature on infrastructures in transition, the focus is usually on the reordering of power relations between the triad of service providers, users and regulators. Figure 2.1 provides a typical representation of this relationship, distinguishing between strong and weak modes of influence. Studies of liberalization and privatization have plotted shifts in the relative influence of state agencies and utility companies, or in the relationship between the provider and the consumer (Newbery, 1999; Finger and Allouche, 2002; Page and Bakker, 2005). Research on technological innovation in infrastructure systems has explored how state-led regulatory or financial incentives can promote the uptake of new technologies by both infrastructure providers and users (Jamison and

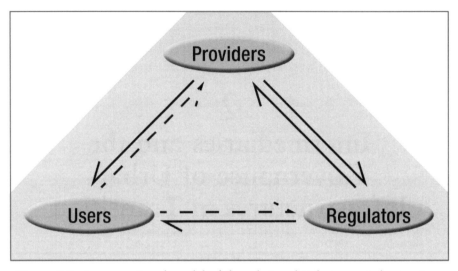

Figure 2.1 *A conventional model of the relationship between infrastructure providers, users and regulators*

Rohracher, 2002). Work on changing consumption patterns has also focused on the utility–user interface in highlighting shifts in actor roles and relations (Southerton et al. 2004; Summerton, 2004; Wissen and Naumann, 2006).

By contrast, relatively little attention has been paid as yet to the roles of other actors of infrastructure governance who do not fit neatly into one of these three categories of provider, user or regulator. This is surprising given that one of the distinctive features of the current transformation of infrastructure systems is that it has brought forth a range of new actors performing new tasks (Coutard, 1999; Graham and Marvin, 2001; Guy et al, 2001). As markets open up, services diversify and alternative technologies gain credence, specialists are emerging to perform a wide range of functions not previously required or recognized. Many of these actors are working in-between the service providers, users and regulators, often with the capacity to reorder relationships between these groups. Examples range from business consultants or research organizations 'translating' novel environmental regulations into practice to non-profit agencies brokering new forms of market regulation, from information campaigns encouraging greater resource efficiency to innovation networks improving communication flows between technology providers and users. Common to all these actors is the intermediary nature of the work they do. Whether facilitating dialogue, providing guidance, bridging gaps, advocating reform or pioneering novel forms of interaction, their arenas of action are defined by their 'in-betweenness', cutting across the provider–user–regulator triad.

This chapter explores how intermediary organizations of this kind are products of the shifting governance of urban infrastructures, but also how they themselves are instrumental in reconfiguring power relations.[1] The aim of the chapter is twofold: firstly, to demonstrate how the governance concept can be applied to explain the contexts of emergence and modes of operation of intermediaries in the energy and water sectors; and, secondly, to illustrate how the study of intermediaries can substantiate our understanding of the shifting governance of socio-technical networks today. To this end, the chapter begins by exploring various meanings of intermediaries and intermediation in a range of literatures, justifying the interpretation selected for the book. The subsequent section demonstrates how the governance concept can be used to provide guidance for understanding the political dimensions to intermediary emergence and intermediary work. Against this conceptual backdrop, the chapter then sets out the core challenges to the governance of socio-technical networks in Europe today, as deduced from the rich literature on infrastructures in transition. These governance challenges are portrayed in terms of changing relations between the state and the utility, between service provider and user, between infrastructure and urban systems, and between infrastructure and the environment. The relevance of each of these four governance challenges for the emergence and operation of intermediary organizations is elaborated, drawing on examples for illustration. The chapter concludes by summarizing the main findings, and demonstrating how the study of intermediaries can provide an empirical focus to the often poorly substantiated study of shifting governance structures and processes today.

Intermediaries as boundary organizations

The term 'intermediaries' is used in a variety of literatures to describe organizations operating in-between other actor groups, but there exists no common conceptual understanding or even an agreed definition of what intermediaries are (see Chapter 1 in this volume). As Gustedt (2000) has argued, intermediaries in the field of regional development can be distinguished not only by their organizational form, but also in terms of their function (mediating, informing, connecting, coordinating and so on) and the stage of their development. What is distinctive to all of them, though, is the relational work that they perform and their positioning in-between other actors, or between actors and artefacts such as a technology.

These characteristics resonate with the concept of 'boundary organizations' developed by Guston, Miller and others to describe 'those social arrangements, networks, and institutions that increasingly mediate between the institutions of "science" and the institutions of "politics"' (Miller, 2001, p482; see Guston, 2001). Miller argues that these relationships – particularly in international politics – are not static, but highly dynamic, requiring what he terms 'hybrid management' to put the 'elements together, take them apart, establish and maintain boundaries between different forms of life, and coordinate activites taking place in multiple domains' (Miller, 2001, p487). Whilst the boundary organizations' concept is limited to bridging two arenas (politics and science), van Lente et al (2003) are interested in intermediaries operating not just bilaterally, but across multiple relations. This broader notion of 'systemic intermediaries' is useful for highlighting the complexity of many intermediaries' relationships, but also the importance of certain intermediaries that are critically positioned to work across multiple forms of social organization.

In contrast, Marvin and Medd prefer to emphasize the intentionality behind intermediation, focusing on 'strategic intermediaries', who are ones 'deliberately positioned to act in between by bringing together and mediating between different interests' (Marvin and Medd, 2004, p84). This emphasis on deliberation is of particular relevance for addressing the governance dimensions to intermediation. Governance is implicit also in the term 'intermediary space', also coined by Marvin and Medd to describe 'a context where the apparently firm boundaries between production and consumption can be questioned, broken down, reworked and actively reconstructed by intermediaries' (Marvin and Medd, 2004, p82). This notion of an intermediary space resonates with Selle's work on organizations working in the space 'between market, state and private households..., a special "world" in which the diverse values, ways of acting, and organizing principles of the surrounding spheres are brought together' (Selle, 1994, p66, translation T.M.). We take up this idea of intermediary space to analyse, in the following section, how the governance concept can contribute to our understanding of how intermediaries emerge out of changes to conventional modes of governance and, in turn, shape these changes themselves.

Governance perspectives on intermediation

Governance has become an important concept for capturing the growing complexity of institutional structures, political processes and social relations involved in the collective pursuit of public, common or individual interests. The burgeoning literature on governance is a response to a perceived need to broaden the study of governing beyond the arenas of formal government institutions to include more informal and less visible ways in which collective goals are advanced (Jessop, 2002; Benz, 2004; van Kersbergen and van Waarden, 2004; Mayntz, 2005). Common to all research into governance, rather than government, is an interest in looking beyond purely top-down explanations of the exercise of power to broader forms of socio-political coordination between public and private actors, which cut across the realms of state, market and civil society (Le Galès, 1998; Gualini, 2002).

Governance research suffers, however, from three major shortcomings. Firstly, there exists no universally accepted definition of what governance is: Rhodes alone has identified seven frequent uses of the term, ranging from 'new public management' to governing through networks (1997). Secondly, a governance theory does not (yet) exist: only various sets of conceptual constructs, each staking out the parameter of a particular interpretation and application of the term. Thirdly, there is a dearth of empirical evidence to back up (or dispute) the various conceptualizations of governance. In drawing inspiration for our research on intermediaries, we acknowledge these shortcomings, but, at the same time, recognize how the governance debate is challenging traditional notions of collective action. In this section we explore four dimensions of this debate – presented as dualities – which are particularly relevant because they address issues of context, relations, deliberation and impact so central to the study of intermediaries and intermediation.

New realities and new perspectives

Common to all governance research are two fundamental characteristics which distinguish it from past studies of government. On the one hand, governance studies are interested in analysing *new realities* of governing. There is a general preoccupation with 'new arrangements for partnership and collaboration between government organizations, business groups and community groups of various kinds' (Healey et al, 2002, p11). This is based on the acknowledgement that we are experiencing a significant shift in the scope, scale and style of collective action in pursuit of common and public interests. On the other hand, governance studies are applying *new perspectives* to the collective pursuit of political interests. They (rather belatedly) recognize that the process of governing – in the past as well as today – is more complex than hitherto assumed. In particular, governance research rejects the clear conceptual division between the state, the market and civil society familiar to traditional policy analyses in favour of a more relational, fluid and contingent approach to political collective action (Mayntz, 2005).

This overarching interest of the governance literature in revealing both new realities and new perspectives of political collective action reflects powerfully our own interest in applying the concept of intermediaries to the social organization of socio-technical networks. On the one hand, we set out to identify and analyse what we understand to be an emergent phenomenon in the organization of water and energy services: the growing significance of actors operating across the traditional spheres of provision, use and regulation as well as between technologies, nature and the city. Although not denying the existence of intermediation of this kind in the past, we claim that the extent and importance of intermediaries represents a 'new reality' in the governance of socio-technical networks. The triad of providers, users and regulators was always an over-simplistic representation of the social organization of socio-technical networks (see Figure 2.1). In today's context of institutional, economic and technological restructuring, it is seriously outdated, blind to the new actors and actor constellations emerging from the transition process. On the other hand, we are using the concept of intermediation, as with the governance debate, to pursue a 'new perspective' on familiar structures and processes. Applied as a heuristic device, the concept of intermediation can stimulate a novel, relational way of thinking about how infrastructure services are organized. Here the dynamic relations between components and actors of a socio-technical system, rather than a static model of clear-cut responsibilities, take centre stage. This leads us to the second dimension of the governance debate: on actor relations.

Generic term or specific model?

Opinion in the literature is divided over whether 'governance' is a generic term applying to all modes of collective action in pursuit of common goals or, rather, a distinct counter-model to traditional forms of government (see Healey et al, 2002). Proponents of the former would subscribe to the broad definition of 'governance' by the Commission on Global Governance as the sum of all ways in which individuals, public agencies and private organizations govern their common affairs in a continuous process of negotiation and cooperation (1995). Here, the interest lies in using governance as a heuristic device to explore multiple interactions between the realms of hierarchy (state), the market and civil society (Pierre, 2000; Healey et al, 2002; Mayntz, 2003; Blatter, 2005). For proponents of the latter interpretation, 'governance' refers solely to forms of networked political action beyond the traditional sphere of government (Rhodes, 1997; Héritier, 2002; Fürst, 2003, 2004). The interest here lies in exploring how forms of 'network governance' can pursue collective goals more effectively than public agencies alone.

For the purpose of our study of intermediaries we embrace the former, non-normative understanding of governance. Rather than focusing just on selected forms of network governance (with or without state involvement), we are concerned with what Bob Jessop has aptly defined as 'the resolution of (para-)political problems (in the sense of problems of collective goal-attainment or the realisation of collective purposes) in and through specific configurations of governmental (hierarchical) and extra-governmental (non-hierarchical) institutions, organisations and practices' (Jessop, 1995, p317). What is important from this governance perspective is less the interactions within a network than 'the way social networks weave in and out of the formal institutions of government and develop guidance mechanisms within themselves' (Healey, 1997, p205). This broader understanding of governance is highly significant for research on intermediaries. It directs attention not simply on the interactions between members of a social network, but on the relational work intermediaries perform between a far wider range of actors, policy fields and action arenas. They are not merely 'filling in' existing contexts of action, but are actively engaged in generating and sustaining new forms of interaction themselves.

Product of necessity or design?

A further distinction in the literature revolves around whether new governance forms are a product of necessity or design. For some commentators, governance is a direct product of structural changes to the global political economy. As the influence of international markets and business grows – it is argued – so the power of state authorities declines, resulting in a reconfiguration of power relations between public agencies, private companies and civil society, finding expression in new forms of governance (Jessop, 1995; Brenner, 1999). Others dispute the inevitability of this process, with its determinist undertones, and argue that governance is strongly shaped by recognition of the inadequacies of what Enrico Gualini calls 'self-centred political–administrative patterns of agency' (2002, p32). Governance in this sense is, rather, a product of deliberation, to create multi-level and multi-actor forms of coordination better suited to policy development and delivery.

The issue of intentionality behind governance structures and processes is highly relevant to intermediary research, as we noted earlier when referring to strategic intermediaries. Although strategic intermediary organizations are created deliberately to address a particular deficit or exploit a particular opportunity, we should not be blinded into assuming this is the norm. Some organizations assume intermediary functions only gradually, some perform intermediary roles different to those for which they were established, whilst others are even unaware they are acting as intermediaries. When researching intermediaries we need to consider, therefore, not only those organizations created deliberately to fulfil a particular intermediary function, but what intermediary functions are being performed, by whom and in what context.

Beneficial or detrimental impact?

It follows from the above that opinion in the literature is divided over whether or not governance is inherently beneficial. Many proponents of new modes of network governance see these as a valuable addition to the body politic or, more specifically, as a complement to hierarchical government, with the capacity to raise the effectiveness of processes of governing and involve actively a wider range of actors. It is in this context that some commentators speak of 'good governance' (Evans et al, 2005). By contrast, sceptics use the governance concept to highlight the increasing influence of commercial interests over state policy (John and Cole, 2000). They criticize in particular the lack of democratic accountability, and the exclusivity and selectivity of many forms of governance, in practice (Stoker, 2000). In this context, we need to consider instances of 'governance failure' as a parallel to market or state failure (Jessop, 1998).

Just as these more critical studies emphasize that new governance arrangements are not politically benign, we need to avoid pre-judgemental views of intermediaries as being independent arbiters. Medd and Marvin (2008) stress that intermediaries are not neutral or arbitrary, but play a role in ordering and defining relationships. Their acts of intermediation are inherently political in the broad sense of involving the articulation and pursuit of particular goals between actors of diverse influence and capacity. We need to consider intermediaries, therefore, as political players in their own right pursuing a variety of interests like any other actor. Equally, we need to contemplate the potentially negative impacts of intermediaries, whether in failing to perform intermediary functions, in causing unintended negative effects or in using their position to prevent – rather than facilitate – exchange. Nor does being well-positioned and well-connected protect intermediaries from failure.

Intermediary space

To conclude this appraisal of the governance debate and its relevance to intermediary research, we address the notion of 'intermediary space'. As Figure 2.2 illustrates, the space in which intermediaries operate is not bounded by a network organization, nor is it restricted to interactions between human actors. In the case of urban infrastructure, it exists at the interface not only between human actors – such as providers, users or regulators – but also between the city and nature or the city and its infrastructure, as we shall see in the following section. The governance perspective helps us understand intermediation as attempts to reorder these relations. It also sensitizes us to the highly political nature of this process of reordering.

How relations are being reordered in urban infrastructures today and what roles intermediaries are playing is the subject of the following section.

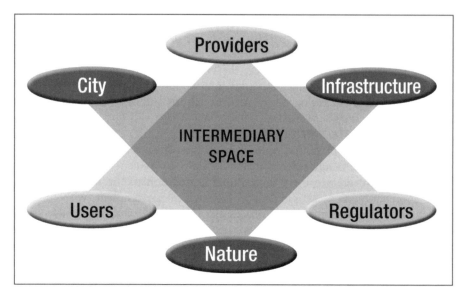

Figure 2.2 *Intermediary space in urban infrastructure systems*

The shifting governance of socio-technical networks and the emergence of intermediaries

In the introduction to his edited volume *The Governance of Large Technical Systems*, Olivier Coutard argues that the governance concept is a valuable tool for unpacking the set of regulatory, policy and organizational changes currently affecting socio-technical networks (1999). In this section we explore how the governance of socio-technical networks is changing in Europe today and how these shifts are creating openings for intermediary organizations.

Infrastructures in transition

The current transformation of urban infrastructure systems in Europe comprises a number of generic trends already well documented in the literature and requires only a brief summary here (see Coutard, 1999; Graham and Marvin, 2001; Guy et al, 2001; Coutard et al, 2005). The *liberalization* of European markets for electricity and gas services has created a more competitive business environment, and raised the relative importance of efficiency and customer relations in utility strategies. The parallel (but distinct) trend towards the *privatization* of utility companies or services has reduced the influence of public agencies as former owners. Both developments have led to the emergence of new market actors and – though for different reasons – greater consumer interest and involvement in service provision. Alongside organizational fragmentation and actor diversification, however, a parallel process of *economic concentration* can be observed, marked by company mergers and the growing globalization of energy and water markets. The *regulation* of utility services has also changed dramatically since the early 1990s. Whilst governments – national and local – have lost influence over direct service provision in cases of privatization or commercialization, the powers of regulatory authorities have increased in the field of environmental and climate protection, and, to a lesser extent, consumer protection and market regulation. Here, the growing influence of the EU has strengthened substantially the supranational dimension to the multi-level governance of infrastructure systems in Europe. Shifts in *consumption patterns*, such as the dramatic drop in water consumption in transition countries since 1990 or the growing preference for electricity from renewable energy sources, have generated greater sensitivity to the needs of specific consumer groups and localities. This process is reinforced by growing *technological diversification*, characterized by the wider application of small-scale technologies, especially for electricity generation and heating, but also for water re-use. This has resulted not only in the emergence of a wider range of technology developers, consultants and operators, but also in the increased involvement of users operating their own in-house infrastructures such as solar heating or grey-water systems.

It should be emphasized that these trends differ hugely in intensity between countries, and between sectors, depending on a whole range of geographical, technological, institutional and socio-economic factors (Voss and Bauknecht, 2007). They also do not represent a coherent development trajectory, but occur, rather, in parallel and are in some cases even contradictory. Thus liberalization often leads to economic concentration which reduces competition. Similarly, deregulation is generally accompanied by new forms of regulation (e.g. to ensure competition).

Governance challenges

All of these dimensions of the transformation of urban infrastructure systems have far-reaching implications for their governance. They all involve the re-ordering of relations between core components of socio-technical networks, which invariably involves a reordering of power relations between the actors involved and often a shift in the way collective interests are pursued. Of the manifold governance challenges raised by the trends listed above, four are particularly significant in terms of reordering relations and creating space for intermediaries (see Figure 2.3). In each case we first elaborate the governance challenge and then explore its relevance for the emergence of intermediaries, using examples for illustration.

State–utility relations

The waves of liberalization (and privatization) of utility services across Europe since the mid-1980s have generated considerable academic interest – especially amongst political economists – in issues of ownership and regulation. The governance challenge here is about how to pursue public sector interests under competitive market conditions (e.g. Newbery, 1999, on the UK electricity and gas sectors; Finger and Allouche, 2002, on the water sector). Identifying a paradigm shift in modes of state intervention 'from ownership to oversight' (Abbate, 1999, p115), these contributions are interested in exploring alternative ways in which public bodies, often no longer providing utility services

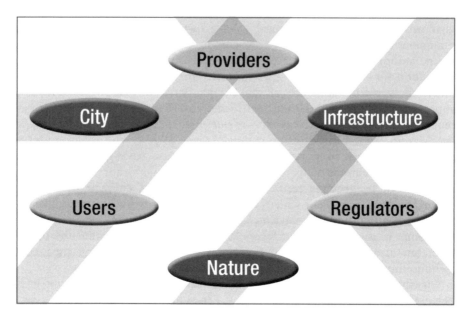

Figure 2.3 *Intermediary emergence along reconfigured relations*

themselves, can influence infrastructure development and service provision. For many commentators, however, these alternatives – such as fiscal incentives or collaborative planning – are insufficient to control the environmental, social and economic negative externalities associated with infrastructure systems (Coutard, 1999; Rochlin, 2005). For instance, Gandy (1997) uses the case of New York City to illustrate how the political-organizational reordering of water supply in the early 1990s undermined traditional 'municipal managerialism' and replaced it with a fragmented form of governance, resulting in piecemeal, ad hoc responses to environmental problems.

In contexts of this kind, intermediaries can emerge as products of market restructuring, as a response to new modes of regulation or to fill institutional gaps resulting from reforms. As power relations between service regulators and providers shift and as new policy agendas emerge, certain organizations are positioning and presenting themselves as intermediaries with the ability to exploit opportunities which these changes are bringing. Marvin and Medd see a direct link between the unbundling of integrated infrastructure networks and their selective rebundling by intermediaries (2004). One such example is the Berlin Centre of Competence for Water (KWB), an intermediary network created as part of the privatization package of the city's water utility in 1999, and dealt with in detail by Timothy Moss and Ulrike von Schlippenbach in Chapter 7 of this book. Another example is the French organization Service Public 2000, set up in 1996 by the French Mayors Association (AMF) and the National Federation for the Management of Local Public Utilities (FNCCR) to advise local authorities on how to negotiate contracts with private water companies.[2] The function of this intermediary is to help offset the strongly asymmetrical relationship between powerful water companies and the small communes they serve.

Provider–user relations

A second strand of research on infrastructure reconfiguration addresses how trends towards market competition, service differentiation and consumer engagement are changing the conventionally limited and largely one-directional relationship between the utility and the service user. Some commentators have challenged the widespread assumption that liberalization brings more choice to consumers (Summerton, 2004). The potential benefits for consumers, it would appear, depend on their relative value to the utility, with strategically important users being 'cherry-picked' for special services and low-value customers being subject to 'social dumping' (Guy et al, 1999; see, for Eastern Germany, Wissen and Naumann, 2006; for England and Wales, Page and Bakker, 2005). Other commentators argue for a more in-depth appraisal of how modes of production and consumption influence one other, and how this interaction is currently changing (Southerton et al, 2004; Trentmann, 2006). The governance challenge in this case is to respond to both the threats and the opportunities which this reordering of utility–user relations presents to issues of consumer protection and user empowerment. In this context we need to appreciate how utility–consumer relations are also being affected by changing patterns of resource consumption and new modes of self-provision (e.g. solar-powered electricity generation, re-use of water).

These changes to provider–user relations and growing public awareness of infrastructure systems are stimulating the emergence of intermediary organizations capable of liaising between utilities and consumers, whether household or commercial. These can range from advisory groups and information campaigns on resource use or pollution, to training and educational programmes for targeted consumer groups. Regional energy agencies in Austria provide one such example, building up and stabilizing new relations between farmers, manufacturers and consumers around biomass-based systems for heating and power generation in rural communities (Rohracher and Späth, 2008). Another example is the organization Sustainable Water Environment in Lancashire (SWEL), which liaises between the UK's Environment Agency (EA) and small and medium-sized enterprises (SMEs) in the region over solutions for water pollution problems. SWEL has proved highly successful: firstly, by maintaining strict confidentiality in its dealings with each party; and, secondly, by 'translating' EA policy to local businesses in ways that reflect their interests (Medd and Marvin, 2008 and Chapter 9 of this book).

Infrastructure–city relations

It is widely acknowledged that the development of a locality and its infrastructure systems are inextricably linked. However, only since the mid-1990s have significant steps been made to link urban studies and technology studies in researching the interdependencies of urban and infrastructure development (Hommels, 2005).[3] What governance issues are at stake here is reflected in the much-cited comment by Susan Star: 'Study a city and neglect its sewers and power supplies (as many have), and you miss essential aspects of distributional justice and planning power' (1999, p379). Infrastructure systems are both a product and a medium of the political economy of a locality (Kaika and Swyngedouw, 2000; Gandy, 2004). This is most prominently illustrated by the 'splintering urbanism' thesis developed by Stephen Graham and Simon Marvin (2001), who argue that new logics of urban and infrastructure politics are accentuating socio-spatial disparities in utility services (for a critique, Coutard, 2005; Coutard and Guy, 2008). At the same time, scholars are keen to highlight new ways of shaping the city–infrastructure interface to beneficial effect, whether through the growing sensitivity of utilities towards the changing geographies of infrastructure systems (Guy et al, 1996), ways of improving linkage between infrastructure planning and urban development (Ennis, 2003), or a better understanding of how infrastructure transformation is contextualized locally (Guy et al, 2001; Monstadt, 2007).

This literature directs us towards intermediation at the interface between infrastructures and the city. It suggests we need to explore how certain organizations are recognizing the need to relate the development of infrastructure systems to the development of the city or region they serve, and how they are positioning themselves to advance this relationship. The close interdependence of technologies, infrastructure systems and spatial development is addressed by several of the intermediaries studied in the EU project on which this chapter is based. One of these is the consultancy BULPLAN, based in Sofia, which supports local authorities, developers and utilities with studies and advice on how to plan urban development in ways which take adequate consideration of the limited water resources of the Sofia region, the investment needs of the infrastructure networks and the effects of management restructuring to water services (Moss and Wissen, 2005). Other intermediaries operate across different levels of social organization, from the household to the region and beyond. They introduce spatial sensitivity into infrastructure development by being able to transcend boundaries of a geographical kind. This is the distinguishing intermediary feature of the Mersey Basin Campaign (MBC), a broad partnership of government, business and community organizations of the Mersey basin which has proved successful in accessing different forms of funding and enrolling actors from local to regional levels in the common interest of improving the environmental quality of the river Mersey (Medd and Marvin, 2008; and Chapter 9 of this book).

Infrastructure–environment relations

The central importance of infrastructure systems for improving the natural environment and contributing to sustainable development is a fourth strand of debate on the governance of socio-technical systems in transition (Coutard et al, 2005). From a political ecology perspective, the current renewal, modernization and (selective) extension of infrastructure systems in Europe present a window of opportunity for re-thinking radically how infrastructures are planned, and what services are required so as to take greater account of today's policy objectives for environmental and climate protection (Coutard et al, 2005; Loske and Schaeffer, 2005; Pehnt et al, 2006). The governance challenge here is to identify institutional frameworks and modes of interaction, which encourage more sustainable use of natural resources and energy through technological innovation and altered practices (Jamison and Rohracher, 2002; Rohracher, 2002). Rohracher (2002) argues, for instance, that strategies for sustainable socio-technical systems require better coordination between actors on the supply side and greater enrolment of consumers in innovation processes.

This fourth governance challenge – on infrastructure–environment relations – focuses attention on how intermediaries can, for instance, connect environmental objectives to technical applications. A good example is the environmental consultancy CookPrior in the North East of England, which specializes in matching innovative technical solutions to specific business contexts of wastewater management by means of close interaction and 'translation' between technology providers and users (analysed in detail by Beveridge and Guy in Chapter 6 of this book). The British company Glassarc works, rather, at the interface between technologies and buildings.[4] Using its good connections to suppliers of water conservation technologies, Glassarc encourages key decision makers on construction projects to consider applying these technologies.

Conclusion

This chapter has argued that intermediary organizations and the often hidden work which they perform are highly significant for the shifting governance of today's urban infrastructure systems. We have used the governance concept to frame an exploration of the political nature of intermediaries and intermediation, focusing on four core dimensions of the governance debate. Firstly, the governance perspective helped identify and explain the emergent phenomenon of intermediaries as a 'new reality' of actors operating across the traditional spheres of water and energy provision, regulation and consumption, but also as a 'new perspective' on modes of governance, challenging conventional models of how water and energy services are organized. Just as the governance concept leads us to consider less familiar processes and structures of collective action, so the notion of intermediaries encourages us to look beyond the provider–regulator–user triad when investigating the governance of infrastructure systems in transition. Secondly, the non-normative, generic understanding of governance applying to all modes of collective action in pursuit of common goals is useful for understanding intermediaries not simply as central figures in a social network, but as actors capable of reconfiguring relations between diverse actor groups, as well as between different arenas of action and spatial contexts. Thirdly, the debate on intentionality in the governance literature is highly valuable in distinguishing between intermediaries that are created deliberately to meet a strategic purpose and those that are fulfilling intermediary functions, sometimes without being aware that they are doing so. The function of intermediation is, therefore, more significant than determining whether an actor is, or is not, an intermediary. Fourthly, the governance debate sensitizes us to the dangers of assuming that intermediary activity, by virtue of being relational, is inherently benign. Intermediaries are not independent, impartial bodies, but political players like any other, even when bridging interests or facilitating interaction.

Whilst a governance perspective can thus raise our understanding of the politics of intermediation, the empirical research in this book illustrates how the study of intermediaries can, conversely, help substantiate our understanding of the governance of socio-technical networks in transition. If governance is about looking beyond simple, functional distinctions between the state, the market and civil society, then the study of intermediaries is instrumental in revealing what happens at the more open and blurred interfaces between the public and the private, the regulator and the regulated. As traditional boundaries between actor groups are being eroded or redefined, intermediaries would appear to play an important role in communicating across cultures of compliance (state), of competition (market) and of collaboration (civil society) (see Healey et al, 2002). The boundary work of intermediaries relates not solely to the 'conceptual trinity of market-state-civil society' (Jessop, 1995, p310), but also to other dimensions, as the empirical examples in this book illustrate. Governance settings are today increasingly trans-scalar, cross-sectoral and multidimensional (Gualini, 2002; Blatter, 2005). This means that, to be effective, key actors need to operate across different scales of governance (e.g. EU, national, regional, local), different policy fields (e.g. water, energy, regional development, research) and different modes of communication (e.g. informational, persuasive, receptive). The study of intermediaries at these various interfaces, we conclude, can deliver important insights into the nature of this boundary work so crucial to governance studies.

Acknowledgements

This chapter is a shortened and revised version of the paper 'Intermediaries and the governance of sociotechnical networks in transition', published by Pion Ltd in *Environment and Planning A*, 2009, vol 41, pp1480–1495. The author is grateful to the publishers for granting permission to republish in this revised form. He would also like to thank the members of the EU-funded project 'Intermediaries', in particular Simon Marvin, Simon Guy and Will Medd, for the many stimulating discussions on researching intermediaries and comments on this paper.

Notes

1   The research presented in this paper is based on an international research project on intermediary organizations in the water sector, funded by the EU under the 5th Framework Programme Research, entitled 'New intermediary services and the

transformation of urban water supply and wastewater disposal systems in Europe'; see http://www.irs-net.de/intermediaries/. The final report is available under http://www.irs-net.de/texte/intermediaries/DetailedReport.pdf. Published results include: Marvin and Medd, 2004; Beveridge and Guy, 2005, 2009; Medd and Marvin, 2008; Moss, 2009.

2 A notable exception is the earlier work by urban historians and historians of technology on the development of Large Technical Systems (Hughes, 1983; Tarr and Dupuy, 1988).

3 See www.sp2000.asso.fr, accessed on 13 September 2010.

4 See www.glassarc.com, accessed on 13 September 2010.

References

Abbate, J. (1999) 'From control to coordination. New governance models for information networks and other large technical systems', in O. Coutard (ed) *The Governance of Large Technical Systems*, Routledge, London/New York, pp114–129

Benz, A. (2004) 'Einleitung: Governance – Modebegriff oder nützliches sozialwissenschaftliches Konzept?', in A. Benz (ed) *Governance – Regieren in komplexen Regelsystemen. Eine Einführung*, VS Verlag für Sozialwissenschaften, Wiesbaden, pp11–28

Beveridge, R. and Guy, S. (2005) 'The rise of the eco-preneur and the messy world of environmental innovation', *Local Environment*, vol 10, no 6, pp665–676

Beveridge, R. and Guy, S. (2009) 'Governing through translations: Intermediaries and the mediation of the EU's Urban Waste Water Directive', *Journal of Environmental Policy & Planning*, vol 11, no 2, pp69–85

Blatter, J. (2005) 'Metropolitan Governance in Deutschland: Normative, utilitaristische, kommunikative und dramaturgische Steuerungsansätze', *Swiss Political Science Review*, vol 11, no 1, pp119–155

Brenner, N. (1999) 'Globalisation as reterritorialisation: The re-scaling of urban governance in the European Union', *Urban Studies*, vol 36, pp431–451

Commission on Global Governance (1995) *Nachbarn in einer Welt. Der Bericht der Kommission für Weltordnungspolitik*, Stiftung Entwicklung und Frieden, Bonn, p4

Coutard, O. (1999) 'Introduction. The evolving forms of governance of large technical systems', in O. Coutard (ed) *The Governance of Large Technical Systems*, Routledge, London/New York, pp1–16

Coutard, O. (2005) 'Urban space and the development of networks: A discussion of the "splintering urbanism" thesis', in O. Coutard, R.E. Hanley and R. Zimmermann (eds) *Sustaining Urban Networks. The Social Diffusion of Large Technical Systems*, Routledge, Abingdon, pp48–64

Coutard, O. and Guy, S. (2008) 'STS and the city: Politics and practices of hope', *Science, Technology and Human Values*, vol 32, pp713–734

Coutard, O., Hanley, R.E. and Zimmermann, R. (eds) (2005) *Sustaining Urban Networks. The Social Diffusion of Large Technical Systems*, Routledge, Abingdon

Ennis, F. (ed) (2003) *Infrastructure Provision and the Negotiating Process*, Ashgate, Aldershot

Evans, B., Joas, M., Sundback, S. and Theobald, K. (2005) *Governing Sustainable Cities*, Earthscan, London

Finger, M. and Allouche, J. (2002) *Water Privatisation. Trans-National Corporations and the Re-Regulation of the Water Industry*, Spon Press, London/New York

Fürst, D. (2003) 'Regional Governance zwischen Wohlfahrtsstaat und neo-liberaler Marktwirtschaft', in I. Katenhusen and W. Lamping (eds) *Demokratien in Europa. Der Einfluss der europäischen Integration auf Institutionenwandel und neue Konturen des demokratischen Verfassungsstaates*, Leske and Budrich, Opladen, pp251–268

Fürst, D. (2004) 'Regional governance', in A. Benz (ed) *Governance – Regieren in komplexen Regelsystemen. Eine Einführung*, VS Verlag für Sozialwissenschaften, Wiesbaden, pp45–64

Gandy, M. (1997) 'The making of a regulatory crisis: Restructuring New York City's water supply', *Transactions of the Institute of British Geographers*, vol 22, pp338–358

Gandy, M. (2004) 'Rethinking urban metabolism: Water, space and the modern city', *City*, vol 8, no 3, pp363–379

Graham, S. and Marvin, S. (2001) *Splintering Urbanism: Networked Infrastructures, Technological Mobilities, and the Urban Condition*, Routledge, London

Gualini, E. (2002) 'Institutional capacity building as an issue of collective action and institutionalisation: some theoretical remarks', in G. Cars, P. Healey, A. Madanipour and C. de Magalhaes (eds) *Urban Governance, Institutional Capacity and Social Milieux*, Ashgate, Aldershot, pp29–44

Gustedt, E. (2000) *Nachhaltige Regionalentwicklung durch intermediäre Organisationen?*, Ibidem, Stuttgart

Guston, D.H. (2001) 'Boundary organizations in environmental policy and science: An introduction', *Science, Technology & Human Values*, vol 26, no 4, pp399–408

Guy, S., Graham, S. and Marvin, S. (1996) 'Privatized utilities and regional governance: The new regional managers?', *Regional Studies*, vol 30, no 8, pp733–739

Guy, S., Graham, S. and Marvin, S. (1999) 'Splintering networks. The social, spatial and environmental implications of the privatization and liberalization of utilities in Britain', in O. Coutard (ed) *The Governance of Large Technical Systems*, Routledge, London/New York, pp149–169

Guy, S., Marvin, S. and Moss, T. (eds) (2001) *Urban Infrastructure in Transition. Networks, Buildings, Plans*, Earthscan, London

Healey, P. (1997) *Collaborative Planning. Shaping Places in Fragmented Societies*, Macmillan, Basingstoke

Healey, P., Cars, G., Madanipour, A. and Magalhaes, C. de (2002) 'Transforming governance, institutionalist analysis and institutional capacity', in G. Cars, P. Healey, A. Madanipour and C. de Magalhaes (eds) *Urban Governance, Institutional Capacity and Social Milieux*, Ashgate, Aldershot, pp6–28

Héritier, A. (2002) 'Introduction', in A. Héritier (ed) *Common Goods. Reinventing European and International Governance*, Rowman & Littlefielde, Lanham, pp1–12

Hommels, A. (2005) 'Studying obduracy in the city: Toward a productive fusion between technology studies and urban studies', *Science, Technology, & Human Values*, vol 30, no 3, pp323–351

Hughes, T. (1983) *Networks of Power. Electrification in Western Society, 1880–1930*, John Hopkins University Press, Baltimore/London

Jamison, A. and Rohracher, H. (eds) (2002) *Technology Studies and Sustainable Development*, Profil Verlag, Munich/Vienna

Jessop, B. (1995) 'The regulation approach, governance and post-Fordism: Alternative perspectives on economic and political change?', *Economy and Society*, vol 24, no 3, pp307–333

Jessop, B. (1998) 'The rise of governance and the risk of governance failure: The case of economic development', *International Social Science Journal*, vol 155, pp29–45

Jessop, B. (2002) 'Governance and meta-governance in the face of complexity: On the roles of requisite variety, reflexive observation, and romantic irony in participatory governance', in H. Heinelt, P. Getimis, G. Kafkalas, R. Smith and E. Swyngedouw (eds) *Participatory Governance in Multi-level Contexts: Concepts and Experience*, Leske and Budrich, Opladen, pp33–58

John, P. and Cole, A. (2000) 'When do institutions, policy sectors and cities matter? Comparing networks of local policy makers in Britain and France', *Comparative Political Studies*, vol 33, no 3, pp248–268

Kaika, M. and Swyngedouw, E. (2000) 'Fetishizing the modern city: The phantasmagoria of urban technological networks', *International Journal of Urban and Regional Research*, vol 24, no 1, pp120–138

Kersbergen, K. van and Waarden, F. van (2004) 'Governance as a bridge between disciplines: Cross-disciplinary inspiration regarding shifts in governance and problems of governability, accountability and legitimacy', *European Journal of Political Research*, vol 43, pp143–171

Le Galès, P. (1998) 'Regulations and governance in European Cities', *International Journal of Urban and Regional Research*, vol 22, no 3, pp482–506

Lente, H. van, Hekkert, M., Smits, R. and Waveren, B. van (2003) 'Roles of systemic intermediaries in transition processes', *International Journal of Innovation Management*, vol 7, no 3, pp247–279

Loske, R. and Schaeffer, R. (eds) (2005) *Die Zukunft der Infrastrukturen. Intelligente Netzwerke für eine nachhaltige Entwicklung*, Metropolis-Verlag, Marburg

Marvin, S. and Medd, W. (2004) 'Sustainable infrastructures by proxy? Intermediation beyond the production-consumption nexus', in D. Southerton, H. Chappels and B. van Vliet (eds) *Sustainable Consumption. The Implications of Changing Infrastructures of Provision*, Edward Elgar, Cheltenham, pp81–94

Mayntz, R. (2003) 'Governance im modernen Staat', in A. Benz (ed) *Governance. Eine Einführung*, Dreifachkurseinheit der FernUniversität Hagen, Hagen, pp71–83

Mayntz, R. (2005) 'Governance-Theorie als fortentwickelte Steuerungstheorie?', in G.F. Schuppert (ed) *Governance-Forschung: Vergewisserung über Stadt und Entwicklungslinien*, Nomos, Baden-Baden, pp11–20

Medd, W. and Marvin, S. (2008) 'Making water work: Intermediating between regional strategy and local practice', *Environment and Planning D*, vol 26, pp280–299

Miller, C. (2001) 'Hybrid management: Boundary organizations, science policy, and environmental governance in the climate regime', *Science, Technology & Human Values*, vol 26, no 4, pp478–500

Monstadt, J. (2007) 'Urban governance and the transition of energy systems: Institutional change and shifting energy and climate policies in Berlin', *International Journal of Urban and Regional Research*, vol 31, no 2, pp326–343

Moss, T. (2009) 'Intermediaries and the governance of sociotechnical networks in transition', *Environment and Planning A*, vol 41, pp1480–1495

Moss, T. and Wissen, M. (2005) 'Making senses of diversity. A synergy report on an inventory of 113 intermediary organisations of water management in Europe', unpublished manuscript

Newbery, D.M. (1999) *Privatization, Restructuring, and the Regulation of Network Industries*, MIT Press, Cambridge, MA/London, pp199–290, 343–384

Page, B. and Bakker, K. (2005) 'Water governance and water users in a privatised water industry: Participation in policy-making and in water services provision: A case study of England and Wales', *International Journal of Water*, vol 3, no 1, pp38–60

Pehnt, M., Cames, M., Fischer, C., Praetorius, B., Schneider, L., Schumacher, K. and Voss, J.-P. (2006) *Micro Cogeneration. Towards Decentralized Energy Systems*, Springer, Heidelberg/New York

Pierre, J. (2000) 'Introduction: Understanding governance', in J. Pierre (ed) *Debating Governance*, Oxford/New York, pp1–10

Rhodes, R.A.W. (1997) *Understanding Governance. Policy Networks, Reflexivity and Accountability*, Open University Press, Buckingham, PA

Rochlin, G.I. (2005) 'Networks and the subversion of choice: An institutionalist manifesto', in O. Coutard, R.E. Hanley and R. Zimmermann (eds) *Sustaining Urban Networks. The Social Diffusion of Large Technical Systems*, Routledge, Abingdon, pp205–228

Rohracher, H. (2002) 'Managing the technological transition to sustainable construction of buildings: A socio-technical perspective', in A. Jamison and H. Rohracher (eds) *Technology Studies and Sustainable Development*, Profil Verlag, Munich/Vienna, pp319–342

Rohracher, H. and Späth, P. (2008) 'Neue Chancen ungleich verteilt – Räumliche Ausdifferenzierungen bei der Energieversorgung im ländlichen Österreich', in T. Moss, M. Naumann and M. Wissen (eds) *Infrastruktursysteme und Raumentwicklung. Zwischen Universalisierung und Differenzierung*, oekom-Verlag, Munich, pp225–248

Selle, K. (1994) *Was ist bloss mit der Planung los?*, Dortmunder Beiträge zur Raumplanung 69, Dortmund

Southerton, D., Chappells, H. and Vliet, B. van (eds) (2004) *Sustainable Consumption: The Implications of Changing Infrastructures of Provision*, Edward Elgar, London

Star, S.L. (1999) 'The ethnography of infrastructure', *American Behavioural Scientist*, vol 43, no 3, pp377–391

Stoker, G. (2000) 'Urban political science and the challenge of urban governance', in J. Pierre (ed) *Debating Governance*, Oxford University Press, Oxford, pp91–109

Summerton, J. (2004) 'The new "energy divide": Politics, social equity and sustainable consumption in reformed infrastructures', in D. Southerton, H. Chappells and B. van Vliet (eds) *Sustainable Consumption: The Implications of Changing Infrastructures of Provision*, Edward Elgar, London, pp49–64

Tarr, J.A. and Dupuy, G. (eds) (1988) *Technology and the Rise of the Networked City in Europe and America*, Temple University Press, Philadelphia, PA

Trentmann, F. (2006) 'The modern genealogy of the consumer. Meanings, identities and political synapses', in J. Brewer and F. Trentmann (eds) *Consuming Cultures, Global Perspectives, Historical Trajectories, Transnational Exchanges*, Berg, Oxford/New York, pp19–69

Voss, J.-P. and Bauknecht, D. (2007) 'Der Einfluss von Technik auf Governance-Innovationen: Regulierung zur gemeinsamen Nutzung in Infrastruktursystemen', in U. Dolata and R. Werle (eds) *Gesellschaft und die Macht der Technik.*

Sozioökonomischer und institutioneller Wandel durch Technisierung, Campus, Frankfurt/New York, pp109–131

Wissen, M. and Naumann, M. (2006) 'A new logic of infrastructure supply: The commercialization of water and the transformation of urban governance in Germany', *Social Justice*, vol 33, no 3, pp20–37

3
Systemic Intermediaries and Transition Processes

Harro van Lente, Marko Hekkert, Ruud Smits
and Bas van Waveren

Introduction

Policy-makers and scholars argue that Western societies are confronted with the need for major changes in agriculture, energy supply, the knowledge infrastructure, water management, transportation and many other important sectors in order to reach a sustainable future. These changes have a time horizon of at least one generation, and invoke developments and interactions within and between many different domains of society. The issue of stimulating and managing such processes has raised a lot of attention. In policy circles, the terms 'transition' and, accordingly, 'transition management' are used to capture the envisioned long-term and complex changes to more sustainability (Rotmans et al, 2000). The transition to a sustainable society is a dauntingly complex issue, both politically and theoretically. It includes exploration and stimulation of new ways of production and consumption, new types of regulation and, probably, new types of institutions to coordinate the various efforts. One example is the efforts to develop more sustainable energy production and consumption, which require huge adaptations in terms of technology, infrastructure and legislation (Jacobbson and Johnson, 2000). Such transition processes involve many risks and require initiative and creativity. Yet experiences are limited, as are the insights into how these processes should be designed, organized and implemented.

As we are dealing with multiple domains and simultaneous socio-economic changes, system approaches appear to be promising here, since they analyse the interaction between the parties involved and the resulting collective performance. In the last decade, progress has been made with the 'innovation systems approach', which investigates the interplay between various parties (Lundvall, 1992; Nelson, 1993; Edquist, 1997). The approach rejects linear models of innovation and stresses the interdependencies between scientific, technological, economic and political activities. The focus has been on the institutions that support and express the interdependencies and which together build up 'systems of innovation'. Metcalfe (1995) defines an innovation system as:

> *that set of distinct institutions which jointly and individually contributes to the development and diffusion of new technologies and which provides the framework within which governments form and implement policies to influence the innovation process. As such it is a system of interconnected institutions to create, store and transfer the knowledge, skills and artefacts which define new technologies.*

Innovation systems, as illustrated in Figure 3.1, comprise industrial firms, universities and research institutes, political arrangements that support innovation and intermediary organizations that function as a broker between the various parties.

In this chapter we build on the systems of innovation approach to address the intellectual challenges posed by complex and long-term transitions. Our focus is on a crucial ingredient of any system of innovation: the intermediary organizations that connect, translate and facilitate flows of knowledge. We are especially interested in the emergence of a new type of intermediary organization that operates at network or system level, in contrast to the more traditional intermediaries that tend to focus on bilateral relations (knowledge transfer) and the support of individual organizations (management support of small and medium-sized firms). We will call these new types of organizations 'systemic intermediaries', and our key question is how systemic intermediaries actually and potentially contribute to transitions.

We will proceed in three steps: Firstly, we will elaborate the actual and potential roles of systemic intermediaries in innovation systems. We will characterize the ongoing changes in innovation systems and discuss the rise of a new type of intermediary that functions in networks instead of one-to-one

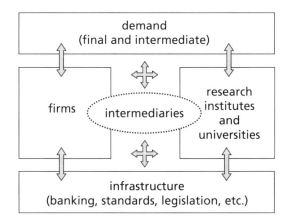

Figure 3.1 *Building blocks of innovation systems*

mediation. Secondly, we address the issue of management of transitions and discuss the possibilities that intermediaries in general, and systemic intermediaries in particular, offer. On the basis of a phase model of transition, possibilities for support of transition processes are assessed and, in particular, the possibilities of systemic intermediaries to do so. Given the characteristics of transitions, what would it imply for policy initiatives to make use of systemic intermediaries? What roles could they have in the management of transitions, and how should these be stimulated? Finally, we will corroborate our arguments in a case study of the recent Californian moves towards a cleaner automotive technology. We will describe the features of the desired future system, the current initiatives taken and the envisioned steps ahead. The analysis includes the opinions and expectations of the relevant players in the energy innovation system concerning the future use of new automotive technology and new energy infrastructures. In particular, we pay attention to the emerging strategic alliances in the car manufacturing industry that focus on the development of low (LEV) and zero emission vehicles (ZEV) and the concomitant infrastructures.

Changing innovation systems and systemic intermediaries

Transitions to more sustainable ways of production and consumption involve, by definition, long-term and complex changes in the way firms, research institutes, public agencies, intermediaries and others operate and innovate. Indeed, transitions involve major changes in innovation systems. Reportedly, already changes in innovation systems are visible and they are appropriate to consider for our purposes. In this section we will summarize the findings and argue that, due to the changing characteristics of innovation systems, the role and function of intermediaries is changing too.

According to many authors, over the last few decades innovation systems have been going through a period of rapid change (Gibbons et al, 1994; Barré et al, 1997; Lundvall and Borras, 1998; Smits and Kuhlmann, 2002). Reported changes refer to the nature of innovation processes (more science-based and more inter- and multidisciplinary): the growing importance of the soft side of innovation, increasing costs and the concomitant growing need for choices, the growing number and variety of actors and the related increasing role of users, and the blurring borders between the public and private domain and between governmental levels (Gibbons et al, 1994; Lundvall and Borras, 1998; Kuhlmann et al, 1999). In the interrelated development of innovation practice, theory and policy, Smits and Kuhlmann distinguish three major trends: the end of the linear model and the rise of interactive and iterative approaches; a reinforcement of the systems approach; and increasing uncertainty, with a concomitant increasing importance of learning processes.

From this analysis they derive five systemic functions that should be addressed in the management of present-day innovation systems (Smits and Kuhlmann, 2002). Firstly, the management of interfaces, which aims at transferring knowledge, at building bridges and at stimulating the debate; furthermore, the management of interfaces is not only limited to bilateral contacts, but also focuses on chains, networks and at system level. Secondly, the building and organizing of (innovation) systems involves construction and deconstruction of (sub)systems, initiating and organizing discourse, alignment and consensus; also, the management of complex systems, prevention of lock-in, identification and facilitation of prime movers and ensuring that all relevant actors involved are part of this function. Thirdly, a platform is provided for learning and experimenting; for example, learning by doing, learning by using and learning by interacting, resulting in learning at the system level. Fourthly, an infrastructure is provided for strategic intelligence such as foresight and technology assessment and building links between these sources, aiming at stimulating synergy and enhanced efficiency, improving accessibility for all relevant actors and stimulating the development of the potential to produce strategic information tailored to the needs of actors involved. Fifthly, stimulating demand articulation, strategy and vision development involves stimulating and facilitating the search for possible applications, developing instruments that support discourse, vision and strategy development.

Smits and Kuhlmann continue their argument with an analysis of the portfolio of policy instruments and show that in industrialized countries the portfolio tends to be dominated by three types of instruments: financial (subsidies, tax schemes), diffusion oriented (technology transfer, mobility of researchers) and managerial (support of management of small and medium-sized enterprises (SMEs) involved in innovation processes). Since these instruments only cover a limited part of the five systemic functions, they argue that the development of instruments that facilitate the five systemic functions should be stimulated further. They coin these instruments 'systemic instruments' to distinguish them from instruments that primarily focus on individual organizations and/or bilateral relations. By the same token, we argue that 'systemic' intermediaries are needed. Systemic intermediaries, as we introduced them above, function primarily in networks and systems (unlike hard and soft intermediaries, which operate primarily in one-to-one interactions), primarily operate in the public, public–private, but not exclusively in the private domain, and focus on support at a strategic level. Whereas financial and diffusion instruments tend to belong to the traditional hard intermediaries and management instruments to soft intermediaries, systemic instruments should be related to systemic intermediaries.

We consider the following systemic processes as key elements of ongoing innovation and transition processes:

1   Articulation of options and demand, which includes the stimulation of technological variety and the search for possible applications. It also includes the awareness of possible futures.
2   Alignment of actors and possibilities, by initiating and strengthening linkages between the various parts of the innovation system. It includes the building and sustaining of networks and the facilitation of interfaces.
3   Support of learning processes, by enhancing feedback mechanisms and by stimulating experiments and mutual adaptations.

Table 3.1 *Characterization of roles of intermediaries*

Intermediary	Ownership	Objective	'Hard' or 'soft'	Funding	Initiative and relationship	Type of service	International
1. Knowledge-intensive business services (KIBS)	Private	Profit by support of clients	Both management (soft) and engineering (hard) services	Fees charged to (mainly individual) clients	Usually the client possible after advertising by KIBS, on a project basis, and mostly one-to-one	Very diverse	Many KIBS have practices in more than one country. Otherwise often willing to work abroad
2. Research and technology organizations	Semi-public	Supplying largely technical knowledge to industry, non-profit	Largely 'hard'	Considerable government funding and additional income from industry	Often own programmes for which funding is sought, on long-term projects with possible industry participation, one-to-one or to many	Applied technical knowledge	Sometimes difficult due to public funding, although increasingly funding in international (e.g. EU) context
3a. Industry associations	Independent associations (controlled by members)	Support of the industry, non-profit	Both 'hard' and 'soft'	Membership fees (or government subsidies)	From the association and from the industry, support is always available for the entire industry (i.e. not exclusive)	Various	Often national, but, in the case of some industries, international (e.g. aviation, automotive)
3b. Chambers of Commerce	(Local) government	Support commercial activity within its geographic area	'Soft'	Annual fees of businesses in its area and fees for additional services	Advertises services, but whether these are used depends on businesses, repeated short-term relationship	Support, training	Occasional help to international business when investing in the Chamber's region
3c. Innovation centres	(Local) government	Support or facilitate innovation	'Hard' and 'soft', with emphasis on the latter	Largely government funding	Approaches businesses and will work with many	Support, training, network building	Occasionally
3d. University-liaison offices	University	Earn additional income for university	Often 'hard'	University and industry	Takes initiative for cooperation, both exclusive and if possible with group of firms	Brokerage of applicable (science-based) knowledge	Often international, but contested in relation to national funding

The three key processes – articulation, alignment and learning – summarize the challenges posed by changing innovation systems; these activities are increasingly required at a network or system level. In Table 3.1 we characterize the roles of intermediaries in terms of the three key functions.

We should add at this point that roles of intermediaries will depend highly on the context. Indeed, one of the most important characteristics of the innovation systems approach is the recognition of the fact that each national innovation system is unique because of historical path dependencies (Edquist, 1997). For instance, in the USA coordination tends to occur through regulation and norms, whereas in the Netherlands the emphasis is on deliberations and consensus, which favours the instrument of covenants (the so-called Polder model; also known as the Rhineland model). The notion of path dependency has major consequences for the transferability of instruments, and by this for the whole concept of 'best practices' (Smits and Kuhlmann, 2002). Policy instruments should be in line with the characteristics of the innovation system, which will differ – sometimes quite considerably – from other innovation systems. In addition, instruments never provide ready-made solutions, but create at best the conditions that facilitate learning processes which, again, are highly context specific and difficult to transfer. Yet, experiences from one innovation system may serve as a source of inspiration for other innovation systems, as they will often face the same types of problems and challenges.

Four phases of transitions and systemic intermediaries

In this section we return to the issue of transition management and the potential contribution of systemic intermediaries. In order to do so we need to be more specific about transitions and transition management; that is, long-term systemic changes. As a first approach we will use the analogy of the well-known life cycle of industrial innovation (Tidd et al, 2001) and suggest that transitions can be said to occur in phases: exploration, take-off, entrenchment and stabilization. We are aware that this is a dangerous step. An analysis in terms of phases seems a step backwards and a denial of the progress made in the 'systems of innovation' literature. Notably, a key element in this tradition was the deconstruction of the linear model: what appeared to be linear and sequential was always a reconstruction in hindsight of a far more complicated, iterative, multi-linear process with many feedback loops. Yet, we think that phases, as a first ordering, can be useful, provided we take account of the insights about complexity, multi-linearity, feedback and co-evolution that technology and innovation studies have brought to the fore. An additional reason to introduce these phases is to better link up with the political discussion on transitions (Rotmans et al, 2000).

Consequently, we can have a closer look at the various issues and activities in the four phases of transition processes. In the following we will briefly describe these phases in terms of the key activities and processes, and suggest different roles for systemic intermediaries. Table 3.2 summarizes the main characteristics of transition processes in terms of the four distinguished phases

Table 3.2 *Systemic intermediary activities and intervention in transition phases*

	Exploration	Take-off	Embedding	Stabilization
Key notions	Search processes Creative destruction Heuristics Paradigms	Lock-in Niches Strategic niche management Dominant design Hybrid innovations Bandwagons	Momentum Building new networks Deconstructing obsolete networks Alignment Enrolment Socio-technical regimes Learning by doing	Incremental change Learning by using Economies of scale Creative destruction
Key activites	Awareness New Combinations Identification of major trends	Mobilization of relevant actors Development of coherent transition goals Support new technologies Identify niches Identify lock-in dangers	Standards Alignment Enrolment Interrelatedness Creative destruction and construction	Reflection on new goals Identify major trends Awareness
Possible roles of systemic intermediaries	Articulation of societal needs Define arenas Stimulate research Develop visions of the future Make variety in options visible Advice	Vision development Systems approach Create niches Identify bandwagons Agenda building Analysis Advise	Strategy development Clearing-house Standardization Pilot projects Project management Preventing strategic games Analysis Advice	Define new arenas Make variety in options visible Articulation of societal needs Analysis Advice
Possible instruments	Awareness technology assessment (TA) Foresight exercises Delphi methods Scenario methods	Scenario workshops (GDSS) Subsidizing Building simulations Back-casting methods Delphi methods	Strategic TA Constructive TA Strategic workshops (GDSS) Standardization Delphi methods	Delphi methods Awareness TA Foresight exercises

Note: GDSS is Group Decision Support System, a dedicated ICT application to support decision making

that are introduced above. Furthermore, the roles of systemic intermediary organizations and potential instruments are listed.

Exploration and articulation

Typically, in the exploration phase new options and varieties emerge, together with the awareness that new directions are needed. A key element here is the multitude of search processes, within laboratories and universities and between stakeholders. Innovation studies show that these search processes are non-linear: various routes and options are suggested and tried.

The search is guided by past successes and experiences, thus limiting the 'search space' and giving rise to paradigms and trajectories (Dosi et al, 1988). One of the characteristics of the exploration phase is the combination of, on the one hand, eagerness to find out what is possible and, on the other hand, resistance to change existing configurations. A second characteristic of the search processes is the relatedness of innovations. Typically, we see in the exploration phase a growing awareness of possible new, encompassing societal goals, such as a sustainable energy system or a more balanced agricultural food production.

Systemic intermediaries in this phase basically can have three functions: (1) to enhance the articulation of societal needs (that ask for a transition); (2) to make the variety of technical options more visible; and (3) to identify possible stakeholders. They sketch, as it were, the 'arena for transition'. Possible instruments here are awareness technology assessments (to define technical possibilities and societal needs), foresight exercises (to sketch technological futures), and Delphi and scenario methods.

Take-off: competition and niches

When new possibilities have been defined and explored and new futures have been expressed, a competition between trajectories can be expected. In the case of transitions and system innovations, more is at stake than the succession of product ranges; it is rather a system change. System changes often involve a change in technological paradigms (Dosi et al, 1988); that is, changes in established ways of thinking and designing. A paradigm is defined as a set of rules, examples and strategies that have proved to be successful in the past and that condition the following steps. It indicates what the relevant problems are and how to solve them, in principle. Often, a dominant design appears, that guides and inspires so-called technological trajectories (Sahal, 1981).

A great danger of the competition between the established and the new system is what the evolutionary economist calls the lock-in phenomenon (Arthur, 1988). A central concept here is the logic of 'increasing returns to adoption', which indicates that the value of a technology increases when it is adopted more widely. Sources of the lock-in are the interrelatedness of technology and the importance of learning by using, economies of scale and other characteristics of systems of technology. In the lock-in situation, thus, the established system has gained an advantage on the basis of its history, not on the basis of technical superiority. An important activity therefore, in the take-off stage, is to detect possible lock-in situations. Often, however, the lock-in situation cannot be undone without great efforts and expenses, due to sunk investments. In these circumstances it is useful to think about protected spaces or niches (Vergragt, 1988; Kemp et al, 1998) in which the new technology can be introduced. In the strategic niche management approach, a sequence of niches is designed to make learning by using possible (Rip et al, 1995).

In the take-off stage, two types of activities in which systemic intermediaries could be involved are crucial. On the one hand, the new system should get a critical mass of stakeholders, by sketching relevant futures; on the other hand, it is important to identify promising niches or to create them. Possible instruments are scenario workshops, simulations, technological road mapping, strategic niche management and back-casting projects.

Entrenchment: momentum and irreversibilities

When the various socio-technical developments of a new system are connected and reinforce each other, the new system may become irreversible: there is no way back. The various strands of development have become so intertwined that the system has a life on its own, as it were. When individual actors (such as firms) stop their support, others will continue their efforts. Thomas Hughes, in his monumental *Networks of Power* (1983), has coined the term 'momentum' to account for the life on its own of electricity networks, and his diagnosis appears to hold in many other technological systems. Irreversible developments do not go automatically in the right direction, though, and often there is a considerable space for intervention, by firms or governments. One opportunity for intervention is the legal framework, including environmental regulation and international treaties. Another opportunity, important for firms, are standards. In this phase, learning processes are crucial: Do stakeholders succeed in profiting from experiences and interactions? Here the strategic game in which they are involved is important: it may propel developments intensively or may hinder them severely.

An important role for systemic intermediaries in this stage could be to organize strategic workshops – supported by strategic technology assessments – in order to articulate and align the various perspectives and activities. Systemic intermediaries also could play an important role in identifying and preventing frustrating strategic games. Likewise, standardization should be followed critically: standardization opens ways for new innovations, but closes ways, too, that exceed the frameworks of the standard.

Stabilization: time for a change?

New systems may become so entrenched in current routines, infrastructure and legal frameworks that they have become an established system in themselves. They have become robust and can only with considerable costs and effort be made undone. Most changes will be incremental and build on economies of scale. Probably, new routes need to be explored that fall beyond the scope of the newly established system, just like in the exploration stage. In fact, in due course the question is warranted whether it is time for a new change. Systemic intermediaries should raise this question and use the same instruments as in the exploration stage.

A transition to a clean transport system

In this section we apply our arguments for the need of systemic intermediaries and their potential roles in transition processes to a relevant transition case study. In this case study we seek to illustrate that systemic intermediaries can play an important role in transition processes.

We have chosen to focus on the transition to a clean transport system and more specifically on the introduction of ZEV (which are vehicles that meet automobile emission standards as set in the LEV programme of the state of California) to replace current automotive technology in California, for three reasons. Firstly, there has been a strong increase in intensity regarding the development of low and zero emission technology in the last decade (Frenken et al, 2004), and recently a significant amount of activities have been carried out to bring these new technologies to the Californian market. The first steps of a transition process seem to be taken. These activities are the result of the LEV programme that is mandated by the Californian Air Resources Board (CARB). In this programme, CARB approved standards for LEV and ZEV that would apply from 1994 to 2003. These standards were based on the progressive introduction of transitional low emission vehicles, LEV and ultra-low emission vehicles. Furthermore, the LEV programme stated that 2 per cent of passenger cars produced and offered for sale in California in 1998 should be ZEV and this percentage was to rise gradually to 10 per cent in 2003. In 1998, CARB approved new proposals that eliminated the 1998–2003 requirements, but led to a strengthening of the regulations after 2004. As a reaction to the CARB mandates, three major options for the future car system are being developed, which are likely to be among the technologies that compete for substituting the existing internal combustion engine paradigm. The three technologies concern electric vehicles (EV), hybrid vehicles (HEV) and fuel cell vehicles (FCV).

Secondly, the leading Californian market for these types of vehicles shows the presence of a powerful systemic intermediary fulfilling roles as described in this paper. This systemic intermediary is the California Fuel Cell partnership (CaFCP), a collaboration of different actors (oil companies, car manufacturers, automotive technology developers, governmental groups) working together to demonstrate vehicle technology, fuel infrastructures, and to explore paths to commercialization. This partnership was established in January 1999.

Thirdly, a transition towards a clean transportation system is interesting to study because the transport sector is an important consumer of energy, and will therefore also be an important target for transition management initiatives and (inter)national sustainability programmes.

In the analysis we will focus on the three roles for systemic intermediaries: (1) articulation of options and demand; (2) alignment between various actors and activities; and (3) learning processes at system level.

Articulation of options and demand

In the search for zero emission car technology, several technologies are being developed by the main car manufacturers to compete in the future with the traditional internal combustion engine vehicle (ICEV), namely the EV, the HV and the FCV.

EV have an electromotor powered by a battery. It has the advantage that the electromotor has absolutely no emissions during use. Disadvantages are long recharge times and limited radius of action. Hybrid vehicles combine an electric engine and a classic internal combustion engine. It seems a typical transition technology. It has the disadvantages of not being a ZEV, but is much more efficient than the classic internal combustion engine. FCVs have the advantages of both the EV and the internal combustion engine: the car uses an electric engine and is therefore very efficient, but is also able to take in gaseous and/or fluid energy carriers, which eliminates the use of batteries. By establishing the CaFCP, articulation took place by focusing the entire mission of the partnership on one propulsion technology: the fuel cell. This choice is most likely based on the advantages of fuel cell technology on the one hand and on the difficulties in bringing this technology to the market on the other. For successful integration of this technology in the current transport system, a strong coalition of actors is necessary to develop, test and commercialize this technology. None of the participants of the CaFCP can do this by itself.

The development process of FCVs focuses on three types of vehicles: FCVs fuelled with hydrogen, methanol or conventional fuels such as gasoline (Frenken et al, 2004). To understand the implications of the fuel choice for the transition to an FCV-based transportation system, we need to discern the difference between car technology, infrastructure and environmental performance. The best fuel for a fuel cell is hydrogen. Therefore, when hydrogen is used as a fuel for an FCV, it can be fed directly to the fuel cell, and no complicated steps are necessary to create hydrogen on board the vehicle. In terms of car technology, this is the simplest process. In terms of environmental performance, hydrogen scores well due to the absence of harmful emissions produced by the vehicle (hydrogen is converted into water vapour). Furthermore, model results indicate that in well (oil drillings) to wheel (end use in the car) calculations, hydrogen is the most efficient fuel (Ogden et al, 1999). However, in terms of infrastructure, the use of hydrogen is complicated due to the introduction of a new fuel that is gaseous under normal circumstances, that needs to be compressed heavily when used, and therefore has specific handling characteristics.

The interest in gasoline is based on the fact that the current fuel-infrastructure can be maintained to fuel the FCVs. A disadvantage is the complex design of the FCV since much technology is needed to convert gasoline into hydrogen. When gasoline is used in an FCV, the environmental performance is better than that of internal combustion vehicles, but harmful emissions are still emitted from the vehicle.

The advantage of methanol is that it can be produced from biomass and that the carbon-to-energy ratio is low. In terms of environmental performance, methanol, could be a very suitable fuel when produced from renewable resources. Well-to-wheel models show that when fossil fuels are used to produce methanol, the efficiency of the methanol FCV is the lowest of the three options (Ogden et al, 1999). Just like gasoline, the fuelling of methanol requires a complex fuel conversion unit in the car in order to produce hydrogen. The adaptations in infrastructure are much smaller than for hydrogen, since methanol is a liquid that can be handled in the same way as gasoline. However, much work needs to be done to create an extra fuelling system next to the current fuel systems that are used by cars.

The three FCV types thus differ in terms of the advantages of the three technologies and the degree of change that is implied. The main relative advantage of the FCVs is their environmental performance. Some studies claim that optimized hybrid internal combustion engines are more efficient than fuel cell vehicles. Often these studies neglect the fact that fuel cells are only at the very beginning of their learning curve. High-efficiency gains can be expected when massive amounts of fuel cell vehicles are brought to the market.

To describe the necessary changes in the innovation trajectory of these FCVs, in Figure 3.2 we distinguish between the technical and organizational complexity.

In terms of required organizational changes, the hydrogen FCV is considered as most complex and the gasoline FCV as least complex. The necessary change in the fuel infrastructure is large for hydrogen (gaseous fuel, handling of pressurized gas, new fuelling equipment, new trucks, new pipelines, different know-how) and small for gasoline FCVs (no change in fuel infrastructure). For methanol a new infrastructure needs to be developed as well, but since methanol is a liquid, the infrastructure strongly resembles the current fuel infrastructure. Next to the infrastructure aspects, introduction of any FCV will require changes in know-how of vehicle technology in repair facilities, and users will experience different driving characteristics. In terms of technological complexity, the gasoline and methanol FCVs are most complicated due to the onboard reforming of the fuels. All three vehicle types are of course complex because they require new electric drive trains. The onboard storage of hydrogen is also different from traditional technology, but is considered less intricate than onboard reforming.

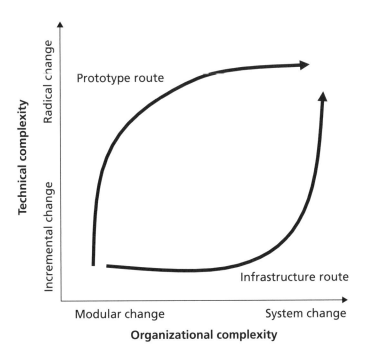

Figure 3.2 *Positioning of three FCVs in terms of technical and organizational complexity*

After choosing fuel cell technology, the CaFCP articulated further options and demand by commissioning the study 'Bringing fuel cell technology to the market: Scenarios and challenges with fuel alternatives'. Based on this report and a round table discussion, the CaFCP decided that the first FCVs demonstrated in the market initially will use hydrogen as their fuel source (CaFCP, 2001). In addition, the CaFCP is currently generating public awareness for the vehicles in outreach events and verifying public perceptions with annual surveys. The CaFCP sees the generation of public awareness, confidence and enthusiasm for FCVs as the primary method to build a positive image, and to support a customer demand for the vehicles (CaFCP, 2001).

Now that we know that the CaFCP has selected one of the potential options to develop further, the question arises whether this decision is really made by the partnership or whether it is simply an extension of the individual strategies of the participants. We analysed the individual strategy of the main participants by means of a patent analysis, by which we study the dynamics of the research focus regarding new car technology for the past 20 years (from Frenken et al, 2004). Based on this patent analysis, we can conclude that at system level no choice has been made by the car producers for a specific fuel for FCVs. The development process still seems to be in the divergent phase.

Based on this, we can conclude that the efforts of the CaFCP really differ from the strategies of the individual partners. Their focus is on a diverging development strategy, while their coordinated action in the CaFCP strongly focuses on one single option that is developed further.

Alignment between actors

The Californian case shows an increasing alignment between actors. The alignment processes that take place within the CaFCP are illustrated in Figure 3.3, which gives an overview of the participants in the CaFCP.

Figure 3.3 illustrates that four actor groups collaborate in the partnership: fuel cell producers, car manufacturers, oil companies and government bodies. Note that in this collaboration most elements of an innovation system can be recognized: technology development, conversion of technology into marketable products, compatibility of technology with infrastructure and regulation. Around the activities of the CaFCP, four types of alignment processes can be distinguished. Firstly, the setting up of the partnership is an alignment process in itself. It creates a common vision of future goals, it frames expectations regarding potential routes and creates awareness that more than one party is needed to successfully introduce FCVs in the market. Secondly, the activities within the collaboration have led to alignment. The centralized decision-making process regarding new experiments stimulates consensus on the important bottlenecks that need to be solved and on the best options to do so. Thirdly, the CaFCP is a dynamic partnership as new actors may join. The number of actors has grown over the last two years and this reinforces the alignment between a growing number of actors. Fourthly, alignment processes occur between the CaFCP and other actors that have an important role to play in the successful implementation of FCVs. These actors are related to the partnership as associate partners; these include two

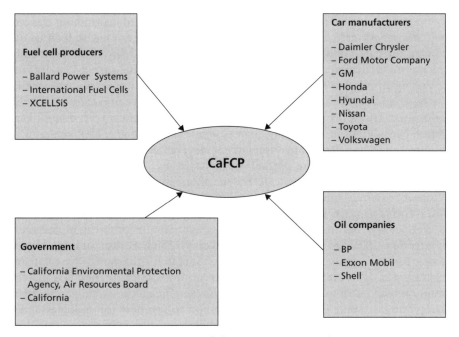

Figure 3.3 *Overview of the participants in the CaFCP*

hydrogen gas suppliers, three hydrogen-fueling stations, one methanol fuel supplier and three bus transit agencies.

Learning processes

In the Californian partnership, important learning processes take place and are indeed seen by the partnership itself as crucial ingredients. All four main goals of the partnership relate to learning. The first goal is to 'demonstrate vehicle technology by operating and testing the vehicles under real world conditions in California', and intends to create learning processes about vehicle performance, such as radius of action, filling behaviour, driving behaviour and reliability. These test data are important input parameters in the technology development process. The feedback loop of experiment data ensures learning processes necessary for successful technology development. Goal two is to 'demonstrate the viability of alternative fuel infrastructure technology', and refers to learning processes about the interaction between fuel cell technology and fuel infrastructure. These learning processes are of the utmost importance to make a large-scale introduction of FCVs possible. They concern the behaviour of hydrogen gas in transport, filling and storage in cars. Hydrogen is stored cryogenically at very low temperatures and is converted to gaseous hydrogen (under very high pressure) to deliver the fuel to vehicles. Also, the handling of methanol needs experimentation since the acute toxicity of the chemical requires extreme care when handled. The third goal, to 'explore the paths to commercialization', requires learning processes about potential problems and solutions. And, finally, goal four is to 'increase public awareness, preparing the market for commercialization'. This requires feedback mechanisms to learn about the created awareness at a certain time. The education programme is focused on proving the capabilities, benefits, reliability and affordability of fuel cell technology for vehicular uses. Learning processes are necessary to adapt the marketing strategy to the general opinion on fuel cell technology by the public.

In summary, in the commercial introduction of fuel cell technology in the Californian transport sector the CaFCP plays an important role. The CaFCP can be considered, in our terms, as a systemic intermediary, as it operates at system level in its attempts to stimulate the development of technologies, infrastructure and markets. The partnership is based on a voluntary collaboration of actors. The establishment of the partnership is not due to profitable prospects or environmental concern, but relates to the regulation of the state of California that has set strict norms regarding the introduction of clean vehicle technology. This so-called zero emission mandate forced car manufacturers to introduce ZEVs to the California market by 2003. Due to this mandate a strong common interest in a successful introduction programme by car manufacturers was created. The Californian prototype route has led to the situation that car manufacturers do not have sufficient knowledge about the energy infrastructure and aim for cooperation to test new technologies under real-world conditions. Therefore, the establishment of a partnership could be successful. Without the regulation measures of the state of California, however, it is unlikely that a similar partnership, with the same drive for success, would have emerged in the short term. This case, therefore, also shows that systemic intermediaries can be successful in bringing strategic innovations and transition processes closer (especially in the prototype route), but that it is unlikely that they can speed up the process without strong urgency of the key actors in the transition process. Systemic intermediaries are a catalyst in a chemical reaction, as it were. They speed up reactions that thermodynamically are feasible. However, if the thermodynamics of a reaction are not right, no catalyst will be able to get the reaction going to form a stable new product. This suggests that success of systemic intermediaries may be larger in the prototype route since it involves large initial investments of the individual stakeholders, which increases their commitment and urgency.

Conclusions

In this chapter we introduced the notion of systemic intermediaries in order to highlight the emergence of a new type of intermediary organization that seeks to function at system or network level, in contrast to traditional intermediary organizations that operate mainly bilaterally. Their emergence is relevant in the light of the challenges that arise from so-called transitions to more sustainable production and consumption. In many domains these long-term and complex socio-technical changes require the coordinated effort of industry, policy-makers, research institutes, intermediary organizations and others.

In order to study the complex interplay of these parties we used the systems of innovation framework, which stresses the interactions and interconnections in innovative trajectories. A review of recent changes in innovation systems points to the need of more systemic efforts and clarifies the potential of a new type of intermediary. The articulation of needs and options, the alignment of relevant actors, and the support of processes of learning and experimenting, were identified as major functions of systemic intermediaries.

We specified these functions, and the concomitant roles, through a phase model of transitions, in which we identified key activities and processes, which, in their turn, suggest systemic efforts and, consequently, possible roles and instruments for systemic intermediaries. The four phases require different forms of articulation, alignment and learning.

More extensively, we analysed the Californian initiatives towards introduction and diffusion of LEVs and ZEVs, and discussed the important role of the CaFCP in this process. We conclude that CaFCP has been powerful in its articulation, alignment and learning activities, and can indeed be seen as a systemic intermediary. We also note that its relative success benefits from urgency that has been built up by the strict Californian legislation. In addition, the Californian route via huge initial investments in new technological solutions adds to the commitment of the participants to support and accept coordinated efforts. To put it in more general terms, the efforts of systemic intermediaries in encompassing systemic innovations are useful and probably necessary, but not sufficient. The management of transitions asks for this new type of intermediary, but their efficacy will depend on the specific make-up of the innovation system at stake.

Acknowledgements

This is a substantially shortened and revised version of 'Roles of systemic intermediaries in transition processes', *International Journal of Innovation Management*, vol 7, no 3 (September 2003) pp1–33. We are grateful for permission to publish this revised version.

References

Arthur, B. (1988) 'Competing technologies', in G. Dosi (ed) *Technological Change and Economic Development*, Pinter, London and New York, pp590–607

Barré, R., Gibbons, M., Maddox, J., Martin, B. and Papon, P. (1997) *Science in tomorrow's Europe*, Economica International, London

California Fuel Cell Partnership (2001) 'CaFCP position paper', CaFCP, Sacramento, CA

Dosi, G. et al (1988) *Technical Change and Economic Theory*, Pinter, London and New York

Edquist, C. (ed) (1997) *Systems of Innovation: Technologies, Institutions and Organization*, Pinter, London

Frenken, K., Hekkert, M.P. and Godfroij, P. (2004) 'R&D portfolios in environmentally friendly automotive propulsion: Variety, competition and policy implications', *Technological Forecasting and Social Change*, vol 71, no 5, pp485–507

Gibbons, M., Limoges, C., Nowotny, H., Schwartzman, S., Scott, P. and Trow, M. (1994) *The New Production of Knowledge: The Dynamics of Science and Research in Contemporary Societies*, Sage Publications, London

Hughes, T.P. (1983) *Networks of Power: Electrification in Western Society 1880–1930*, Johns Hopkins University Press, Baltimore, MD

Jacobsson, S. and Johnson, A. (2000) 'The diffusion of renewable energy technology: an analytical framework and key issues for research', *Energy Policy*, vol 28, no 9, pp625–640.

Jacobsson, S. and Bergek, A. (2004) 'Transforming the energy sector: The evolution of technological systems in renewable energy technology'. *Industrial and Corporate Change*, vol 13, no 5, pp815–849

Kemp, R., Schot, J. and Hoogma, R. (1998) 'Regime shifts to sustainability through processes of niche formation: The approach of strategic niche management', *Technology Analysis and Strategic Management*, vol 10, no 2, pp175–195

Kuhlmann, S., Boekholt, P., Georghiou, L., Guy, K., Heraud, J-A., Laredo, P., Lemola, P., Loverdidge, D., Luukkonen, T., Polt, W., Rip, A., Sanz-Menendez, L. and Smits, R. (1999) *Distributed Intelligence in Complex Innovation Systems*. Final report of the Advanced Science and Technology Policy Planning Network (ASTPP), Karlsruhe, http://mpra.ub.uni-muenchen.de/6426/1/Final.pdf (accessed 15 September 2010)

Lundvall, B.A. (ed) (1992) *National Systems of Innovation: Towards a Theory of Innovation and Interactive Learning*, Pinter, London

Lundvall, B. and Borras, S. (1998) *The Globalising Learning Economy: Implications for Innovation Policy*, Office for official publications of the European Communities, Luxembourg

Metcalfe, J. (1995) 'The economic foundations of technology policy: Equilibrium and evolutionary perspectives', in P. Stoneman (ed) *Handbook of Economics of Innovation and Technology Change*, Blackwell, Oxford, pp409–512

Nelson, R.R. (ed) (1993) *National Systems of Innovation*, Oxford University Press, Oxford

Ogden, J.M., Steinbugler, M.M. and Kreutz, T.G. (1999) 'A comparison of hydrogen, methanol and gasoline as fuels for fuel cell vehicles: Implications for vehicle design and infrastructure development', *Journal of Power Sources*, vol 79, no 2, pp143–168

Rip, A., Misa, T.J. and Schot, J. (1995) *Managing Technology in Society*, Pinter, London

Rotmans, J., Kemp, R., van Asselt, M., Geels, F., Verbong, G. and Molendijk, K. (2000) *Transities & Transitiemanagement: De Casus van een Emissiearme Energievoorzieing*, International Centre for Integrative Studies, Maastricht

Sahal, P. (1981) *Partners of Technological Innovation*, Addison-Wesley, Reading, MA

Smits, R. and Kuhlmann, S. (2002) 'Strengthening interfaces in innovation systems: Rationale, concepts and (new) instruments', Report prepared on behalf of the EC STRATA Workshop 'New challenges and new responses for S&T policies in Europe', session 4: 'New instruments for the implementation of S&T policy', Brussels, 22–23 April

Tidd, J., Bessant, J. and Pavitt, K. (2001) *Managing Innovation: Integrating Technological, Market and Organizational Change*, 2nd edn, Wiley, Chichester

Vergragt, P.J. (1988) 'The social shaping of industrial innovations', *Social Studies of Science*, vol 18, pp483–513

4
Cities Mediating Technological Transitions

Mike Hodson and Simon Marvin

Introduction

Cities have historically been powerfully shaped by the development of key infrastructural technologies. Complex socio-technical systems of water, energy, transport, communications and waste make the concept of the contemporary city possible (Graham and Marvin, 1996, 2001). While there have been dramatic changes in the social organization of infrastructure and drivers shaping its development, the physical infrastructure of the city is often slow to change. Cities face the challenge of shaping complex technological transitions – refitting new and often hybrid energy infrastructures, laying new ICT systems over old infrastructures, through road pricing and control technologies, introducing decentralized new and renewable technologies into centralized systems (see Graham and Marvin, 1996; Guy and Marvin, 2001; Guy et al, 2001). Yet we lack a systemic way of understanding the role of places in shaping such socio-technical transitions (Eames et al, 2006; Hodson and Marvin, 2006).

Technological transitions (TT) and transition management (TM) approaches have generated considerable interest in academic and policy circles in recent years (Rotmans and Kemp, 2002; Geels, 2004; Kemp and Loorbach, 2005), where, in terms of a loose definition, a 'transition can be defined as a gradual, continuous process of structural change within a society or culture' (Rotmans et al, 2001, p2). The development of these approaches may be seen as a response to the complexities, uncertainties and problems which confront many Western societies, in organizing 'sustainably' various aspects of energy, water and transport infrastructure. The systemic nature of this challenge highlights the involvement – in the functioning of a particular system and any subsequent transition – of multiple actors or 'stakeholders' across different local, national and international levels of activity. With this in mind, such problems become difficult to 'solve' and 'solutions' are seen to require systemic innovation, rather than individual or episodic responses. The point being that 'these problems are system inherent and the solution lies in creating different systems or transforming existing ones' (Kemp and Loorbach, 2005, p125).

While transitions approaches acknowledge the interplay and interpenetration of different landscape (macro), regime (meso) and niche (micro) levels, they say little explicitly about the role of the city and regional scale in processes of transition. This is problematic to us for three reasons. Firstly, a significant level is not explicitly nor adequately dealt with in an approach that does take the need for multi-level analysis seriously. Secondly, responsibilities for key aspects of technology, innovation and competitiveness policy have been devolved from the nation state to city and regional scales. Finally, at the city and regional scale, significant efforts are now being made to shape strategically technological transitions through strategic intermediaries that mediate relations systemically between technological potentials and local context. Consequently, a key scale is currently inadequately conceptualized or perhaps at worst missing from an approach that is generating new insights into technological transitions.

The contribution we want to make to the debate is to develop an understanding of the role of the urban and regional scale within technological transitions. Critically, we ask in what ways and to what extent cities and regions can shape technological transitions. We address this question in the following steps: section two (Understanding transitions approaches and cities and regions) compares the treatment of level within two broad multi-level approaches to technological change; section three (Sensitizing technological transitions to cities and regions) examines how cities and regions shape transitions by focusing on the critical role of place-based intermediaries that are established to work between technological possibilities and local context; section four (Understanding intermediaries, cities/regions and technological transitions: the case of London's hydrogen economy) then takes the example of hydrogen energy economy development in London as a means of exploring London's emerging systemic transition, and the role of strategic intermediaries in building visions and translating these into action; and finally, we offer conclusions around the key question of the extent to which cities and regions can shape technological transitions.

Understanding transitions approaches and cities and regions

This section compares and contrasts the treatment of level within two multi-level approaches to technological change – first through technological transitions and second through urban and regional governance approaches – in order to start building an enlarged conceptual understanding of the active role of place within technological transitions.

Multiple levels within technological transitions

TT is a multi-level approach that focuses on three interconnected levels – the landscape, regime and niche to 'understand the complex dynamics of socio-technical change' (Geels, 2002a, p1259). Firstly, the concept of landscape is important in seeking to understand the broader 'conditions', 'environment' and 'pressures' for technological transitions – such as economic growth and climate change that operate at the macro level (Geels, 2002b). Secondly, the concept of regime operates at the meso level, and relates to existing technologies being intertwined within a configuration of institutions, practices, regulations and so on that impose a logic, regularity and varying degrees of path dependencies on technological change. These can include scientific knowledge, engineering practices, regulatory requirements, institutions and infrastructures (Hoogma et al, 2002). Finally, there are socio-technical niches operating at a micro level which are understood as 'protected spaces in which actors learn about novel technologies and their uses' (Geels, 2002b, p365).

Technological transitions are premised not on radical regime shifts, but through a 'stepwise process of reconfiguration' (Geels, 2002a, p1272). Regime shifts may take place over a considerable period of time. Geels (2002a, p1262) points out that TT involves the linking of 'multiple technologies', and that the use and development of innovations in different domains and contexts see an accumulation of niches – an important mechanism in gradual regime shift. Early linkages between niche and regime may rely on 'link up with established technologies, often to solve particular bottlenecks' (Geels, 2002a, p1271). There is an important focus on ideas of technological add-on and hybridization, where existing and new technologies 'form some sort of symbiosis' (Geels, 2002a, p1271).

Although we are sympathetic to technological transitions' commitment to a multi-level analysis and its insights into managed socio-technical change, we have also struggled to conceptually and empirically understand the role of cities and regions in transitions. While the multi-level approach is useful in understanding the distributed nature of technological transitions, our critical concern is that institutions, social interests and knowledge are often assumed to be 'out there' (Geels, 2004, p902). Place is implicit within the threefold division of landscape, regime and niche. This then begs the questions of whether cities and regions can establish their own regimes within which niches and transitions are able to exist.

Bringing cities and regions to technological transitions

We can find ways of addressing these questions by stepping outside the TT framework to look at the implications of more critical approaches to technological change that specifically address the urban and regional. Consequently, TT would clearly benefit from an appreciation of 'multi-level governance' and the politics of scale in understanding attempts to shape transitions in place. Key to this is the development of a conceptual framework that permits us to analyse the entangled relations and interactions of governance at different scales which inform potential transitions. This is particularly significant in times of increased 'globalization' and neo-liberalism, where the changing role of the state and issues of multi-level governance raise a whole series of issues not only about how we might think about the city and region, but also the interrelationships between regions: the local, national and supranational. How do we understand cities and regions through multi-level governance in relation to the place-based shaping of technological transitions?

Critical to understanding these shifts are changes in the international economy, through the reconfiguration of national and international financial and political institutions (see Aglietta, 1979) over the last three decades that have generated neo-liberal pressures for increased 'competitiveness', 'entrepreneurialism' and 'innovation'. This raises issues related to both governance and technology; in particular, the changing role of the nation-state is important, where we are seeing a shift from the Welfare State to a Competitive State (Jessop, 2002). The competitive state has a 'concern with technological change, innovation and enterprise and its attempt to develop new techniques of government and governance to these ends' (Jessop, 2002, p96).

These structural shifts have three significant implications for our understanding of cities and regions in technological transitions. Firstly, to highlight the pervasiveness of notions of 'competitiveness', and the ways in which this is manifest in wider 'pressures for' city and regional transformation through science, technology and innovation (see Fuller et al, 2004). Cities and regions develop positions on technological potentials to position themselves in the global race for economic competitiveness. Secondly, city and regional analyses need to take account of a complex interplay of relationships at various political scales. Critically, this requires 'an appreciation of the complex geometry of power and the political and cultural struggles through which societies assume their regional shape' (MacLeod and Jones, 2001, p670). Cities and regions are differentially positioned within existing social, political, economic and ecological relations (see Bulkeley and Betsill, 2005), which delimits their capacity to shape technological transitions. Finally, cities and regions are clearly constructed in an unfolding and structured set of social, political and economic relationships. This highlights the importance of seeing city and regional development in relation to technological transitions not only through the lens of 'endogenous' institutional interrelationships, but also in terms of the influence of, and relationships with, the nation-state. Cities and regions actively and strategically work both internally and externally in developing the resources, networks and relationships to actively shape technological transitions.

In summary, landscape pressures (e.g. macro economic trends, climate change, resource constraints) are interpreted in city and regional contexts through the collective anticipations, responses and reactions to these types of pressures of networks of institutions and individuals. These networks inform the re-envisioning of places. We should understand this not in respect of a naive emphasis on free agency, but in terms of the prior trajectories – the logics or path dependencies in other words – of city and regional contexts and the networks that constitute them. In this view the role of cities and regions in transitions is linked to their capability to adapt and transform through reconfiguring and adjusting urban and regional institutions of governance to technological transitions. The key question this raises is: What are the implications of this analysis of the re-emergence of cities and regions for our understanding of technological transitions?

Sensitizing technological transitions to cities and regions

A 'multi-level governance' approach allows us to refocus on three sets of issues that are currently weakly conceptualized and understood within existing TT approaches (see, for instance, the sympathetic critique by Berkhout et al, 2003).

Firstly, there is the issue of the dominance of normative visions – a key step in transition processes – and the degree of problematization that is often lacking from transitions accounts. The critical insight from the 're-emergence of cities and regions' is the prevalence of the particular visions perhaps most powerfully embodied in the notion of the race for technological progress and economic competitiveness. This means that the processes through which visions are produced require a focus on whose views inform such visions and, importantly who is excluded, underpinned by what forms of expectations and aspirations.

This second issue, then, relates to what is often seen as a key shortcoming of transitions approaches – understanding the negotiations and unfolding relations of actors in transitions. Working through cities and regions allows us to look more critically at processes of interaction across scales in a way that can acknowledge differential positioning, power relations and varying capacities and potential for adapting local contexts.

Finally, it also adds to our understanding of the role of government in 'creating the conditions' for transitions. Although the nation-state is still important, so also, increasingly, are various other levels and scales of governance that are related often in complex and different ways in various contexts. We increasingly need to acknowledge the role of city and regional scales in shaping technological transitions as part of a wider devolution of responsibility, but not necessarily powers, to reshape the technological and economic competitiveness of places.

Mediating between cities/regions and technological transitions

Cities and regions often develop specialist intermediaries (Marvin and Medd, 2004) who seek to shape relationships strategically between technology and local context. Intermediaries position themselves to have a particular role in literally intermediating between sets of different social interests (and technology), to produce an outcome that would not have been possible, or as effective, without their involvement. The role of intermediaries in shaping technological transitions has been examined by van Lente et al (2003) (see Chapter 3). Within a transitions context, intermediaries play key roles for three reasons. Firstly, intermediaries play an important role as brokers, by connecting, translating and facilitating flows of knowledge between different parties (van Lente et al, 2003). Secondly, they cite a variety of organizations that function as intermediaries: knowledge-intensive business services, research and technology organizations, and so on. Finally, they argue that due to the changing characteristics of innovation systems, namely a move to systemic transitions, so too there is a shift towards the emergence of 'systemic intermediaries'. In contrast to intermediaries that work primarily in one-to-one interactions – that is, bi-laterally – these new systemic intermediaries work at the network level and offer support at the strategic level. The functions that these intermediaries perform will broadly involve 'articulation of options and demands', 'alignment of actors and possibilities' and support 'learning processes'. The critical issue for us is how place-based systemic intermediaries established by cities and regions attempt to purposively shape and manage technological transitions.

Intermediaries in cities and regions: how do they work?

With the increasing responsibilities devolved to cities and regions to shape technology and innovation, specialist network intermediaries are being developed within places to shape technological transitions. These intermediaries are usually cross-sectoral in composition, network-based (rather than bi-lateral), with a focus on a broad technological sector (rather than a single technology), and can be characterized as transition managers within a particular local context. There are two key sets of activities that characterize their work. The first is the work involved in developing place-based images of technological transitions. Intermediaries develop a collective but particular understanding of existing city and regional contexts (either from 'within' or 'outside' the city and region), and they position themselves between technological possibilities and local contexts to rethink city and regional contexts through technological transitions. In doing this, they identify (multiple) points of intervention within existing and new systems of provision (between systems of production and consumption). In the language of transitions they develop a 'vision' of a transition of the city or region, which takes (a particular) account and attribution of city and regional history, and outlines a vision of transition. Visions are not fixed and will change over time with the variety of social interests that become involved.

The second role is in the governance of place-based transitions. Intermediaries build social networks of actors who either position themselves favourably in relation to the debate or who are positioned by the intermediary. These actors can operate at various scales (local, national, international scales) and may be public or private, governmental or non-governmental. The potential involvement of multiple actors needs acknowledgement that they are embedded in particular institutional settings with associated institutional enablement and constraints, and views of the city or region, in pursuing their expectations (i.e. they are not 'free agents'). This raises the possibility of a variety of expectations (see van Lente, 1993) of city and regional technological transitions from multiple institutional positions. In short, intermediaries 'manage' processes and governance of city and regional transitions.

Understanding intermediaries, cities/regions and technological transitions: the case of London's hydrogen economy

Our argument is that transitions unfold in particular places and that places are differentially positioned in terms of their ability to inform transitions. The concept of systemic intermediaries allows us to address the extent to which particular places – here cities and regions – strategically shape technological transitions. In doing this, we suggest that understanding the early stages of transitions in particular cities and regions mean we address the following three issues. Firstly, outlining the vision that has been developed for a particular place-based transition. Secondly, to understand the negotiations of these visions including the social actors involved and the expectations from different positions embodied in them – this requires a focus not only on 'endogenous' relationships within cities and regions, but also on the 'exogenous' relationships with national government, private capital and so on. Finally, both these steps require a focus on the mediation so we are interested in the role intermediary organizations play between visions and territorial manifestations of these visions.

We approach these three issues through a case study of recent attempts to position London as a hydrogen energy economy.[1] There have been numerous attempts to define the hydrogen economy (see Rifkin, 2002; Romm, 2006), which may be broadly understood as the widespread use of hydrogen as a fuel for transport, heat and electricity generation, and there have been enthusiastic attempts to develop a hydrogen economy in the London City region (Mayor of London, 2004a).

Outlining two emerging visions

Our focus is now on outlining the two dominant emerging visions of attempts to re-imagine London through hydrogen: (1) 'the progressive urban governance of London'; and (2) 'the politics of the showcase city'.

Emerging vision 1: envisioning the progressive urban governance of London

New governance arrangements since 2000, and in particular the role of the mayor Ken Livingstone,[2] has seen Livingstone keen to position London as a world leader in re-fashioning 'progressive' urban governance through a series of statutory and non-statutory strategies that address issues of climate change and air quality (Mayor of London, 2002), noise (Mayor of London, 2004c), economic development (Mayor of London, 2005), energy (Mayor of London, 2004a) and transport (Mayor of London, 2001). A central issue in terms of energy strategy was increasing renewable energy generation at the expense of fossil fuels, with an emphasis on 'cleaner' energy generation including encouraging community-level and small-scale combined heat and power (CHP) systems. In particular, the mayor focused on the introduction and increased 'take-up' of 'cleaner' road vehicles, 'cleaner fuels' and 'low emission zones' in specified parts of London, and, in the 'longer term', increasing take-up of zero emission vehicles, which would include hydrogen fuel cell vehicles. This 'inward' focus also sat alongside a more 'outward'-facing view of London positioning itself as a 'world leader' and making 'London a leading city for sustainable energy' (Mayor of London, 2004a, p8).

A senior policy advisor to the mayor with a close understanding of the mayor's thinking on these issues argued: 'He [the mayor] wanted to be at the forefront of the world. He wanted to be seen as the city in the world that's leading on the hydrogen economy.'[3] In being an 'early mover', however, a substantial amount of work is required to realize this objective (Mayor of London, 2004b). In particular, the proposal is that transport, which accounts for around 20 per cent of energy consumption in London, could underpin the development of a hydrogen economy, particularly given the large number of fleet vehicles and public transport. This could exploit the 'large potential market for hydrogen' (Mayor of London, 2004b, p86) and also the development of re-fuelling infrastructure that 'could "fan out" to the rest of the country' (Mayor of London, 2004b, p86). In this sense, London is represented as not only a 'world leader', but also as a national exemplar of the development of the hydrogen economy.

Emerging vision 2: envisioning the politics of the showcase city

A second, key emerging vision we characterize as the politics of the showcase city focused on how a future London was envisioned by a variety of actors 'exogenous' to the city. The Clean Urban Transport Europe (CUTE) initiative was underpinned by a 'public–private partnership', established at the end of 2001, and involved the demonstration, over two years, of 27 fuel cell-powered buses in nine European cities. The initiative was part-funded by the European Commission and the commercial interests in the partnership. The network built around the initiative was brought together by a large automotive producer, Daimler-Chrysler, and included a central role for the energy provider BP and also BOC as a supplier of hydrogen.

Cities were viewed as places within which combinations of technologies could be demonstrated under 'different operating conditions' to be found in Europe. This would also facilitate the 'design, construction and operation of the necessary infrastructure for hydrogen production and re-fuelling stations'. The types of data to be 'extracted' included 'safety, standardization and operating behaviour of production for mobile and stationary use, and exchange of experiences including bus operation under differing conditions among the numerous participating companies for replication' (European Commission, nd, p2). The London demonstration, which commenced in 2003, included three fuel cell buses operating on the streets of London. In doing this, understanding the politics of the showcase city in London required not only an appreciation of the networks of multinational capital, the European Commission and their expectations and aspirations, but also the relationships that were negotiated with the organizational and institutional context within London, including London Buses and its operator First Group and the Energy Savings Trust.

Intermediaries and negotiating London hydrogen futures

The development of and attempts to translate into action these two visions of hydrogen economy development in London were negotiated within the context of two strategic intermediaries: the London Hydrogen Partnership and a public–private partnership of the CUTE initiative.

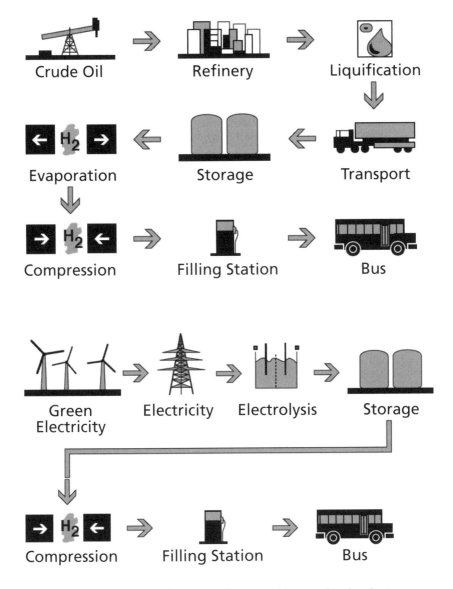

Figure 4.1 *Cities as showcases for assemblages of technologies*

The London Hydrogen Partnership as a strategic intermediary

The vision of London as a world leader in progressive urban governance can be understood in terms of the possibilities and constraints on the relatively new role of mayor to develop strategic agendas of personal interest. This needs to be set within the context where resources available to the mayor were generally low (Rydin et al, 2004) and, crucially, where there was a heavy reliance on central government for funding resources (Sweeting, 2003). With this in mind, the mayor, Ken Livingstone, attempted to define his role particularly through strategies that addressed themes of environmental concern, economic regeneration, social equity and a 'world' leadership role for London. In attempting to move from these aspirations to being, as one of Livingstone's policy advisors told us, 'the city in the world that's leading on the hydrogen economy', there was a key role for policy advisors in 'making it happen'. This required understanding and locating the 'relevant people' in the Greater London Authority (GLA), communicating the mayor's aspirations outlining that 'this is what the mayor wants to happen'.

Fleshing this process out accounts in many ways for the development and structures of the London Hydrogen Partnership (LHP) – which encapsulates many aspects of a strategic intermediary – through which endeavours were being made to develop a London hydrogen economy. Attempts to develop hydrogen and fuel cell initiatives, which address the mayoral agenda, have been undertaken under the auspices of the LHP since April 2002 (LHP, 2002). The LHP was organized (see Figure 4.2) around a steering group (chaired by the Deputy Mayor), a forum (a meeting and networking forum) and five task groups (Stationary Applications; Transport Applications; Infrastructure & Renewables; Safety & Regulation; Skills, Training & Communications), with the broad spread of interest involved providing a context within which London was positioning itself as 'prepared' for the multifarious possibilities of the hydrogen economy.

The underpinnings of the LHP were first of all via 'internal' GLA discussions as to what the 'relevance' of a hydrogen economy might be to the GLA and how might a hydrogen economy be achieved through 'partnership'. The role of 'partnership' was central to the constitution of a London hydrogen economy, where an action plan became the embodiment of and embodied by a broad-base of different social interests. This, according to a GLA official centrally involved in the development of the LHP, placed an emphasis on the drafting and re-drafting of the Action Plan as a 'long-term visioning document ... to try to shape everybody's thinking and bring everybody along'. The view was that an action plan would not only set out what a hydrogen economy could look like and sketch steps to get there, but also be fundamental to ensuring that 'we [achieved] consensus'. This needs to be understood in a context where the role of mayor and the GLA were relatively undefined and required 'getting them [institutions of the GLA] up and running, as much as making any bold or radical policy statements', and that 'this – as much as any genuflection on Livingstone's part – is ensuring that he pursue an ideologically uncontroversial policy of co-operation and partnership within London' (McNeill, 2002, p77). This search for 'consensus' captured the interpenetration of actors from various scales of political activity, which included representation from the GLA and national government departments and agencies, business and industry and academia, predicated on and lubricated by the proximity of national, city-regional and multinational political, academic and business interests in the London goldfish bowl.

CUTE: 'public–private partnerships' as strategic intermediaries

The vision of London as a showcase city is informed by a small number of supranational and multinational capital interests. Both Daimler-Chrysler, as a leading automobile producer, and BP, in its role as a petroleum supplier, viewed the CUTE initiative as providing a context within which 'alternative' technologies could be developed, demonstrated and showcased in a variety of urban contexts. For BP, according to a leading member of its Hydrogen Team, 'as an energy company hydrogen presents both a massive opportunity and potentially a massive threat to our business if we don't play it in the right way. So a lot of what we do in the Hydrogen Team is to manage risk for BP.' This was particularly important within the frame and discourse of a competitive 'race' among automobile and petroleum companies, and informed anticipations about future commercial trajectories that hydrogen and fuel cells were seen as one set of technologies among a range of possible future technologies.

In terms of the key role of the European Commission in the CUTE initiative, it had a focus not only on a targets approach to CO_2 emissions reduction, but also in promoting the utilization of hydrogen and fuel cell technologies and in understanding different configurations of technologies in contexts. The coalition of interests brought together in a 'public–private partnership', as a strategic intermediary, was a means of developing and highlighting 'European competitiveness' in what was seen to be a key strategic area, but also in a 'Europe-wide' focus that informed and fed back into

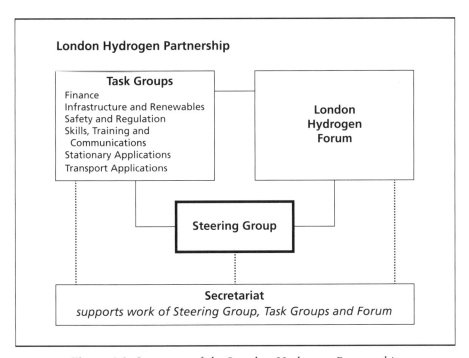

Figure 4.2 *Structure of the London Hydrogen Partnership*

the unfolding development of an EU hydrogen and fuel cells strategy (European Commission, 2003). In undertaking the CUTE initiative, an official from the European Union's (EU's) Directorate-General for Energy and Transport (DGTREN) highlighted the crucial importance of involving multi-national capital in the project, claiming the initiative 'wouldn't have happened at all were it not for the likes of Daimler-Chrysler, and then, later on the energy companies driving it forwards and putting the whole proposal together ... and then putting out to the cities for interest if you like'. The claim was made that multiple fuel cell buses and associated infrastructures needed, in a series of highly 'visible' cities, to be 'tested out' under a 'variety of conditions'.

Consequences: negotiating a vision within London and a vision from outside of London

The key issue these – both competing and complementary – visions of a future London, in relation to the hydrogen economy raise, is in the way in which the strategic intermediary provided the context within which the particular politics and values of multiple social interests were negotiated and translated into a collective view of the role of the city in technological transitions.

Although a vision of progressive urban governance acknowledged the importance of London's position as a world city in a 'globalized' economy, its emphasis was largely on the politics of urban governance 'within' London – or on developing a politics of progressive urban governance, of 'inclusivity' and 'partnership', within a context of globalization. In the case of the hydrogen economy, this was underpinned by a strategic intermediary that attempted to create a context within which various social interests from London's civil society could develop dialogue and a position around translating the hydrogen economy from aspiration into a material reality. In respect of the LHP, this meant bringing together representatives of London's political institutions and regulatory interests, as well as those of public services and academia. It also meant engaging with representatives of multinational capital to develop a progressive urban politics primarily from within London.

Following the setting-up of the LHP there were a small number of material manifestations of hydrogen demonstration projects (e.g. a hydrogen generator powering the Christmas tree lights in Trafalgar Square in 2004), but also a number of cultural events (such as a public lecture by the hydrogen economy 'guru' Jeremy Rifkin). Yet in many ways attempts to affect a move from a vision to 'delivering' on the agenda of progressive urban governance was seen as problematic. This was largely due to a 'limited engagement' by multinational capital, in the view of a GLA official closely involved in the development of the GLA or the over inclusivity of the GLA according to a representative of multinational capital who sat on the LHP. The GLA official told us that the private sector 'see the public sector putting the majority of the funding in and they know when to come into make things happen. And in a sense the wrong people have been in the room for that.'

One view from the Multinational Corporation (MNC) representative was to claim, pejoratively, that the LHP was a 'talking shop'. This source blamed the inclusivity of an array of social interests in developing a future London hydrogen economy and a 'lack of financial resources' allocated to the initiative, and suggested that the hydrogen economy was a 'big boys' game'; the strong inference being one of the desirability and indeed necessity of a narrowly instrumental view of a London hydrogen economy as the domain of multinational capital, rather than of engaging with the inclusivity of a politics of progressive urban governance. This highlights the difficulties faced by a strategic intermediary, such as the LHP, which seeks to hold together a wide variety of social interests with multifarious sets of values and expectations within a context where, given the relative limitations on resources of the mayor, initiatives need to be attractive to multinational capital.

In contrast to a politics of progressive urban governance, it is helpful to see the public–private partnership of the CUTE project as a strategic intermediary which largely, though not exclusively, produced a vision of a future London hydrogen economy from the 'outside' or external to London. The public–private partnership around CUTE brought together a small number of supranational political and multinational capital social interests. The significance of this is that their interests were by and large not deeply embedded in institutions in London. London was seen as a showcase – a test-bed to test out technologies.

The notion of what we would characterize as a test-bed is interesting in that it also appeals to the competition among 'world' and European cities in attracting such demonstrations. In this respect, according to a DGTREN official: '[Daimler-Chrysler] invited all the [participating] cities to explain to them what they intended to do.' There was, furthermore, a view of cities as 'laboratories' where there is:

> [what] we call an assessment framework for the project which is like in a laboratory. You don't start messing around with elements and liquids and things in the laboratory [without defining] how you are going to measure all the reactions that are going to happen in this place that you are doing the experiment and how you are going to monitor all that.

Cities in this view of the hydrogen economy were seen as colonies of corporate capital and sites for the 'dropping in' of technologies; the point being that cities were competing to be colonized by corporate interests, competing to render the politics of the city subject to a degree of abdication to corporate interests, who viewed cities as laboratories within which reactions could be measured, extracted and utilized to inform a next generation of technological artefacts. This view of the city fails to acknowledge possibilities of local agency.

The significant issue is the extent to which different social interests that constitute the city from within are able to envision and enact their collective view of the future of the city, the extent to which those external to the city are able to shape visions and actions in respect of the future of the city, and/or the extent to which these two positions are negotiated. Critically, hitherto, there has been strictly limited overlap and coupling between these two intermediaries which crucially perform different intermediary roles, where: (1) in the case of the LHP, social interests within the city actively mediate between technological possibility and the city to try and reshape London's energy infrastructure from within; and (2) the CUTE public–private partnership intermediary largely acts as a conduit for social interests outside of the city to reshape London's transport infrastructure and views the city as a recipient of socio-technical change. Where there have been overlaps it has not been through formal collaboration between the two intermediaries, but through less-formalized links between social interests from each of the intermediary contexts. This has included, for example, the mayor's highly public support for the CUTE initiative in London, representatives from BP and BOC sitting on the Steering Group of the LHP, and through London Buses – who are responsible for achieving the environmental targets and standards for the bus fleet as required by the Mayor's Air Quality Strategy – working with the bus operator First London and BP on the CUTE project in London.

Conclusions

This chapter has examined whether cities can shape technological transitions and, if so, to what extent these can be regarded as strategic or systemic in orientation. In addressing this question we have acknowledged the strengths, but also identified a number of shortcomings of technological transitions approaches, particularly in terms of the treatment of cities and regions which are often the places where transitions take place and are often actively shaped by territorial priorities. The focus on exploring the possibilities of cities and regions shaping technological transitions, we have suggested, is particularly important in view of the contemporary 're-emergence' of cities and regions as scales of political activity in a period when we are seeing a degree of 'hollowing out' of nation-states, and a re-articulation of relationships between the national and other scales of political activities. The chapter has developed a synthesis between transitions literatures with those of multi-level governance. This enabled us to highlight the continuous pressure on cities and regions constantly to rethink their economic futures strategically. Pushing this further, we detailed the emerging role of strategic intermediaries as a fruitful focus for researching the ways in which cities and regions not only seek to re-think their futures strategically, but do so in relation to visions of systemic technological transitions. There are four key conclusions.

Firstly, we have undertaken a detailed case study of London that systematically and critically examines the complex relations between technological possibilities and urban context, which are embodied in visions, and the types of interrelationships and the different forms of knowledge which strategic intermediary organizations selectively 'bundle together'. Central to these activities and practices is the formation of relationships both inside and outside London across a range of different scales of governance from the neighbourhood, to city-region, national state and supranational, as well as with multinational capital.

Secondly, we have clearly demonstrated the simultaneous co-existence of different visions of urban futures in relation to the 'same' set of energy technologies. This highlights the key role of particular and political social interests, their views of the city and its future transition through particular technologies, and the organizational forms of strategic intermediaries in creating the context through which these social interests and their visions can be held together. Strategic intermediaries seek to hold together these visions, which are at times in tension with each other, in order effectively to manage internal and external expectations and political networks.

Thirdly, the large world cities such as London, with well-established governance structures, in our view, seek to position themselves (and are positioned by national governments) as transition managers rather than as managers of a bundle of niche experiments. While cities may organize a series of local niche experiments, we argue that world cities also seek to engage with and put pressure on regimes to create more conducive and supportive environments for their urban transition, and also actively seek to influence landscape pressures. For instance, London has active relationships with national government, positioning itself as a national and international exemplar of the hydrogen economy (Hodson and Marvin, 2007). London is actively positioning itself as the national exemplar and is also positioned by national government as a national exemplar, that actively shapes national and regional energy policies and priorities. Through the coalitions built with other world cities and multinational capital, the hydrogen bus initiatives could be significantly extended if current plans are successful.

Finally, having highlighted a central role for strategic intermediaries and the work they perform in producing visions of urban socio-technical futures, a future research agenda should engage with these issues through comparative work with world cities such as London, but also explore what the role of strategic intermediaries is in envisioning futures of medium-sized and smaller cities. However, comparative work could usefully examine these issues.

Acknowledgements

This is a shortened and revised version of a paper by Hodson, M. and Marvin, S. that first appeared in 'Cities mediating technological transitions: Understanding visions, intermediation and consequences', *Technology Analysis & Strategic Management*, vol 21, no 4, pp515–534. We are grateful for permission to publish this in revised form. We also gratefully acknowledge the support of both the UK Sustainable Hydrogen Energy Consortium, funded through the UK EPSRC, and the CREATE Acceptance project, funded through the European Commission's Sixth Framework Programme, in undertaking this work.

Notes

1   Research took place in two phases. First between January 2004 and January 2005 and then in August 2006, and included 18 interviews with leading officials in the GLA and in national government departments, at local and supranational scales, and also included interviews with industrialists and consultants. Additionally, we

drew on a rich body of policy and organizational documentation – both in terms of those in the public sphere and some internal organizational/departmental documents made available to us on the basis that content and names were not directly drawn upon – and of a number of websites. We undertook further observational work and a series of informal discussions at a series of 'relevant' workshops.

2   Ken Livingstone was replaced as mayor by Boris Johnson in May 2008.

3   All quotes have been anonymized as agreed, in negotiations to undertake interviews, with interviewees.

References

Aglietta, M. (1979) *A Theory of Capitalist Regulation: The US Experience*, Verso, London

Berkhout, F., Smith, A. and Stirling, A. (2003) 'Socio-technological regimes and transition contexts', Working Paper Series, SPRU, University of Sussex, Brighton

Bulkeley, H. and Betsill, M. (2005) 'Rethinking sustainable cities: Multilevel governance and the "urban" politics of climate change', *Environmental Politics*, vol 14, pp42–63

Eames, M., McDowall, W., Hodson, M. and Marvin, S. (2006) 'Negotiating generic and place-specific expectations of the hydrogen economy', *Technology Analysis and Strategic Management*, vol 18, nos 3–4, pp361–374

European Commission (2003) *Hydrogen Energy and Fuel Cells: A Vision of Our Future*, European Commission, Brussels

European Commission, nd. *Clean urban transport for Europe general introduction brochure*, Brussels: European Commission

Fuller, C., Bennett, R. and Ramsden, M. (2004) 'Local government and the changing institutional landscape of economic development in England and Wales', *Environment and Planning* C, vol 22, pp317–347

Geels, F. (2002a) 'Technological transitions as evolutionary reconfiguration processes: A multi-level perspective and a case study', *Research Policy*, vol 31, pp1257–1274

Geels, F. (2002b) 'Towards sociotechnical scenarios and reflexive anticipation: Using patterns and regularities in technology dynamics', in K. Sørensen and R. Williams (eds) *Shaping Technology, Guiding Policy: Concepts, Spaces and Tools*, Edward Elgar, Cheltenham, pp359–387

Geels, F. (2004) 'From sectoral systems of innovation to socio-technical systems. Insights about dynamics and change from sociology and institutional theory', *Research Policy*, vol 33, pp897–920

Graham, S. and Marvin, S. (1996) *Telecommunications and the City*, Routledge, London

Graham, S. and Marvin, S. (2001) *Splintering Urbanism: Networked Infrastructures, Technological Mobilities and the Urban Condition*, Routledge, London

Guy, S. and Marvin, S. (2001) 'Constructing sustainable urban futures: From models to competing pathways, impact assessment and project appraisal', *Journal of the International Association for Impact Assessment*, vol 19, no 2, pp131–139

Guy, S., Marvin, S. and Moss, T. (eds) (2001) *Urban Infrastructure in Transition: Networks, Buildings and Plans*, Earthscan, London

Hodson, M. and Marvin, S. (2006) 'Reconnecting the technology characterisation of the hydrogen economy to contexts of consumption', *Energy Policy*, vol 34, pp3006–3016

Hodson, M. and Marvin, S. (2007) 'Transforming London/testing London: Understanding the role of the national exemplar in constructing "strategic glurbanisation"', *International Journal of Urban and Regional Research*, vol 31, no 2, pp303–325

Hoogma, R., Kemp, R., Schot, J. and Truffer, B. (2002) *Experimenting for Sustainable Transport: The Approach of Strategic Niche Management*, Spon Press, London

Jessop, B. (2002) 'The future of the capitalist state', Polity, Cambridge

Kemp, R. and Loorbach, D. (2005) 'Dutch policies to manage the transition to sustainable energy', in F. Beckenbach, U. Hampicke and C. Leipertet (eds) *Jahrbuch Ökologische Ökonomik: Innovationen und Transformation*, vol 4, Metropolis, Marburg

Lente, H. van (1993) 'Promising technology: The dynamics of expectations in technological developments', PhD thesis, University of Twente, Enschede

Lente, H. van, Hekkert, M., Smits, R. and Waveren, B. van (2003) 'Roles of systemic intermediaries in transition processes', *International Journal of Innovation Management*, vol 7, no 3, pp247–279

London Hydrogen Partnership (LHP) (2002) 'London Hydrogen Partnership action plan' (2nd draft), GLA, London, http://www.fuelcellmarkets.com/content/images/articles/hydrogen_action_plan2(1).pdf

MacLeod, G. and Jones, M. (2001) 'Renewing the geography of regions', *Environment and Planning D: Society and Space*, vol 19, pp669–695

Marvin, S. and Medd, W. (2004) 'Sustainable infrastructures by proxy? Intermediation beyond the production-consumption nexus', in D. Southerton, H. Chappells and B. van Vliet (eds) *Sustainable Consumption: The Implications of Changing Infrastructures of Provision*, Edward Elgar, Cheltenham

Mayor of London (2001) *The Mayor's Transport Strategy*, GLA, London

Mayor of London (2002) *Cleaning London's Air: The Mayor's Air Quality Strategy*, GLA, London

Mayor of London (2004a) *Green Light to Clean Power: Highlights of the Mayor's Energy Strategy*, GLA, London

Mayor of London (2004b) *Green Light to Clean Power: The Mayor's Energy Strategy*, GLA, London

Mayor of London (2004c) *Sounder City: The Mayor's Ambient Noise Strategy*, GLA, London

Mayor of London (2005) *Sustaining Success: The Mayor's Economic Development Strategy*, GLA, London

McNeill, D. (2002) 'Livingstone's London: Left politics and the world city', *Regional Studies*, vol 36, no 1, pp75–91

Rifkin, J. (2002) *The Hydrogen Economy: The Creation of the World-Wide Energy Web and the Redistribution of Power on Earth*, TarcherPutnam, New York

Romm, J. (2006) *The Hype About Hydrogen: Fact and Fiction in the Race to Save the Climate*, Island Press, Washington, DC

Rotmans, J. and Kemp, R. (2002) 'Managing societal transitions: dilemmas and uncertainties: The Dutch energy case-study', Workshop on the 'Benefits of climate policy: Improving information for policy makers', 12–13 December, OECD, Paris

Rotmans, J., Kemp, R. and Asselt, M. van (2001) 'More evolution than revolution', *Foresight*, vol 3, no 1, pp1–17

Rydin, Y., Thornley, A., Scanlon, K. and West, K. (2004) 'The Greater London Authority – a case of conflict of cultures? Evidence from the planning and environmental policy domains', *Environment and Planning C*, vol 22, no 1, pp55–76

Sweeting, D. (2003) 'How strong is the Mayor of London?', *Policy and Politics*, vol 31, no 4, pp465–478

PART II

INTERMEDIARIES IN NETWORK TRANSITIONS

Timothy Moss

Introduction

Working within the conceptual framework set out in Part I, the chapters in Part II present case studies of intermediaries in action relating to different dimensions of network transitions and different infrastructure systems. The line of argument developed so far in the book is that an ongoing complex process of change in the ways urban infrastructures are provided, regulated and used is creating space for intermediary organizations to emerge and re-order actor relations. Their interventions across and between the classic actor triad of service provider, regulator and user are, we have argued, significant for three overarching reasons. Firstly, intermediary organizations are affecting changes to the governance of urban infrastructure. By mediating new relations between actors, technologies, institutions and so on, they are re-ordering traditional power constellations around utility services. Secondly, intermediaries act as forces for innovation in socio-technical systems generally characterized by strong path dependency and resistance to change. Especially interesting are those intermediaries which act strategically to reconfigure relations between different components of a socio-technical system in order to advance particular interests. Thirdly, we have argued the importance of place in understanding how intermediaries emerge and work. Cities and regions are not merely the geographical backdrop for intermediary activities; they are intricately involved in influencing the kinds of intermediaries that emerge, what objectives they pursue, how they operate and, ultimately, what impact they have. All three dimensions – governance, innovation and place – are critically important for the environmental implications of intermediation. It is our contention that intermediaries possess huge potential to shape the use – and non-use – of natural resources and energy via the infrastructure systems which capture, transform and supply them.

The case studies in this section focus on intermediaries as products and expressions of network transitions, and their impact on the governance of socio-technical systems. They each address the following questions:

1   How are current network transitions stimulating the emergence of intermediary organizations?
2   How are these organizations themselves mediating network transitions?
3   In what ways are they generating new modes of governance for urban and regional infrastructures?

Each of the chapters addresses one universally acknowledged dimension of network transitions particularly pertinent to governance issues: market liberalization (Rohracher), environmental regulation (Beveridge and Guy), privatization (Moss and von Schlippenbach) and technological innovation (Randles and Mander). Each of these transition dimensions creates different kinds of opportunity (or necessity) for intermediation and generates different kinds of intermediary organizations and activities. The chapters also each focus on one sector of (urban) infrastructure: electricity supply and use (Rohracher), wastewater treatment and disposal (Beveridge and Guy), water supply (Moss and von Schlippenbach) and air transport (Randles and Mander). Each of these infrastructure sectors is facing particular governance challenges within the general framework of network transitions. In the following chapters, characteristic challenges are selected for detailed analysis of how intermediaries are intervening to address them.

The first chapter in this section, by Harald Rohracher, is about the creation and coordination of consumer choice for green electricity by intermediary organizations. It presents a case study on the role of environmental and other non-governmental organizations (NGOs) in Germany and Switzerland in establishing green electricity labels following the liberalization of energy markets. These labels set sustainability standards for electricity from renewable energy – for instance, by specifying which types of biomass may be used for electricity generation under the labelling scheme and setting up accreditation and evaluation procedures. Such green electricity labels serve as a 'boundary object' between electricity generators, suppliers, consumers and regulators, and have the potential to shape the transformation of the energy system by creating and articulating demand for specific electricity products, and mediating the establishment of socio-technical constituencies around green electricity generation and use. The chapter illustrates how NGOs are playing a vital role in defining and negotiating such standards, enrolling and aligning supply- and demand-side actors, communicating with a wider public and building trust for the respective products, establishing links with regulators, and shaping policies for renewable electricity at national and European levels. In essence, their intermediary function lies in translating between the different logics of demand, supply and regulation, and in creating new links between incumbent and new actors in the electricity sector.

The second chapter, by Ross Beveridge and Simon Guy, investigates the role of intermediaries in translating environmental regulation into practical applications of wastewater management. It takes a specific example of how the European Union's (EU) Urban Wastewater Directive sparks the pursuit of new environmental standards in wastewater practices in the North of England. The case study follows the work of one intermediary organization – an environmental consultancy – in mediating between technology providers and (industrial) users to develop an environmentally and economically sustainable response to the regulatory requirements. Designed as a study of environmental innovation, the chapter conceives of innovation – in accordance with actor network theory – as being a highly contingent process of 'translation' through which actors' interests and identities, their practices and – in this case – the Directive itself are re-represented and re-ordered through the construction of new actor networks. From such a perspective, governance of the water sector is shown to be a highly contested, unpredictable business shaped by situationally specific negotiations and compromises. Crucially, the case study reveals the importance of intermediation in this process of realignment. Working at the interfaces between a range of actors and the Directive, intermediaries become integral to the ways in which objects and practices are translated and innovation achieved – or not.

The third chapter, by Timothy Moss and Ulrike von Schlippenbach, studies intermediation as a product of privatization in the water sector. It analyses the intermediary role of the Berlin Centre of Competence for Water (KWB), a network of business, research and government organizations established as part of the partial privatization of the Berlin Water Utility, with the purpose of coordinating and promoting water research in the Berlin region. From a governance perspective this case is intriguing in terms of the redistribution of power and influence in a post-privatization context. The KWB was designed as a new mode of public–private collaboration to help offset the loss of public sector influence incumbent to the privatization deal. The chapter contrasts the original expectations of the KWB's members with the realities of the KWB in action, focusing on its multiple intermediary functions. Three dimensions of intermediation are investigated: how the KWB operates between diverse actor groups; between different policy fields; and between different territorial scales. The chapter analyses how successful the KWB has proved in operating as a forum for exchange and joint activities on water research, promoting innovative applications in water management and stimulating market opportunities in water R&D for the Berlin region.

The fourth chapter, by Sally Randles and Sarah Mander, explores how market intermediaries are influencing air travel in the UK. The study is set in the context of increasing numbers of journeys by airplane and the total passenger distance travelled per annum on the one hand, and a regulatory imperative to significantly reduce CO_2 emissions from air travel on the other. The chapter takes a novel perspective on this conundrum by investigating the market intermediaries (such as the media, the Internet, a network of travel agents and so on) which sit between the provision and 'consumption' of air travel, exerting affective powers on both in ways which, the authors argue, are currently invisible to the policy gaze. Market intermediaries, because of their strategic 'in-betweenness', have the profound potential to drive up levels of consumption, even as policy-makers try to bring levels down. This chapter is, therefore, illustrative of the environmentally detrimental effect of certain intermediaries who undermine policy attempts to reduce aviation emissions.

5
Constructing Markets for Green Electricity: The 'Soft Power' of Intermediaries in Transforming Energy Systems

Harald Rohracher

Introduction

Over the past two decades, electricity markets in Europe and many other countries have been substantially re-regulated – from vertically integrated, usually publicly owned monopolies to more market-like structures with a separation of generation, supply and grid operation, and the privatization of utilities. Under this principle, suppliers have the choice to offer a diversified portfolio of electricity products (differentiated by price or origin; e.g. from renewable energy carriers), while consumers – in theory at least – have the freedom to choose their supplier and product on the market. Breaking up the hierarchically integrated structure of past electricity systems, however, also leads to higher fragmentation of the sector and an increased number of actors involved (independent generators, new sellers and re-sellers, and so on).

In this chapter, I will argue that this proliferation of new actor constellations, business models and products also generates demand for new forms of coordination and intermediation activities. While this demand is met by consultants, knowledge brokers and new types of knowledge-intensive business services (e.g. sorting out profitable consumer groups and designing specific product offers, acting as match-makers between industry customers and supply companies, or aggregating information for regulators and other actors), the new organization of the sector also opens new spaces for more strategic forms of normatively or policy-driven intervention through intermediation activities. The specific case I will investigate is the attempt by various non-profit organizations (environmental, research, consumer) to construct new markets for electricity from renewable energy carriers ('green electricity') by bringing actors together in new networks, establishing new 'calculative practices' for the evaluation of these specific goods (Callon and Muniesa, 2005) and orienting the market towards specific normative aims. Such 'strategic intermediaries' (Medd and Marvin, 2006) thus not only seize new business opportunities within the electricity sector, but also have long-term political perspectives to shape or transform the sector (or parts of it) towards aims such as sustainability.

This chapter centres on the establishment of green electricity labels by non-profit organizations aiming at a more sustainable electricity system as such an example of strategic, market-oriented intermediation, activities and as a specific form of non-state governance (Cashore, 2002). The aim of such labels is to provide guidance and transparency for consumers overwhelmed by heterogeneous and often non-transparent green electricity offers, and consequently to set in place conditions for a growth of this market segment by inducing new green electricity generation capacities and the articulation of demand for such products. This requires innovative organizational solutions to establish a new nexus between producers and consumers, to mediate between different interests and also between different ideas about what green energy means.

The underlying research question of this chapter is whether 'electricity labelling' can be analysed as an element of a broader re-organization of infrastructure systems towards more market-like relationships between its constituents. Does the new institutional context of electricity systems also reshape the 'opportunity space' for non-commercial, intermediary actors pursuing broader environmental or social goals such as greening the electricity system? While under the former regulatory structures such goals would have rather been pursued by political lobbying and the organization of public resistance, one may expect that action now shifts towards strategic intervention into markets by environmental organizations and other NGOs.

Although the establishment of electricity labels does not have a particularly urban dimension to it, we will, however, see that urban and regional utilities often were the strongest supporters of such labelling schemes from the supply side. The urban context often provided better opportunities to create new socio-technical arrangements of green electricity supply and demand around these labels, and was thus often more effective in creating incentives for an urban transition of electricity systems.

A crowded policy space: governance by regulation and non-state governance in the electricity market

Initiatives for the introduction of green electricity labels have to relate to a complex institutional environment of electricity market regulation, public support schemes for renewable energies and green electricity product offers by various electricity suppliers. With respect to the complex interactions of policies and regulations in the electricity system, I will follow Sorrell (2003), who analyses the overlaps and interactions of UK climate change policy as a 'crowded policy space'. The term 'policy space' was originally introduced by Majone and denotes:

*a set of policies that are so closely interrelated that it is not pos-
sible to make useful descriptions about one of them without
taking the other elements of the set into account... In an already
crowded policy space, solutions beget new problems in the form
of policy overlaps, jurisdictional conflicts and unanticipated consequences (Majone, 1989, pp158–159).*

This section will sketch out the crowded space of renewable electricity policies
which sets the scene for attempts of intermediary organizations to shape the
market for renewable electricity.

While energy market liberalization in the European Union (EU) has been
mainly driven by the aim of creating a European electricity market with
increased competition and economic efficiency, environmental policy aims
have given rise to the establishment of an additional and equally complex set
of regulations. Many of these regulations have been tailored to fit the 'liberalization framework', but they also show the limits of the idea of self-regulation
in the electricity market via price signals and competition when it comes to
societal aims such as climate-change mitigation and sustainability.

To achieve self-imposed targets for the future share of renewable electricity, two sets of regulatory measures have been introduced at EU and national
level. The first set comprises instruments to increase market transparency with
respect to electricity from renewable energy sources (and thus is fully in line
with liberalization efforts), while the second (and so far much more effective)
set of measures introduces technology-specific financial support mechanisms
to protect growing niche markets for renewables and to make them more competitive with established generation technologies in the long run.

The instrument of Electricity Disclosure (introduced in 2003) obliges electricity suppliers to display the mix of energy sources of the electricity they sell
to end consumers (Boardman and Palmer, 2003). While such measures look
rather straightforward and simple at first sight, they are often highly complex
in their regulatory implementation. This is partly due to the specific character
of electricity: at the physical level there is no flow of electricity from specific
generation facilities to specific customers, and electricity from renewable
energy sources does not have properties different from nuclear electricity.
What can be traced, though, is either the 'flow of economic transactions',
which may track sales from end consumers back to specific generation plants,
or a separately generated 'flow of green electricity attributes' (e.g. expressed
by certificates), which can be traded independently from the economic transactions of electricity itself. Both cases, however, require a complex and
comprehensive tracking system for electricity to follow the transactions from
wholesale and spot markets to the end consumers, and to avoid 'double counting'; that is, the selling of more green electricity than has been produced.

These regulations allow for the counting, tracking and disclosing of electricity from renewable sources, and fit to a liberalized electricity market
framework. Much more important for the market success of electricity from
renewables, however, are economic incentives which also show wide variations in regulatory details. Setting favourable feed-in tariffs for the production

of renewable electricity is currently the most widespread policy support mechanism for green power in Europe. Nevertheless, even if such support schemes are highly effective, they bear the risk of disconnecting sustainability goals from end consumers (Markard and Truffer, 2006), as the relations between the type of electricity generation and consumption are rather abstract and non-transparent to the electricity consumer, and are not reflected in the electricity products sold.

Market-based instruments such as electricity disclosure set their hopes on the increased articulation of demand because of a highly positive consumer attitude to green electricity (see Eurobarometer, 2006; Diaz-Rainey and Ashton, 2008). This segment of environmentally conscious consumers is targeted by various green power products offered by incumbent suppliers or new market entrants sometimes exclusively producing or selling green electricity. In Germany, for example, more than 140 out of a total of approximately 900 electricity suppliers have launched a green product since the domestic market was opened in 1998 (Bürger, 2007). However, in most cases the market share is rather small and, typically, less than 2 per cent of all electricity customers have switched to a green power product (Willstedt and Bürger, 2006) – though this has to be put into perspective as the total production volume of electricity from renewables is typically less then 10 per cent and the market share of labelled products has often risen significantly since 2006 (and has, for example, doubled in Germany from 2007 to 2008 only). A problem is that many of these products are non-transparent and confusing for consumers, and do not deliver the environmental benefits they claim (Graham, 2006). A typical problem is that they do no more than splitting an existing electricity mix into a green part sold at premium prices and residual 'standard electricity', without in total achieving any environmental benefit. As a consequence, consumer trust in such products is usually rather low (Birzle-Harder and Götz, 2001; Diaz-Rainey and Ashton, 2008). This failure of both regulatory framework and voluntary products to create a transparent green electricity market with environmental benefits is where labelling initiatives come into play. Such labels strive to create new green electricity markets which provide consumers with credible products of high environmental standards and with impacts on the overall generation mix of electricity.

Green electricity labels in practice: setting up a new production–consumption nexus

In this section, two specific examples of green electricity labels are described as a basis for further analysis. The case studies are partly based on the EU project Clean Energy Network for Europe (CLEAN-E) (Bürger, 2007), which was aimed at analysing existing labelling schemes and their interactions with regulatory support policies, and at extending green energy labelling to additional countries. The project provided ample opportunities for interactions with practitioners of labelling organizations participating in the project. In addition, eight semi-structured interviews were conducted with experts involved in setting up and operating two specific labelling schemes in Germany and Switzerland. The qualitative empirical material mainly covers insights into the process, opportunities and barriers of setting up and operating green electricity labels from the perspective of 'labelling insiders', and is the basis for the following descriptions and analyses.

A systematic comparison of existing green electricity labels in Europe and elsewhere shows a broad variety of different designs (Truffer et al, 2001; Willstedt and Bürger, 2006). In many countries several green electricity labels exist, often varying widely in the labelling and monitoring procedures, eligibility criteria (electricity from which type of plants and energy source is acceptable) and other criteria such as additionality.[1] Some eco-labels are operated by state authorities (e.g. Australia), but much more often by non-state actors. Labels can be distinguished by the degree of independence of the certification process. This ranges from (a) first-party certification, wherein organizations generate rules intentionally and report conformance themselves, to (b) second-party certification, where firms and organizations work together to generate rules and report compliance, and (c) third-party certification, where independent bodies set the standards and others report conformance (Pattberg, 2004). Many green electricity labels are no more than 'environmental claims' by utilities. In contrast, the labels we will be dealing with adhere to advanced standards: in terms of third-party certification, in terms of labelling criteria and accreditation procedures, and in terms of sustainability requirements.

Let us turn to two such cases as a specific type of governance of production–consumption relationships by non-state intermediary actors. Both labels, 'naturemade' in Switzerland and 'ok power' in Germany, were among the earliest green electricity labels introduced in the late 1990s, and both try to set advanced standards for environmental labelling of electricity. Moreover, both labels have been exclusively set up by non state intermediary actors and both are involved in creating a joint European standard: Eugene (European Network for Green Electricity), which is, in a way, a meta-label that certifies 'green electricity labels' according to superior environmental standards.[2] Let us first give a short description of the development and organizational forms of these two labels.

The German 'ok power' label

The green electricity label 'ok power' was established at the beginning of the liberalization of the end-consumer market for electricity in Germany in 1998. Expectations were running high at that time that freedom of choice for consumers, combined with growing public sympathy for renewables (Wüstenhagen and Bilharz, 2006), would open a considerable market segment for green power products. At the same time it became clear that many electricity suppliers would offer green products, some of them of dubious quality and with little positive effect on the environment. Nevertheless, contrary to many other countries, the liberalization process in Germany was also accompanied by the emergence of a variety of exclusive green electricity producers and suppliers of varying size. Environmental organizations such as the Worldwide Fund for Nature (WWF) and Greenpeace were heavily campaigning among consumers for switching to green electricity at the start of the liberalization process,[3] and obviously had great interest in securing high environmental standards for these products.

The key actor in setting up the new label was the German 'Institute for Applied Ecology' (Öko-Institut), which is a private institution committed to research-based, environmental policy consulting. Öko-Institut is an example of an intermediary organization, mediating between science (cooperation with research institutes), policy (administration, decision-makers) and the public (providing environmental information for a general audience). Like other research-based intermediaries, Öko-Institut saw its main role in initiating the process and not in operating the labelling organization, and in developing criteria for the eligibility of renewable energy sources.

From the beginning there were two other key institutions on board: WWF Germany, an international environmental organization which already had experience with the successful Forest Stewardship Council (FSC) label to certify timber from sustainable forestry; and Verbraucherzentrale Nordrhein-Westfalen, one of the most active consumer associations in Germany. The three organizations together founded the association (Verein) Energievision e.V., which is the organization still representing, implementing and operating the label.

The regulatory context in Germany is rather specific: Under the Renewable Electricity Act (EEG), very favourable feed-in tariffs for green electricity generators were established which would cover most of the green electricity produced, apart from large hydro-power. The label ok power never was designed in competition to the public support system, but always saw itself as complementary to these feed-in tariffs. Eligibility thus concentrates on generation facilities not covered by the EEG or going beyond EEG in environmental standards (e.g. refurbished and environmentally upgraded hydro-power plants; wind energy in less favourable areas). Moreover, the label allows the inclusion of imported green electricity, thereby linking into the international tradable green certificate system (Renewable Energy Certificate System, RECS) and also linking up with the 'Guarantees of Origin' system used as a proof for the source of green energy; ok power thus has the character of an ecological benchmark for green electricity, showing how strict standards could be applied, but it was never designed as a mass product. Currently, eight electricity products are certified under the ok power label, covering approximately 0.5 per cent of the market share of electricity in Germany. Nevertheless, the volume of electricity certified under this label is growing rapidly, from 0.62TWh (2006) to 1.0TWh (2007) and about 2.7TWh for 2008, which is an equivalent of 760,000 households (http://www.ok-power.de). This means that around a third of German 'green electricity' for households is currently sold according to the ok power standards.

The main task of the labelling organization Energievision is to organize the accreditation process of power products by independent auditors, to continuously improve eligibility criteria and to motivate new suppliers to have their product labelled. However, the limited resources make it difficult to carry out effective promotion campaigns to increase the market share of the label.

Promotion is limited to communicating to the members of the organizations involved and consumers of the electricity companies certified. Another focus, especially of WWF, is on large, international consumers such as Tetra Pak, who can sign up to WWF's Climate Saver programme by, for instance, switching to green power. One success story for ok power was the German Ministry for Environment's choice of an ok power-certified product for its buildings after carrying out a competitive bidding process.

The Swiss 'naturemade' label

Despite many similarities in the idea behind the labels, the Swiss context is quite different from the German one (see Truffer et al, 2003, for a comprehensive discussion of the history and socio-political context of green electricity labelling in Switzerland). The Swiss electricity market has not yet been liberalized and is characterized by a large number of regional and municipal utilities. Still, the expectation of an approaching market liberalization regime has been an important driver for Swiss utilities to differentiate their portfolio and offer green electricity products. In addition, many regional and municipal utilities which do not have to compete on a national or international market still have a strong sense of public service, which also includes environmental responsibility. As a consequence, several municipal utilities had already been offering green electricity products during the 1990s (Wüstenhagen et al, 2003).

While public discourse in Germany had long been dominated by the anti-nuclear energy movement, Switzerland had a long-standing controversy over the further development of hydro-power and its effect on the environment (Truffer et al, 2003). Similar to the German Öko-Institut, one of the main entrepreneurial actors in Switzerland has been a (public) research organization – the Swiss Federal Institute for Aquatic Science and Technology (EAWAG). In 1998, EAWAG launched a transdisciplinary research project on the development of a 'green hydro-power' standard (see Truffer et al, 2003; Truffer, 2007). Along with this research, a labelling organization was established with strong support from the municipal utilities of the city of Zurich and WWF. Similar to Öko-Institut, EAWAG saw its role in initiating the labelling organization and developing criteria with a strong research base, rather than operating a label itself. Indeed, it was more successful than Öko-Institut in detaching itself from the further process.

The labelling organization Verein für umweltfreundliche Energie (VUE) – Association for Environmentally Friendly Energy – was set up in 2000 and launched the green power label naturemade. Eligibility criteria and plant accreditation tools of naturemade and ok power are based on rather different concepts. In general, naturemade puts more emphasis on ecological and plant-specific criteria (probably originating in the hydro-power discussion), while ok power is more oriented to mitigation of climate change and green electricity imports. The market share of naturemade products is somewhere around 0.5 per cent of the total market (or close to half of the green electricity), which is similar to ok power, but also, remarkably, growing (from 325GWh in 2006 to 1776GWh in 2007; see http://www.naturemade.ch). A range of smaller and larger municipal utilities, such as the municipal utilities of Zurich or Geneva, offer various green electricity products (e.g. purely from solar energy) certified under naturemade.

VUE is an interesting example of an intermediary as an 'organization of organizations' (Ahrne et al, 2007), as Swiss electricity companies (and their business associations) and advocacy organizations of renewable electricity generators have been included directly in the labelling organization, along with WWF and consumer organizations. While Germany has strong feed-in tariff regulation, Swiss organizations saw much more need to build up a market for green electricity in the first place and consequently felt required to create sufficient acceptance on the side of producers. About one-third of producers and suppliers are organized within the label, although they also represent quite different positions. Thus, an important design feature is the power balance between interest groups in the board and in committees of the association.

Due to the integration of electricity companies, as well as environmental and consumer organizations, VUE's social dynamic is quite different to the German case. From the beginning, the Swiss green electricity label served also as a means to get hydro-power utilities and environmental organizations – both opponents in the conflict over the further expansion of hydro-power generation – out of a 'prisoners' dilemma' they had been locked in (Truffer et al, 2003). Conflicts of interest could now be resolved within the labelling organization where environmental organizations and the electricity industry were equally represented. While this was a reason for some environmental organizations to keep out of this process, other actors involved went through a learning process, enabling them to find consensual solutions and making use of the know-how distributed between the partners. Still, from time to time, conflicts on various issues emerge which challenge the existence of the association, whether for utilities supporting political initiatives against the ideals of naturemade or environmental organizations launching campaigns which are strongly disapproved by suppliers. However, as the current chairperson points out in an interview, VUE is accepted as a 'container' or protected space, where controversial discussions can take place. Even if consensus cannot be reached, internal discussions are not made public. Looking back at the long history of conflicts over water protection issues in Switzerland, VUE provides one of the first functioning platforms for bringing the conflict parties together at the same table.

Although, like in Germany, consumers are the target group of labels, consumer associations have not been the drivers of the labelling process, a role taken rather by environmental organizations and producers. Boström (2006) points out with the case of organic food labelling in Sweden that consumer associations often lack sufficient resources to fully participate in the labelling procedures, and power is often shifted to the producer side as a consequence. In both cases studied in this chapter, however, consumer associations have been part of the steering group from the beginning and remained active in the labelling process. Although they had limited resources to directly mobilize consumers, they could contribute to the design of the labelling system as representatives of consumer interests and as sources of know-how about the consumer-friendly design of green power. However, there are also examples of consumer-led initiatives: when 4000 customers switched from the municipal utility Badenova in Freiburg to the green electricity provider Energiewerke Schönau, thereby voicing concern about the electricity policy of Badenova, the utility had to overhaul its electricity products and now offers green electricity under the ok power label (Späth and Rohracher, 2009).

The German ok power and the Swiss naturemade labels are two examples of a variety of green electricity labels in Europe. As even these two examples show, not only the design of the labelling procedures differs, but also there are significant variations in the regulatory and economic contexts of the labels, such as the structure of the electricity market, the design and scope of existing regulatory support for green electricity. These 'policy spaces' vary even more if we take further countries into account. In the UK, for example, public certificate schemes (Renewables Obligation Certificates, ROCs) as a green electricity support mechanism leave hardly any space for voluntary labels, though there is an urgent need for third-party certification (Brown, 2005). However, despite these differences, the two labels presented in more detail share many characteristics and to some extent serve as a benchmark for many other labels because of the comprehensive research activities they are based upon, and because of the thorough environmental assessment of generation plants and green power products.

Transforming electricity systems as a process of strategic intermediation

The way the two labels mediate between supply and demand structures in electricity markets is essentially similar in a number of ways: the labelling and accreditation concept; the role of environmental NGOs and research intermediaries as important drivers of the labelling process; their 'soft power' to intervene in markets based on environmental credibility and symbolic capital rather than the economic resources they command; their interdependence with regulatory structures; and the heterogeneous coalitions and assemblies that have to be formed to make the new production–consumption nexus work. In the following, I will concentrate on two specific challenges which ranked high in the interviews with labelling organizations and which appear to be typical for non-state, market-driven, strategic intermediation activities: the re-framing of markets as a simultaneous re-arrangement of socio-technical constellations on the supply and demand side; and the interaction of private and state governance in hybrid governance systems. These two issues are not only core tasks to be dealt with, but they also bring a number of limitations of such activities to the fore.

Intermediaries and the political construction of markets

Establishing green electricity labels is an example of the co-construction of the economy and politics by concerned groups. As Callon points out, economic markets can be defined as socio-technical arrangements whose functioning is based on a set of framings, including price-setting mechanisms. Such market framing constitutes powerful mechanisms of exclusions, choosing 'certain worlds, with their goods, agents and attachments ... above others which are consequently threatened with extinction' (Callon, 2007, p140). In our case, the dominant framing of electricity markets is such that environmental qualities and standards are not reflected appropriately in electricity products and price-setting mechanisms. Environmental, consumer or research organizations act as intermediaries voicing these concerns and trying to change such dominant market framings. They thereby engage in 'normalising practices' or 'activities that contribute to establish guidelines for how a market should be [re]shaped or work according to some [group of] actor[s]' (Kjellberg and Helgesson, 2007, p143). As the cases investigated demonstrate, it is not sufficient to design environmental labels and propose it as a new standard to consumers and producers. To be effective, labelling organizations have to organize new arrangements between environmentally conscious consumers on the one side and socio-technical arrangements of electricity generation and supply on the other.

Facilitating political consumerism

While there is some truth in the power of consumers to shape markets – in our case to induce green electricity offers with their environmental attitudes and willingness to choose such products – the free choice open to consumers in general is not so free at all. If there are no appropriate offers on the market, if product qualities are not transparent, if transaction costs to select and understand such products are high, or if there is mistrust in the products pretending to satisfy particular needs (e.g. for an environmentally friendly form of electricity consumption), individual consumers are highly constrained in their ability to voice demand (Holzer, 2006).

Indeed, surveys and focus group interviews on 'green electricity' (Birzle-Harder and Götz, 2001; Diaz-Rainey and Ashton, 2008; Ipsos_MORI, 2008) reveal that such products are often confusing and non-transparent. As these studies illustrate, environmentally conscious consumers articulate a demand for simple forms of verification that they are making a valid contribution – however small – by buying green electricity products. The crucial issue for this verification is the source and credibility of its authority. Indeed, symbolic capital in the form of credibility, trust and economic independence was seen as a crucial asset by the labelling organizations, interviewed in their effort to mediate between environmental consumer demand and the structure of the electricity supply side.

As Boris Holzer points out in his analysis of political consumerism, it is

> *not the individual consumer [who] exercises power but a rather fragile and ephemeral 'collective' of aggregated and communicated choice. The sociologically interesting question is not whether there are 'real' choices or not, but how a collective choice can be simulated and communicated in an atomistic market economy (Holzer, 2006, pp405–406).*

Green electricity labels can be such a vehicle to collect, aggregate and communicate individual consumption decisions: consumers of certified green electricity collectively express their will to make a contribution to a sustainable energy system. Green electricity labels are part of a particular discourse which identifies problems and proposes solutions for a shift of electricity systems towards sustainability.

Intermediary organizations, such as WWF, or consumer organizations thereby act as 'transmission belts' for turning monetary consumption resources into political power, as these organizations claim to be able to influence the decisions of consumers, and thus to 'borrow' their purchasing power and use 'this social capital as a signalling device in the market' (Holzer, 2006, p406). As a consequence, a relatively small percentage of consumers – and sometimes just the threat of consumer action – can influence an industry (O'Rourke, 2005).

Re-arranging socio-technical systems

The activities of the green power-labelling organizations investigated also demonstrate that their intermediary role goes far beyond the provision of reliable information as a basis for qualified collective consumer decisions. A re-framing of markets means reshaping socio-technical arrangements (Callon, 2007) or changing different types of market practices (Kjellberg and Helgesson, 2007). While labelling organizations can claim to represent and influence certain market shares of environmental consumers, this demand can only be articulated if a sufficient number of suppliers offer green electricity under the respective label. It is thus a core challenge for labelling organizations to develop sustainable product standards and valid accreditation and evaluation procedures, which are at the same time acceptable for a sufficient number of suppliers in terms of generation and transaction costs.

Labelling organizations are thus in a constant process of system building. They have to develop and negotiate socio-technical arrangements at the supply side via the types of technologies and generation facilities eligible under the label, the type of information, reporting and tracking mechanisms (and thus to some extent the internal business processes) they require from suppliers, the actors and procedures for accreditation and evaluation, and so on. Labelling organizations also have to mobilize and align a broad range of actors such as enterprises, NGOs and state actors – each with different logics of action and different types of power resources – and are thus a kind of meta-organization attempting to organize organizations (Ahrne et al, 2007). As Boström points out, the demand for inclusiveness of such standardization organizations creates interesting hybrid organizational forms which are not civil society organizations, nor companies or state bureaucracies (Boström, 2006). They represent social interests, environmental interests and business interests, and are instrumental in achieving a more efficient dialogue among NGOs, industries and state authorities. Labelling organizations are characterized by their ability to overcome particularistic interests and to enhance solidarity, as well as to provide forms for exchange and mutual learning, as we have especially seen in the Swiss example. What we also observe in our cases is the transformation that intermediary organizations themselves undergo in pursuing their aims – as new labelling systems become more insitutionalized and new actors are included in the networks, labelling organizations have to adapt their organizational structure, their access to resources and their role in the maturing socio-technical system.

Mediating between supply and demand side

The bargaining power for system building at the supply side is highly interdependent with the consumption power labelling organizations represent or are at least able to invoke. Thus a key aim of such organizations is to increase the number of consumers supplied under the label and to actively align large 'lead' customers with the labels (such as the German Ministry for Environment or Tetra Pak in our case study).

Aligning large customers follows a different logic to aggregating household consumption decisions. Companies profit from an improved environmental image and their signalling of public accountability. Labels profit additionally from the 'symbolic benefits' of having large corporations on board as a sign of successful and serious market creation. For the case of forest certification (FSC), these large customers were even more important to move the market than household end consumers. As Gulbrandsen points out, forest certification is not driven by consumers' willingness to pay a premium for eco-labelled products, but rather by the requirements of professional purchasers, responding to pressures from environmental organizations (Gulbrandsen, 2005).

Intermediary organizations, as we can observe in the case of green electricity labels, are essential for stitching such arrangements together as a credible, trusted and neutral (in terms of profit interests) mediator. The social power of such organizations thus derives from their symbolic capital ('moral authority') and their specific expertise (Boström, 2006, p352). Labelling organizations thereby act as 'boundary organizations' which 'incorporate' a new type of production–consumption nexus. It is 'crucial to recognise as an important characteristic the stability it induces by successfully internalising the boundary negotiations' (Guston, 2001, p402). This is what we can observe especially in the Swiss case, where electricity generators, environmental and consumer organizations are all part of the intermediating labelling organization, and indeed 'internalize boundary negotiations' about eligibility criteria or required environmental standards. Similarly, Marvin and Medd (2004, p93) point out that 'the emergence of new intermediaries involves a move beyond this divide to appreciate the co-constitution of production and consumption together, not as separate activities but as entwined in new circuits of production and consumption.'

Intermediaries and the creation of hybrid governance systems

The reorganization of markets through the establishment of green electricity labels can be regarded as a 'non-state market-driven governance system' (Cashore, 2002). However, as we have seen, these private endeavours to set up and coordinate a green electricity market are covering only a small market segment and do not substitute state regulatory structures. While it is true that the liberalized electricity market regime has created new unregulated spaces or institutional voids (Burt, 2004) – in our case the possibility of non-transparent electricity product differentiation as a way of competing for customers – government regulation still sets narrow boundaries to the potential of such non-state forms of governance. Green power labels are an attempt to occupy and restructure part of this ungoverned territory of proliferating electricity products by organizing alternative producer–consumer relations around the issue of sustainability and renewable energy sources. However, the bulk growth of green electricity depends on government-driven schemes (such as feed-in tariffs) and will most likely stay so even under optimistic scenarios about the further development of electricity labels (Wüstenhagen and Bilharz, 2006). The new type of green electricity market governance through intermediaries is thus one element of a more complex and heterogeneous governance structure of the electricity sector, and takes shape in close interdependence with the specific national or even regional characteristics of these regulatory systems.

As we have pointed out earlier, the policy space governing renewable electricity development is already crowded by various climate change mitigation measures at international, national and regional level (various Kyoto targets and instruments, EU renewable energy directives, national feed-in tariffs, regional support measures and so on). Electricity labels aiming at additional environmental benefits have to be carefully designed with respect to this policy context to avoid double-subsidies or double counting of the same amount of green electricity produced for different support schemes and targets (see Ölz et al, 2006). As a result, the German ok power label only includes residual electricity not covered by the German renewable electricity law, while the Swiss label is embedded in a completely different electricity market and regulatory structure. In the UK we have already mentioned difficulties in setting up an independent labelling scheme in addition to a government support system already based on Renewables Obligation Certificates (ROCs).

At least in our case non-state governance does not challenge traditional state authority, but rather complements it, and may even form rather coherent hybrid governance systems of state and non-state actors. As we have seen with the example of the German Ministry for Environment procuring green electricity, the state may even lend moral support to non-state labelling schemes (see also Gulbrandsen, 2006). Symbiotic relations may also work the other way round, with labels and labelling organizations having repercussions on the institutional structure of the electricity sector. As we have seen, green labels are often designed as benchmarks or signalling devices of what sustainable product standards could look like, whether state regulated or as part of a voluntary product portfolio of electricity suppliers. The very construct of green electricity, and the way to track and validate it, was first introduced by green electricity companies operating in a symbiotic relationship with environmental NGOs, and then it found its way into EU directives and national regulations (e.g. Guarantees of Origin and tracking systems). Several representatives of labelling organizations also pointed out that green power suppliers, along with labelling organizations and environmental organizations, did play an important role in enforcing the practical implementation of liberalized regulation in the sector which was regularly subverted by incumbent actors. In model law suits these organizations fought for consumer rights and rights to market access.

At a more informal level, labelling can have an impact on the sector also by gradually restructuring actor positions and relationships. As we have seen, labelling organizations are a forum mediating interactions between incumbent and new electricity generators and suppliers, environmental organizations or consumer organizations, and triggering mutual learning effects – for instance, about overlapping interests and possible cooperation frameworks. This is an example of how repeated interaction over time in organized networks comprising a wide range of actors can result in common expectations about proper behaviour, a degree of mutual trust and mutual learning (Boström, 2006). Cooperation experience and personal relationships may also be a basis for further cooperation in other areas (Wüstenhagen et al, 2003). Learning also occurs on the side of users. Even if green power markets alone will not bring about a sustainable electricity system, they may play an important role in renewable energy support because of their potential to increase eco-orientation both on the consumer side and within the utilities (Markard and Truffer, 2006).

While it is difficult to quantify the impact of labels on the growth of green electricity beyond market data of electricity directly supplied under the labels, we can thus find a number of indirect impacts on regulatory structures, actor constellations and orientations resulting from the interrelatedness of state and non-state governance.

Conclusion

Our analysis of green electricity labelling schemes provides an illustration of how the transformation and re-regulation (liberalization) of socio-technical infrastructure systems we are currently experiencing on a world-wide scale is opening spaces for non-state forms of governance. In such market-driven contexts, strategic intermediation activities working in-between the different logics of supply, demand and public policy (regulation) assume a key role for the political construction and re-framing of markets. In our case, the aim of these intermediary activities is to push electricity markets towards a higher share of renewable energy sources. The case presented in this chapter can be read as an example of how in our present societies, where economics and markets are becoming more and more pervasive, civil society strategies for political intervention find new opportunities in the normatively oriented construction and shaping of markets.

With respect to the establishment of green electricity labels as an attempt to reframe energy markets, two main aspects of such strategic intermediation activities have been highlighted: strategic intermediation as normatively oriented market construction faces the task of simultaneously acting as a system builder for new supply-side structures (aligning actors, establishing standards, developing new procedures and collaboration practices, and so on); and as an agent to aggregate, articulate and translate individual consumption preferences. This balancing and simultaneous developing of intertwined supply-and-demand structures is a key intermediation activity of labelling organizations. The second challenge highlighted in this chapter is the integration and adaptation of non-state governance schemes with governmental regulatory systems. Although government regulation turns out to dominate the green electricity market, indirect influences of non-state forms of governance on the regulatory structures and actor orientation in the electricity system could be identified.

The intermediation activities we studied in this paper can indeed be understood as a form of soft power; that is, a capacity to shape and reconfigure energy markets without any formal empowerment to change regulations and framework conditions. Labelling organizations were able to shape the types of choice electricity consumers had by actively reconfiguring the structures of supply and demand in the sector – creating consumer trust in environmental quality standards, persuading large consumers to articulate demand for environmental products, facilitating learning processes of electricity suppliers about opportunities to offer a new type of product, and finally creating new institutions and procedures to stabilize these relations.

Although these activities did not exclusively address urban electricity infrastructures, they are important to understand the transformation of urban energy systems. As the examples of Badenova (which switched to the labelled product under consumer pressure) or the municipal utility of Zurich (which was an early driver for the label in Switzerland) demonstrate, the closer proximity of consumers and producers in the municipal context, as well as the still higher emphasis on public service in contrast to a purely profit-oriented approach, provide a favourable context to such intermediation activities. In the face of the ongoing extension of market structures into further parts of our society and economy, we thus can expect that non-state intermediation activities may become still more important as a strategy of making urban infrastructure systems more sustainable.

Acknowledgements

An earlier version of this chapter was published in *Environment and Planning A*, vol 41, no 8, 2009, pp2014–2028 (Pion, London).

Notes

1   The additionality criterion aims at giving green electricity consumers a guarantee that they support the construction of new renewable energy generation facilities and do not just pay a premium price for existing plants.
2   However, the association EUGENE has meanwhile been dissolved (February 2009), not least due to the difficulties in harmonizing labels which are all closely tailored to national contexts. This substantiates our observation on the close relations and interaction of non-state governance and regulatory contexts.

3   The activity of Greenpeace Germany during the liberalization process of the electricity market is also a highly interesting case of the new roles environmental organizations can take in such a context. The database of people signing up for green electricity during the initial campaign was sold in a bidding process to the electricity supplier with the ecologically best offer. Later on, Greenpeace set up its own green electricity company (Greenpeace Energy) owned by its members (Genossenschaft – the second largest in Germany with about 12,000 members), which today even invests in its own generation capacity.

References

Ahrne, G., Brunsson, N. and Tamm Hallström, K. (2007) 'Organizing organizations', *Organization*, vol 14, no 5, pp619–624

Birzle-Harder, B. and Götz, K. (2001) *Grüner Strom – Eine Sozialwissenschaftliche Marktanalyse*, ISOE, Frankfurt

Boardman, B. and Palmer, J. (2003) *Consumer Choice and Carbon Consciousness for Electricity (4CE)*, Final Report to the European Commission, Environmental Change Institute, Oxford

Boström, M. (2006) 'Regulatory credibility and authority through inclusiveness: Standardization organizations in cases of eco-labelling', *Organization*, vol 13, no 3, pp345–367

Brown, K. (2005) 'Green tariffs on the ROCs?', *Ethical Consumer*, vol 95, pp24–27

Bürger, V. (2007) *Green Power Labelling. An Instrument to Enhance Transparency and Sustainability on the Voluntary Green Power Market. Final Report of the CLEAN-E Project under the EU EIE Support Scheme*, Öko-Institut, Freiburg

Burt, R.S. (2004) 'Structural holes and good ideas', *American Journal of Sociology*, vol 110, no 2, pp349–399

Callon, M. (2007) 'An essay on the growing contribution of economic markets to the proliferation of the social', *Theory, Culture & Society*, vol 24, nos 7–8, pp139–163

Callon, M. and Muniesa, F. (2005) 'Economic markets as calculative collective devices', *Organization Studies*, vol 26, no 8, pp1229–1250

Cashore, B. (2002) 'Legitimacy and the privatization of environmental governance: How non-state market-driven (NSMD) governance systems gain rule-making authority', *Governance*, vol 15, no 4, pp503–529

Diaz-Rainey, I. and Ashton, J.K. (2008) 'Stuck between a ROC and a hard place? Barriers to the take up of green energy in the UK', *Energy Policy*, vol 36, no 8, pp3043–3051

Eurobarometer (2006) *Attitudes towards Energy. Special Eurobarometer*, European Commission, Brussels

Graham, V. (2006) *Reality of Rhetoric? Green Tariffs for Domestic Consumers*, National Consumer Council, London

Gulbrandsen, L.H. (2005) 'The effectiveness of non-state governance schemes: A comparative study of forest certification in Norway and Sweden', *International Environmental Agreements*, vol 5, pp125–149

Gulbrandsen, L.H. (2006) 'Creating markets for eco-labelling: Are consumers insignificant?', *International Journal of Consumer Studies*, vol 30, no 5, pp477–489

Guston, D.H. (2001) 'Boundary organizations in environmental policy and science: An introduction', *Science, Technology & Human Values*, vol 26, no 4, pp399–408

Holzer, B. (2006) 'Political consumerism between individual choice and collective action: Social movements, role mobilization and signalling', *International Journal of Consumer Studies*, vol 30, no 5, pp405–415

Ipsos_MORI (2008) *Consumers' View on Renewable and Low Carbon Supply Tariffs*, Ofgem, London

Kjellberg, H. and Helgesson, C.-F. (2007) 'On the nature of markets and their practices', *Marketing Theory*, vol 7, no 2, pp137–162

Majone, G. (1989) *Evidence, Argument, and Persuasion in the Policy Process*, Yale Univ. Press, New Haven

Markard, J. and Truffer, B. (2006) 'The promotional impacts of green power products on renewable energy sources: direct and indirect eco-effects', *Energy Policy*, vol 34, pp306–321

Marvin, S. and Medd, W. (2004) 'Sustainable infrastructures by proxy? Intermediation beyond the production–consumption nexus', in D. Southerton, H. Chappells and B. van Vliet (eds) *Sustainable Consumption: The Implications of Changing Infrastructures of Provision*, Edward Elgar Publishing, Cheltenham

Medd, W. and Marvin, S. (2006) 'Ecology of intermediation', in K. Green and S. Randles (eds) *Industrial Ecology and Spaces of Innovation*, Edward Elgar, Cheltenham

Ölz, S., Bürger, V., Draeck, M., Rohracher, H., Ruggieri, G., Vrolijk, C. and Green, J. (2006) *Interaction of Green Power Labelling with Renewable Energy Policies*. A report prepared as part of the EIE project CLEAN-E, Öko-Institut, Freiburg

O'Rourke, D. (2005) 'Nongovernmental organization strategies to influence global production consumption', *Journal of Industrial Ecology*, vol 9, nos 1–2, pp115–128

Pattberg, P. (2004) 'Private environmental governance and the sustainability transition: Functions and impacts of NGO-business partnerships', in K. Jacob, M. Binder and A. Wieczorek (eds) *Governance for Industrial Transformation. Proceedings of the 2003 Berlin Conference on the Human Dimension of Global Environmental Change*, Environmental Policy Research Centre, Berlin, pp52–66

Sorrell, S. (2003) *Interaction in EU Climate Policy. Final Report*, European Commission, Brussels

Späth, P. and Rohracher, H. (2009) *The 'Eco-Cities' Freiburg and Graz: The Social Dynamics of Pioneering Urban Energy & Climate Governance*. Paper presented at the Workshop 'Urban Transitions/Technological Transitions: Cities and Low Carbon Transitions, SURF, Manchester

Truffer, B. (2007) 'Wissensintegration in transdiziplinären Projekten', *GAIA*, vol 16, no 1, pp41–45

Truffer, B., Markard, J. and Wüstenhagen, R. (2001) 'Eco-labeling of electricity – strategies and tradeoffs in the definition of environmental standards', *Energy Policy*, vol 29, pp885–897

Truffer, B., Bratrich, C., Markard, J., Peter, A., Wüest, A. and Wehrli, B. (2003) 'Green Hydropower: The contribution of aquatic science research to the promotion of sustainable electricity', *Aquatic Sciences – Research Across Boundaries*, vol 65, no 2, pp99–110

Willstedt, H. and Bürger, V. (2006) *Overview of Existing Green Power Labelling Schemes*. A report prepared as part of the EIE project CLEAN-E, Öko-Institut, Freiburg

Wüstenhagen, R. and Bilharz, M. (2006) 'Green energy market development in Germany: effective public policy and emerging customer demand', *Energy Policy*, vol 34, pp1681–1696

Wüstenhagen, R., Markard, J. and Truffer, B. (2003) 'Diffusion of green power products in Switzerland', *Energy Policy*, vol 31, pp621–632

6
Innovation to Intermediaries: Translating the EU Urban Wastewater Directive

Ross Beveridge and Simon Guy

Introduction: innovation to intermediaries

To achieve environmental improvements there is an urgent need, we are told, for more innovation. As the Chief Executive of Water UK (the association representing UK water and wastewater suppliers at national and European levels) said in a speech that innovation is needed

> *to support policy development and to support the implementation of solutions... And of course by innovation we aren't just talking about new equipment and plant but: joined up policy formulation and development from EC directives to UK legislation; better ways of implementing UK and EC legislation and policies by regulators and operators; and better overall solutions for the environment, economy and society (Taylor, 2005).*

With these objectives in mind, academics, campaigners and policy-makers have explored the relative merits of a range of policy and regulatory frameworks, institutional structures and 'best practices'. While these issues are clearly important, such studies rarely tell us much about the mundane realities of actually *achieving* environmental innovation, of reforming water practices 'on the ground'. This chapter addresses this gap by exploring the processes through which environmental improvements are sought and why they are difficult to achieve. We do this with reference to one of the key mechanisms by which water practices in Europe are governed – the issuing of EU directives. Taking the example of the EU's Urban Waste Water directive (UWW), we trace the ways in which it signals a realignment of actors and practices in pursuit of new environmental standards in wastewater practices in the north of England.

In particular, this chapter investigates a common problem posed by the implementation of the UWW: how can the practices of small-scale, 'low-tech' commercial water users be transformed in the context of limited knowledge and financial resources. In England, much responsibility for the implementation of the UWW lies with the regional water companies, who are responsible for ensuring that their consumers do not discharge untreated wastewater. The water company in turn seeks to regulate the practices of their users. In doing this, however, they provide only an instruction to the users – all wastewater must be treated – but often little guidance as to how this should be achieved.

A 'gap' between regulatory objectives and the capacity of actors to achieve them can emerge as small-scale commercial users of water search for innovative and cost-effective reforms. In such contexts, implementation on the ground becomes problematic and the ultimate realization of regulatory reforms slow and often haphazard.

We argue that, in order to better encourage environmental innovation, it is vital that we move away from attempts to measure, model and promote it, and instead appreciate its contingent and complex nature (Guy et al, 2001). In response, we adopt an approach to innovation influenced by debates in actor network theory (ANT), which directs our gaze at the often complex interactions which occur between actors as they seek to reform practices. That is, we first take an ontological stance, which conceives of the world as being founded upon heterogeneous processes in which the social, technical and natural are relationally enmeshed (Latour, 2005). Secondly, and in particular, we utilize the concept of 'translation', through which we conceive of innovation in the water sector as being about the re-representation and re-ordering of actors through the construction of new networks (Callon, 1986). This is seen as difficult to achieve, being, as it is, contingent upon the interactions of a diverse range of human and non-human actors who are already enrolled in a range of networks themselves. From this perspective, we conceive of the implementation of the UWW, with its attempt to reform water practices as a contested process of translation that must be achieved and re-achieved in highly specific contexts throughout the water sector. Thirdly, within these processes of translation we highlight the emergence of intermediary organizations who perform a range of roles in-between actors and policy, and who are integral to the ways in which objects and practices are translated and reform realized.

This notion of 'intermediation' is a useful means of conceptualizing research into network transitions in contemporary water governance. Over the last few decades the governance of EU water sectors has been transformed, to varying degrees, through processes of privatization, liberalization, internationalization and increased environmental regulation (Guy et al, 2001; Bakker, 2003; Kaika, 2003). Recent research has probed the impacts of such shifts, arguing that new 'intermediary spaces' are emerging in-between regulators, users and providers of water services, and that the (intermediary) actors working within these spaces can be crucial to the configuration of relationships between economy, environment and society (Moss and Medd, 2005; Wissen and Moss, 2005; Moss et al, 2009). Such intermediaries operate along the production–consumption nexus, but they also 'intermediate between different scales, between technologies and different social contexts, between different meanings and between different sets of interests' (Moss and Medd, 2005, p20). They are, therefore, crucial to understanding the complexity of Europe's water sectors. Looking for intermediaries can then often reveal a range of actors – and forms of interaction – often neglected in studies of water sectors, and ultimately illuminate the contests over the roles and values of 'water' in contemporary society to which these dynamics give rise.

Following the work of an environmental consultancy at the interfaces between the directive and some of those it intends to regulate, we reveal the usually unseen, yet integral processes through which an intermediary organization attempts to bring order and agreement to reforming practices – how they seek to facilitate the implementation of environmental regulation. The consultancy was employed by a company that was producing wastewater resistant to standard biological techniques of degradation. This was presenting them with serious problems of disposal and treatment. The client was a drum re-conditioner in the chemical industry: a company which cleaned and re-furbished 45-gallon drums which had been used to store and transport chemicals.

The consultancy can be seen to act as an intermediary on two levels. In broader terms, they are working in-between the regulator (the EU), the producer (the regional water company) and the user (the drum re-conditioner) at the regional scale. More specifically, the consultancy is working in-between actors (and, as we will suggest, technical and natural entities) at the micro-level.

Innovation as translation

How should practices of environmental innovation on the ground be researched? How can an understanding of the ways in which actors respond to and reinterpret environmental regulation be developed? To consider the role of innovators in the process is nothing new. For example, some analysis has focused on organizations and individuals seen as capable of bridging the gap between the interests of the environment and the economy: 'eco-preneurs' (Isaak, 2000, 2002; Schaper, 2002; Walley and Taylor, 2002). Following entrepreneurship studies, eco-preneurship investigates to varying degrees the interactions between the personal/organizational qualities (their skills and beliefs) of such actors and their surroundings (the economic, social, political and technological context). According to this literature, it is through examining these interactions – between the psychological dimension and the socio-economic dimension – that we can identify, conceptualize and promote the forms of innovative business activity which leads to more sustainable economic practices (for a more detailed critique of the literature, see Beveridge and Guy, 2005).

Other approaches, however, choose to see innovation as a less predictable process: one which cannot be reduced to the interactions between personalities and broader external forces; one where the acquisition and implementation of knowledge is convoluted and 'individuals, groups, and institutions embody widely differing perceptions of what environmental innovation is about' (Guy and Farmer, 2001, p140). For example, a more situated approach, informed by sociology and social psychology, instructs us to see innovation processes as fundamentally conversational (Fonseca, 2002) and, as such, iterative and averse to attempts at planning or ordering. In this view, the material representations of innovation, such as new technologies, emerge through 'ordinary, everyday work conversations' (Fonseca, 2002, p5), in which actors look to resolve conflict through identifying solutions to emergent problems. 'In other words, new order emerges in disorder, that is, diversity and what seems like wasteful interaction' (Fonseca, 2002, p8). Here the importance of location and the use of language within it become paramount to environmental innovation. Stories, for example, 'use language to frame what has happened to a set of characters in a particular time and place' (Eckstein, 2003, p14). Such discursive approaches show how language is vital for framing beliefs, shaping debates and outlining courses of action (see Hajer, 1995).

But while this focus on the language and strategies of communication is useful for understanding innovation, such approaches often neglect the ways in which human actors interact with 'things' around them – such as technologies and nature – and that such interactions have constitutive effects on both people and things: 'actants' can 'recast or reconstruct themselves, their interests and their worlds' as they enter into relations with one and another (Freeman, 2007, p6). In order to better explore these processes, we turn to ANT and, in particular, the concept of translation.

Briefly, ANT has its roots in the sociological study of science and technology, though it has made in-roads into other disciplines including organization studies, geography and politics (Fine, 2005). It aims to understand how organizational practices emerge and are stabilized, and how they are sustained over time and distance. This is to be revealed by looking at the construction of 'actor-networks'. The premise behind the metaphor of the actor-network is that all action is contingent. Indeed, entities achieve their very form as a consequence of the relations in which they are situated (McLean and Hassard, 2004).

ANT sees social structures as materializing from the interaction of human *and* non-human entities; technologies and nature are potentially active in the formation of social structures, and can thus be seen to be actors too. Stepping back slightly from ANT's 'symmetrical' approach to the human and non-human, we prefer, following Hacking (1999a, 1999b) and Murdoch (2001, 2003), to retain a sense of the unique human qualities which emerge in these networks, such as the power of communication and reflection, and shape motivations for action. Thus our case study retains an emphasis on how social processes often order arrangements of heterogeneous elements (Murdoch, 2003, p265). In other words, the distinction here is that heterogeneous relations may mediate social action, but the distinctiveness of human qualities can often be seen to act as a 'driver' for change in the socio-technical–natural world (Murdoch, 2003, p275).

From an ANT-inspired perspective, the achievement of 'network transitions' would be seen as the outcome of a process of translation (of new environmental regulation in the case studied here). This process of translation describes the struggle between the objectives and strategies of human actors, and the performance of technical and natural actors. Through this struggle actors are displaced, re-defined, and then re-assembled and re-ordered, through the creation of a new network of relations (Law, 1999). Importantly, ANT stresses that this process is neither predictable nor controllable, as new knowledge and practices can only be achieved through the construction of relationships between actors.

In this view, innovation moves away from a linear, predictable model, in which change emerges almost inevitably once 'non-technical barriers' have been removed. Instead, attempts at establishing new arrangements, of enrolling actors in a new network, are constantly being resisted or redefined according to the competing visions and practices of actors (Mclean and Hassard, 2004). As Latour says of socio-technical systems undergoing change, what we see is 'uncertainty, people at work, decisions, competition, contro-versies' (Latour, 1987, p4). Thus the process of translation is about reaching a settlement on the often conflicting priorities of a variety of actors, such as designers, regulators, accountants and consumers (Kaghan and Bowker, 2001, p264). It is the actor(s) who can 'firmly associate a large number of elements' to their vision of the innovation, and 'dissociate as speedily as possible ele-ments enrolled by other actors' who succeed and have power in networks (Callon and Latour, 1981, p292; see also Callon et al, 2002).

Translation through intermediation

It is within these contested processes of translation that intermediaries emerge. The notion of intermediation has been much discussed and debated in ANT (see Hennion, 1989; Callon, 1991; Latour, 2005). Here, we adopt a loose interpretation of an intermediary, seeing them as being an entity 'that stands at a place in the network between two other actors and serves to trans-late between the actors in such a way that their interaction can be more effectively coordinated, controlled, or otherwise articulated' (Kaghan and Bowker, 2001, p258). Intermediaries therefore work to translate between actors in contexts where relationships are unstable and decision-making processes difficult. They act as conduits between actors, attempting to resolve disputes: 'intermediaries help the different parties involved in a situation to "improvise" a response that is both sensible and acceptable under the cir-cumstances' (Kaghan and Bowker, 2001, p258). As such they can play integral, if sometimes 'unseen', roles, assisting the actors between whom they are operating to achieve their objectives. The form these intermediaries take is, of course, a result of the negotiations within which they find themselves. It is dependent on the context within which they become embroiled, as they are ascribed roles according to the negotiations in which they are embedded. As they are playing these roles in-between actors, we conceive of them as playing integral roles in altering practices in the water sector.

Utilizing this notion of intermediation, within a broader ANT perspective, what might we expect from a study of the implementation of the UWW? Firstly, at the most simple level, although the UWW is an attempt to re-order water sector practices, so as to achieve particular outcomes, it obviously has no potential to act in isolation. Although the directive contains elements of coercion – it is a form of regulation which should be conformed to – exactly who should, and in what manner, enforce the directive are dependent upon negotiation: its meaning and form are not 'given'. As such, it needs to be translated into action, to be made real, to become embedded in relations of actors.

So while the EU has the power to set regulatory targets, its success is, in part, contingent upon the capacity of intermediaries to enrol, cajole and even coerce actors into new networks of water practices. We conceive of these intermediaries as bridge-builders, forming and fixing relationships between actors and in the process facilitating translations. They draw in and distribute resources necessary for actors to take action. These intermediaries are integral to the UWW in that they are being produced and reproduced in the translation processes through which it is embedded. As a result they acquire a strategic importance to the successful translation of the UWW and play a crucial role in constructing new governance arrangements in water sectors.

In the case study below we take one such example of how the UWW was translated in the north of England. Our chosen actor to follow is a small commercial consultancy ('Consultancy'[1]) that describes its role as helping organizations resolve water-related, environmental and regulatory problems through the introduction of commercially robust process improvements. Through exploratory discussions with the Consultancy, we first identified a case which revealed the complexity of reforming practices in response to environmental regulation. Through a series of in-depth semi-structured interviews, the Consultancy was encouraged to re-tell the story: first chronologically and later in more detail on specific parts of the process which pointed to the apparent difficulties which arise in a group of actors re-negotiating practices.

The company was formed in 2000 and consists of two directors. Between them they have around 30 years experience in positions covering the following areas: lab-bench analysis; research and development; industrial wastewater treatment; management of all quality aspects of the water cycle; environmental regulation of the water and wastewater sector; conservation and recreation. Such experience gives them the ability to perform in both the technological- and business-focused areas of the water sector. To those actors who are business focused, they 'manage the industrial water cycle and optimize the industrial water cycle; we reduce costs' (Interview, 6 May 2004). To actors in the technological dimension, they emphasize their ability to understand technology and turn it into a commercially successful product: 'we can turn the theoretical knowledge, the abstract, into hard-nosed, on the ground business propositions' (Interview, 6 May 2004). The ability to perform in each of these contexts is essential to their intermediation, their work at the 'interface between the ideas and practitioners', bridging this gap between innovators and practitioners (Interview, 6 May 2004).

Through this case study we aim to show a glimpse of what happens when the UWW, as realized by the EU, circulates through the water sector. We show how it becomes entangled with, among other things, the performance of technologies, the visions and strategies of commercial organizations, and ideas of best practices. In other words, through looking at this chain of actions, from the instructions in the directive to changes in micro-level water practices, we emphasize that 'laws do not apply "themselves", ideas do not spread "themselves": there is work to be done' (Hennion, 1989). In doing so we emphasize that the implementation of EC directives is unpredictable and non-linear, a 'series of iterations' (Hennion, 1989) which serve to underscore the contingency of governing environmental standards at a distance.

Translating the UWW directive in the north of England

The UWW requires all sewage to be treated. Up until the late 1990s, some coastal areas of the UK had only limited screening of sewage to remove the larger particles before the raw sewage was discharged to the sea through a long sea outfall. The drum re-conditioner was based in one such region. The water used to clean the drums would have traces of whatever had been in the drums – so could be contaminated with any form of chemical, in combination with any other chemicals present. It was these traces of chemicals which first linked the drum re-conditioner to the UWW when, during 1998–2000, the regional water company, in an effort to comply with the directive, built a sewage works in this town and began tackling the trade effluent discharges of commercial water users such as the drum re-conditioner. In response to the water company's instructions to reduce discharges, the drum re-conditioner company installed a small treatment plant on their site for around half a million pounds, which reduced the amount of effluent discharged. However, it proved inadequate to deal with the metals in the effluent and did not have the capacity to remove enough of the organic load to satisfy the water company.

The wastewater process proved resistant to the standard biological techniques of degradation employed by the drum re-conditioner. The successful translation of the UWW now becomes dependent on the successful treatment of these resistant, rogue chemicals. They become the problem to be solved, provoking negotiations over how to reform practices. As such practices need to be re-configured and the rogue chemicals are active in this process, they mediate the social action around them. At this point, the Consultancy is ascribed the role of assisting the drum re-conditioner to treat the chemicals, to work between them (with their business practices), the chemicals (with their toxic qualities), the water company (with their demands for a reduction of wastewater) and the overall regulatory standards stipulated by the UWW (treat all forms of wastewater).

Emergence of an intermediary

When the Consultancy was appointed, the drum company was toying with the idea of building another effluent plant, but was naturally keen to find a cheaper alternative. The particular problems faced by the drum re-conditioner were far from exceptional. There are many companies providing similar services in England, while many larger chemical companies perform such tasks on an in-house basis. The difference between this company and many others in the field was that they were fairly small by comparison, and as a result adopted a more low-tech, manual approach: 'The big drum-conditioners tend to be large, very professional companies who have chemists, waste managers and so on involved in the process' (Interview, 17 June 2004). By contrast, cleaning the drums for this company might involve 'a couple of blokes with a hosepipe'. They did not have the overall resources, in terms of knowledge and finances, to deal with the problem in the way those larger companies could (Interview, 17 June 2004). This disadvantage perhaps explains why the drum re-conditioner could not or would not follow so-called best practice in this area, which could have vastly reduced the amount of chemical waste they had to dispose of.

Best practice would dictate that the original users of the drums should remove all of the chemicals in the drums prior to sending them for re-conditioning. This might sound insignificant, but some of the drums were an eighth to a sixth full of waste chemicals, which the drum re-conditioner would then have to dispose of. Secondly, best practice would suggest that the drums should be divided into batches containing the same chemicals so these can then be treated discretely. Neither of these practices was happening at the company.

Some of the drum re-conditioners' problems emerged from relatively simple actions performed – or not – by employees:

> *There was nothing technical about that – it was all very straight-forward... If he'd [company boss] got his systems right, workers trained and sorted at the front end of the process a significant amount of the problem would have been resolved (Interview, 8 July 2004).*

Although 'social' in origin, this problem ultimately required a technological, rather than a change in, social/business practice. Firstly, it is 'all about supplier–customer relationships, because some companies would not want to upset their customers by sending back a dirty drum and telling them to clean it out' (Interview, 8 July 2004). This kind of change, which superficially seems simple, requires a re-alignment of relationships which can only occur through negotiation between the actors involved. This can be a tricky, potentially disruptive process and is thus often avoided. Furthermore, the Consultancy suggest that companies in the chemical sector, dominated as it is by engineers and chemists, tend to feel more comfortable with finding a technological solution to problems: 'Most scientists and engineers will prefer to put a technical solution at the end of the pipe rather than tackle the "people" stuff of business' (Interview, 8 July 2004). This line of thinking explains why the company boss was willing to pay upwards of £2 million for a technological fix – building another treatment plant on the site.

Searching for a solution: development of electrochemical technology

For around a year, the Consultancy sought a means of reducing the amount of resistant chemicals discharged by the company through reforming the processes within the plant, according to the work they were able to do. As they say: 'We were there simply as advisors and had no power to insist they did anything' (Interview, 4 November 2004). Nonetheless, in order to find a solution, they re-interpreted the problem presented by the UWW. Their client was considering an end-of-pipe, technical fix: building a larger effluent treatment plant. The Consultancy thought this 'ridiculous', as the plant would have been 'bigger than their actual factory' (Interview, 13 August 2004). Instead, they turned to a small engineering firm, Company X, developing new technologies.

At the first exploratory meeting with Company X, the Consultancy asked them about a ceramic micro-filter they had been working on which could be used in separation processes. They believed this would be suitable for the client because they used an electrochemical system to clean it, which would ensure its longevity despite the toxic nature of the wastewater being separated. In simple terms, electrochemistry uses electricity to remove impurities from substances, so Company X proposed adapting it and applying it to wastewater to remove resistant pollutants. It is not a new technique, having been developed over 20 years ago to make chlorine gas for sterilizing water. However, this technique had not been truly commercialized in any field, let alone that of wastewater treatment, probably because wastewater from domestic sewage and much trade effluent is fairly biodegradable and can be treated in a relatively standardized form. As the Consultancy say, electrochemistry at this stage was 'stuck in a file in an academic box so it might as well not have existed' (Interview, 13 August 2004).

The Consultancy thought Company X would propose a variation of this filter system: 'wastewater would come in, it would go through a plate, leaving clean water on one side and dirty water on the other'. Instead, Company X came up the idea of creating a highly sophisticated electrochemical destruction system to treat the wastewater. So sophisticated in fact that Director 2 had 'no idea what he was talking about' (Interview, 13 August 2004).

Some description of the inventor in Company X is necessary here, as his mode of working has a major bearing on the development of the technology. To the Consultancy he could be described as the 'archetypal mad scientist'. These characteristics had both positive and negative implications: 'He was a great inventor, but so far off the wall and so impractical that he was very hard to work with. He pissed potential customers off something rotten' (Interview, 13 August 2004). This also made for great tension within Company X as the salesman often felt misled and out of the loop, as the inventor seemed, in his opinion, not to care for the realities and pressures of commerce. The Consultancy endeavoured to act as 'facilitators', employing 'soft skills', 'keeping everyone talking to each other' while the technology was being developed (Interview, 13 August 2004).

Technology trial

Having worked on this idea for a few months, Company X met with the Consultancy to trial the technology at the client's plant. The trials lasted for six weeks and there were 30 or so exercises with the technology. The trials were designed to see how much the chemical oxygen demand (COD) of the effluent was reduced. This is a

> *general measure of pollution. It's a cheap test to do, we could do*
> *it on site, and we could react to results in a couple of hours... The*
> *sample was then sent to a lab to see if the real 'nasties' [the resist-*
> *ant chemicals] had been destroyed (Interview, 13 August 2004).*

In appearance, the technology was fairly rudimentary, a 'Heath Robinson lash-up':

> *You had a tank with anodes and cathodes in it. You put the*
> *wastewater in at one end. You charge up each of the electrodes*
> *and in simple terms the electricity drives the break up of the mol-*
> *ecules. Some of it's done by direct electrical destruction – you put*
> *enough energy in and it splits the molecule. If there's salt –*
> *sodium chloride – present hyper chloride forms which chemically*
> *oxidizes the molecule and makes it fall apart. Those were the two*
> *basic processes. This system hadn't been used for treating waste-*
> *waters in the UK because people couldn't get 'the mix of*
> *everything fast enough' without incurring great costs (Interview,*
> *13 August 2004).*

However, 'to be fair to them it worked. It was the best effluent treatment we had seen in a long time' (Interview, 13 August 2004). In short, the technology looked very promising, taking only two hours to clean the wastewater put into it: 'it worked sufficiently well on day one to make us think it could fly' (Interview, 13 August 2004). This system of treating the waste was not, however, the one they planned to produce and had described to the Consultancy in their first meetings. Clearly, they had done it through accident. By switching the polarity of the electrodes – from positive to negative and back again – they had managed to create the right degree of mix with the molecules firing back and forth according to the changing charges of the electrodes. Originally they had probably imagined that they would 'make what we call a hydroxide generator. Hydroxide is a very powerful oxidizing species – it will destroy anything... But what he'd actually done was improve the conventional process [of mixing]' (Interview, 13 August 2004). So somewhere in the process of creation the system had become markedly different from what its creators had intended it to be: 'It wasn't done logically – you find most things aren't' (Interview, 13 August 2004).

This represented a problem for the salesman of Company X: the inventor was

> *always claiming something would be like this, which would later*
> *change entirely – it was a moveable feast. So operating costs,*
> *amount of electricity required kept changing, which undermined*
> *what the seller was saying to the potential client (Interview, 13*
> *August 2004).*

In other words, the qualities and requirements of the good he was trying to sell kept changing without his knowledge. In turn, this impeded his ability to communicate clearly with the drum re-conditioner and thus hampered his strategy for selling the technology.

Negotiating the sale of the technology

The technology had, under trial conditions, performed. Company X had constructed an electrochemical system which had the potential to destroy previously resistant chemicals. They, along with the Consultancy, had embedded the technology for six weeks within the work processes of the plant, and this new alignment of actors, including of course the company's workers, had seemingly achieved its objective: the rogue chemicals could be treated on site. The Consultancy's role in this process was multiple: to enrol the plant workers in the technology – to re-orientate the workers and processes in the plant so as to allow the technology to become embedded; to change existing patterns of work and forge new ones; to translate the technology into a functioning product in the plant through 'demystifying' it and gaining the support of those who would have to work with it:

> We'd got the works' engineer on board, he was really into it, he was enthused about it, and he was learning to do the tests. The plant operators were beginning to see that if they did something with the drums down here the kit – the secret kit! – worked better. So they were all enthused and fired up for it (Interview, 13 August 2004).

There was obviously one final, crucial step left – a price had to be agreed for the technology. These negotiations are obviously difficult to describe in anything but general terms. For Company X they were about attributing a value to this innovative technology, to the work and thinking behind its development. For the drum re-conditioner, it was about attributing a value not just to the technology, but to the new arrangements of workers and technology within the plant. The managing director (MD) of the company thus also had to decide whether he wanted to embed the technology within new work processes within his plant, which would entail training costs as well as having wider implications on how the plant worked.

The Consultancy participated in these negotiations, but Company X's salesman resisted their attempts to play a more fundamental role. In the Consultancy's opinion this was a mistake, as the salesman was not familiar with the plant: he did not understand how it worked and how the technology would fit into the processes already in operation there. It appears there was something of a culture clash between the MD and the salesman. In blunt terms, the Consultancy believe the MD saw him as a 'bullshitter' (Interview, 13 August 2004). They playfully framed this culture clash in terms of a North–South divide, with the salesman being from the South, though they admit that it was far more than this: 'it was a complete mismatch of both cultures and approach', which led to the salesman making unfounded claims about the plant which the MD saw as nonsense (Interview, 13 August 2004):

> *What he [the salesman] did was make claims about the client's*
> *plant which I would say in 'Northern' terms were beyond real-*
> *ity. God knows what he was thinking. The MD was a good*
> *old-fashioned boots-on, hands-on manager – he was on the site*
> *(Interview, 13 August 2004).*

To the Consultancy, the salesman made the mistake of approaching the negotiations in the way he would have if it had been a large, resource-rich chemical
company. He gave the plant 'a much more finished, mature air than it had'
(Interview, 13 August 2004). He made claims about the technology and the
work practices at the factory which were unrealistic. Unfortunately for him
the MD, because he had been monitoring the trials, knew it: 'how quickly the
technology would work, what its operating costs were, how quickly they could
deliver. And these things weren't being lived up to and the MD knew it!'
(Interview, 13 August 2004):

> *He was talking to a 'back-street' drum conditioner... I mean, if*
> *you go and talk to a big chemical company and talk that stuff*
> *up, dressed in suit and tie, brief case and stuff then fair enough.*
> *But not for this site (Interview, 13 August 2004).*

Ultimately, the MD decided not to buy it, saying that they would prefer to
solve the problem at different stages of the process, but the reality, in the
Consultancy's opinion, was that the salesman had handled negotiations
poorly: 'Cutting a long story short, at the end of the pitch after the salesman
had left, the MD of the company said to us: "do not bring that man back
here"' (Interview, 13 August 2004).

Thus the technology was not translated: not for 'technical' reasons – trials
had proven its worth – but because the MD and Company X's salesman had
contested visions of how practices should be conducted in this area. The salesman seems to have attempted to impose his vision of how the company could
and should work, with the benefit of the new technology, while the MD,
despite seeing the benefits of the technology, was resistant to this imagined
state of affairs. In the process, the Consultancy's intermediary role collapsed.
They were unable to work between these two actors, to find a compromise
between their competing strategies and visions.

Conclusions: intermediaries, innovation and governance

The above case study has provided, through the eyes of an environmental consultancy, a glimpse into the realities of reforming wastewater practices on the
ground. We have argued that, when examining the implementation of environmental regulation and the ways in which actors innovate in response to it,
it is best to view it as a process of multiple translations. It is about getting a
range of actors to realign their preferences, understandings and, in the process,
their practices in very specific contexts. Within these twists and turns, the UWW
takes on different meanings as it becomes contingent upon the interpretations

and actions of different sets of actors. It is shown that these actors constantly have to be rearranged. The actors involved have to work hard to develop new arrangements, to define problems, to forge solutions to them, and to agree roles and relationships through reaching compromises. What we can see from the case study is that reaching consensus from contested contexts is neither easy to achieve nor easy to sustain: in such processes of translation, success is never far from failure.

Seen this way, the implementation of EU directives, in this case of reforming wastewater practices, depended upon negotiation between the technology experts, their technology, the rogue chemicals, the inventor, his invention, the salesman, the on-site workers, their MD, the regional water company, the directive itself and the Consultancy who performed an array of services. By including non-human elements in the analysis, we have gained a sense of how contingent social action is upon non-human entities and that the Consultancy becomes something of an intermediary between actors in the 'co-evolution between social, natural and technological aspects of the world' (Murdoch, 2003, p271).

So what does this tell us about the nature of this 'in-between' work, of intermediation? Although, in our case study, the UWW was not fully translated, mediation between these 'actants' is integral to innovation processes in the water sector. In their own words, they were

> 'resource investigators', 'providers of relevant contacts', and a 'source of specialist knowledge and skills' in the 'technical' and 'business' dimensions of the sector, utilizing their experience of 'business processes and new product development' (Interview, 6 May 2004).

As is shown by the example of the Consultancy, an intermediary is not a role that is defined necessarily by 'size' or 'strength', but by location in-between actors and an ability to mediate across boundaries. This is not to suggest that intermediaries make the process of innovation any less messy, inefficient and iterative. As we have argued, these are the defining features of innovation processes and the position of an intermediary is as fragile as the translation processes within which they are produced: their fate is entirely linked to the outcomes of the negotiations in which they emerge. They have been pictured as struggling to translate between actors, trying to overcome knowledge deficits, misunderstandings, outright disagreements, and in the process construct new identities and practices.

In doing this work of translation, it is important to note that they were not neutral. In fact, as was shown above, they have their own objectives and understandings which shape the contexts within which they work. Such thinking is useful, as it points us to key processes within governance and emphasizes the point that the realization of policy objectives such as EU directives is very much a *translation* of those objectives, a transformation of words into some form of new practice on the ground.

Intermediation is then useful for focusing our gaze on the micro-interactions between actors in the water sector. It highlights the extent to which attempts to alter practices become contingent on these processes: how network transitions emerge from these local sites of translation. However, we should be careful not to suggest that the implementation of such directives occurs within a realm without hierarchy, an ever-fluid site in which political power only exists in the extent to which it can be realized through the assembly and performance of networks of relations.

Instead, this case study revealed two different forms of power at work in this particular example of the implementation of the UWW directive: power as a cause of action and power as an effect, an outcome of action. By accepting that both forms of power can exist within innovation processes – as ANT writers have sometimes accepted (Law, 1991) – we can perhaps negate what has been seen as problematic in ANT's conceptualization of the organization of actor-networks the absence of a sense of broader power structures within which actor-networks evolve (Brown and Capdevila, 1999).

In issuing the directive, the EU is exercising its power over actors; its capacity to compel them to treat all wastewater before discharging it. The directive does then act as an instigator of action, providing actors with an overall objective, setting a trajectory for the processes of translation which we have explored. From this point, the process of giving it content, making it real on the ground, of translating new practices, we can see power from an ANT perspective, dispersed across a range of actors, contingent and an outcome of their negotiations. Through focusing on the work of an intermediary in these processes, this case study shows how the objectives of directives can get lost in the self-organizing dynamics of innovation processes: how it can come to mean very different things as it passes through a series of translations.

This chapter has sought to reveal this oft overlooked dimension to the implementation of directives, exposing in particular how the discreet work of being in-between actors often entails in the process a subtle distortion or manipulation – translation – of other actors' objectives. As such, these intermediaries should be seen as having not only the potential to help and hinder the realization of policy objectives, but to *transform* the meaning of these objectives into viable practices. Perhaps a keener sense of this transformative capacity would shed further light on the uneven implementation of policies and the seemingly opaque processes which underpin policy failure.

Note

1   In the interests of anonymity, organizations and personnel are not referred to by name. Interviews were conducted with the Consultancy in the north of England between May and November 2004.

Acknowledgements

This chapter is based in part on the publication by Beveridge, R. and Guy, S. (2009) 'Governing through translations: Intermediaries and the mediation of the EU's Urban Wastewater directive', *Journal of Environmental Policy and Planning*, vol 11, no 2, pp69–85.

References

Bakker, K. (2003) 'From public to private ... to mutual? Restructuring water supply governance in England and Wales', *Geoforum*, vol 34, no 3, pp359–374

Beveridge, R. and Guy, S. (2005) 'The rise of the eco-preneur and the messy world of environmental innovation', *Local Environment*, vol 10, no 6, pp665–676

Brown, S.D. and Capdevila, R. (1999) 'Perpetuum mobile: Substances, force and the sociology of translation', in J. Law and J. Hassard (eds) *Actor Network Theory and After*, Blackwell, Oxford, pp15–25

Callon, M. (1986) 'Some elements of a sociology of translation: Domestication of the scallops and the fishermen of St Brieuc Bay', in J. Law (ed) *Power, Action and Belief: A New Sociology of Knowledge?*, Routledge and Kegan Paul, London, pp196–233

Callon, M. (1991) 'Techno-economic networks and irreversibility', in J. Law (ed) *A Sociology of Monsters: Essays on Power, Technology and Domination*, Routledge, London, pp132–161

Callon, M. and Latour, B. (1981) 'Unscrewing the big Leviathan: How actors macrostructure reality and how sociologists help them to do so', in K. Knorr-Cetina and A. Cicourel (eds) *Advances in Social Theory and Methodology*, Routledge and Kegan Paul, London, pp277–303

Callon, M., Meadel, C. and Rabeharisoa, V. (2002) 'The economy of qualities', *Economy and Society*, vol 31, no 2, pp194–217

Eckstein, B. (2003) 'Making spaces: Stories in the practice of planning', in B. Eckstein and J. Throgmorton (eds) *Story and Sustainability: Planning, Practice and Possibility for American Cities*, MIT Press, Cambridge, MA, pp211–236

Fine, B. (2005) 'From actor network theory to political economy', *Capitalism Nature Socialism*, vol 16, no 4, pp91–108

Fonseca, J. (2002) *Complexity and innovation in organizations*, Routledge, Abingdon, Oxon

Freeman, R. (2007) *Policy Moves: Translation, Policy and Politics*. Conference Paper, *2nd International Conference in Interpretive Policy Analysis: Research and Practice*, 31 May–2 June 2007, Amsterdam, the Netherlands

Guy, S. and Farmer, G. (2001) 'Reinterpreting sustainable architecture: The place of technology', *Journal of Architectural Education*, vol 54, no 3, pp140–148

Guy, S., Marvin, S. and Moss, T. (2001) *Urban Infrastructure in Transition: Networks, Buildings, Plans*, Earthscan, London

Hacking, I. (1999a) *The Social Construction of What?*, Harvard University Press, London

Hacking, I. (1999b) *Mad Travellers: Reflections on the Reality of Transient Mental Illness*, Free Association Books, London

Hajer, M. (1995) *The Politics of Environmental Discourse: Ecological Modernisation and the Policy Process*, Clarendon Press, Oxford

Hennion, A. (1989) 'An intermediary between production and consumption: The producer of popular music', *Science, Technology and Human Values*, vol 14, no 4, pp400–424

Isaak, R. (2000) *Green Logic: Eco-preneurship Theory and Ethics*, Greenleaf, Sheffield

Isaak, R. (2002) 'The making of the eco-preneur', *Greener Management International, Theme: Environmental Entrepreneurship*, vol 38, pp81–90

Kaghan, W.N. and Bowker, G.C. (2001) 'Out of machine age?', *Journal of Engineering and Technology Management*, vol 18, pp253–269

Kaika, M. (2003) 'The Water Framework directive: A new directive for a changing social, political and economic European framework', *European Planning Studies*, vol 11, no 3, pp300–316

Latour, B. (1987) *Science in Action: How to Follow Scientists and Engineers through Society*, Open University Press, Milton Keynes

Latour, B. (2005) *Re-assembling the Social: An Introduction to Actor-Network Theory*, Clarendon, Oxford

Law, J. (1991) 'Power, discretion and strategy', in J. Law (ed) *A Sociology of Monsters: Essays on Power, Technology and Domination*, Routledge, London, pp132–161

Law, J. (1999) 'After ANT: complexity, naming and topology', in J. Law and J. Hassard (eds) *Actor Network Theory and After*, Blackwell, Oxford, pp1–14

Mclean, C. and Hassard, J. (2004) 'Symmetrical absence/symmetrical absurdity: Critical notes on the production of actor-network accounts', *Journal of Management Studies*, vol 41, no 3, pp494–515

Moss, T. and Medd, W. (2005) *Knowledge and Policy Frameworks for Promoting Sustainable Water Management through Intermediation*, www.irs-net.de/texte/intermediaries/DetailedReport.pdf (July 2009)

Moss, T., Medd, W., Guy, S. and Marvin, S. (2009) 'Organising water: The hidden role of intermediary work', *Water Alternatives*, vol 2, no 1, pp16–33

Murdoch, J. (2001) 'Ecologising sociology: Actor-network theory, co-construction and the problem of human exemptionalism', *Sociology*, vol 35, no 1, pp111–133

Murdoch, J. (2003) 'Co-constructing the countryside: Hybrid networks and the extensive self', in P. Cloke (ed) *Country Visions*, Pearson Education, London, pp263–280

Schaper, M. (2002) 'The essence of eco-preneurship', *Greener Management International, Theme: Environmental Entrepreneurship*, vol 38, pp26–30

Walley, E.E. and Taylor, D.W. (2002) 'Opportunists, champions, mavericks...? A typology of green entrepreneurs', *Greener Management International, Theme: Environmental Entrepreneurship*, vol 38, pp31–43

Wissen, M. and Moss, T. (2005) *Making Sense of Diversity – A Synergy Report on an Inventory of 113 Intermediary Organizations of Water Management in Europe*. Working Paper, Erkner, Leibniz-Institute for Regional Development and Structural Planning, www.irs-net.de/download/SynergyReport.pdf (November 2008)

7

The Intermediation of Water Expertise in a Post-privatization Context

Timothy Moss and Ulrike von Schlippenbach

Introduction

In October 1999 the city-state of Berlin sold a 49.9 per cent share in its water and wastewater utility, the Berliner Wasserbetriebe (BWB), to an international consortium comprising the French water multinational Vivendi (today Veolia), the German multi-utility RWE and the insurance company Allianz. The price tag of DM 3.3 billion (ca. €1.69 billion) was hailed by proponents at the time as 'the greatest sale of assets in the history of Berlin'.[1] The partial privatization of the BWB had been agreed under duress, not least to help relieve the city's chronic public debt, and was a highly controversial decision. Despite the city retaining a majority shareholding in the new company, serious concerns were voiced about the loss of influence of public authorities over a company co-owned and managed by global players, and the effect this would have on the pursuit of social, environmental and technology policy objectives in the city. In order to minimize the negative effects of the partial privatization and to exploit the opportunities created by collaboration with key actors in international water markets, a number of agreements were made as part of the privatization package targeted at protecting jobs, limiting price increases, securing investments in infrastructure and supporting environmental improvements. One of these agreements was to create a joint centre of competence for water management in Berlin – the Kompetenzzentrum Wasser Berlin (KWB) – as a public–private partnership of water utilities (Veolia and the BWB), the Berlin state ministries for science, environment and the economy, the city's universities and research institutes, and business groups.

The following chapter investigates this novel intermediary organization – the KWB – as a window on the urban governance of water expertise in a post-privatization context. The privatization of water services – often accompanied by parallel processes of liberalization and commercialization – has transformed the governance of water and water infrastructure systems across the globe since the mid-1980s. As the growing international literature on water privatization cautions, selling up all or part of the shares of a public water utility can have far-reaching implications for the pursuit of such public interests as water quality, accessibility, affordability, employment and infrastructure investments (Lobina and Hall, 2000; Bakker, 2001; Finger and Allouche, 2002; Bakker, 2003). What this literature on the politics of water privatization has tended to overlook, however, is how water privatization affects the governance of the cities served by these socio-technical networks. Notable exceptions are contributions by Erik Swyngedouw, Maria Kaika and others, who have demonstrated not only some of the far-reaching impacts which water privatization can have on decision-making processes and policy priorities in cities, but also how water privatization projects are themselves influenced by urban political discourses and developments (Swyngedouw et al, 2002; Swyngedouw, 2004; Frank and Gandy, 2006).

Instances of water privatization in Germany are particularly pertinent from an urban governance perspective, given that the provision of water services there is the legal responsibility of local authorities (Kluge and Libbe, 2006; Wasserkolloquium, 2008). Many of Germany's larger cities – including the capital Berlin – have a tradition of municipal provision of water services dating back well into the 19th century (Mohajeri, 2006; Kluge and Scheele, 2008). The partial privatization of the Berlin Water Utility (BWB) – Germany's largest water utility – has, therefore, wide-ranging implications for the governance of the city-state. This aspect, however, has generally not been the focus of the literature on the BWB privatization case.

This chapter focuses on one component of the privatization deal – the creation and operation of the KWB – to investigate how and in what ways the governance of water expertise in the city has been affected by this new organization. Three questions guide the research. Firstly, what expectations of the KWB did the city's government departments, water utilities, water researchers and water-related businesses hold at its creation, and how far have these expectations been fulfilled? Secondly, what and whose interests does the KWB promote? Thirdly, in what way does the KWB function as an intermediary organization, working across diverse actor constellations, policy fields and spatial contexts?

The chapter is structured around these three questions. We begin by setting the emergence of the KWB in the context of recent utility restructuring in Berlin, drawing on documentary evidence and recent studies of the partial privatization of the BWB. The main section – based on face-to-face interviews and telephone interviews with leading participants and the KWB's own publications – analyses how the KWB works, comparing the expectations of the main actors involved with the realities of the network in operation. These empirical findings are then interpreted in terms of intermediation in urban water management, focusing on the nature of intermediation between actors, between policy fields and between territorial scales. We finally assess the performance (to date) of the KWB, critically assessing how far the KWB represents a new mode of water governance in Berlin.

The KWB as a product of the privatization process

The partial privatization of the BWB was motivated primarily as a means of raising money to help offset the city's huge and rapidly rising public debt (on the BWB privatization case, see Hecker, 2001; Wolfers, 2004; Lanz and Eitner, 2005; Monstadt and von Schlippenbach, 2005; Ochmann, 2005; Beveridge and Hüesker, 2008; Beveridge, 2010; Hüesker, 2010).[2] Under the privatization deal, the city-state of Berlin retained a 50.1 per cent share of the Berlinwasser Holding and of the BWB. The successful consortium of Vivendi (Veolia), RWE and Allianz paid DM 3.3 billion (ca. €1.69 billion) for 49.9 per cent of both entities. In 2002, Allianz sold its shares to Veolia and RWE. Beyond the sale price, a number of contractual agreements were made to advance certain policy interests. These included a moratorium on water price increases until 2004, a job protection guarantee for 6400 posts for 15 years and an investment pledge of €2.5 billion over the following ten years, as well as less specific agreements on job creation in the region, international cooperation and support for the BWB by its new shareholders.

At the time, the deal was heralded as a coup by the two main political parties, the CDU and SPD, then in a coalition government. Apart from the sale price, they were particularly keen to emphasize the strategic potential of the alliance with global players for strengthening the BWB, Berlin's expertise in water management and the city's economic development. The CDU's economics spokesman told the city parliament in July 1999:

> *Those who are familiar with developments in the international water market ... appreciate the strategic importance of this decision. Together with the consortium and the Berlin Water Utility we will use Berlin as a base for strategic expansion towards Eastern Europe (Abgeordnetenhaus-Drucksache 13/66, p4805, translated by the authors).*

His colleague from the SPD added:

> *We expect the Berlin Water Utility to be commercially active not only internationally but also in Germany. The whole water sector will soon be restructured in Germany... It will be up to the Berlin Water Utility to get involved here and shape developments, thereby securing jobs in the city (Abgeordnetenhaus-Drucksache 13/66, p4812, translated by the authors).*

This positive appraisal is reflected in subsequent analyses by financial and legal consultants. Focusing on the issue of water pricing, Benedikt Wolfers concludes that the case of the partial privatization of the BWB illustrates 'how the public interest in fair water pricing, and in health and environmental protection can be reconciled with the private investors' interest in receiving an adequate return for their investment' (Wolfers, 2004, p123). This contrasts sharply with the conclusion of Klaus Lanz and Kerstin Eitner: 'Berlin is a graphic example that profit expectations and public interest in a sound and stable water sector are very difficult to reconcile' (2005, p219). They and other commentators are highly critical of the loss of influence of the city-state of Berlin over such core issues as water prices, infrastructure investments, environmental protection and the distribution of BWB profits (see also Ochmann, 2005; Hüesker, 2010). The KWB – which is barely referred to by these studies of the privatization deal – was, therefore, created against the backdrop of considerable concern over the future pursuit of public interests via the BWB, but also widespread hope that the BWB, with its new partners, could play a more prominent role in international water markets.

The KWB: intermediating in a post-privatization context

Establishing a network for water expertise in Berlin

In the course of the negotiations over the partial privatization, the idea arose of developing a centre of competence for water management which linked research expertise in the Berlin region with that of the successful bidding consortium, to be funded by the latter as part of the privatization package. The proposal, it appears, came originally from the Senate Department for Science and was then fleshed out by leading figures at the Technical University of Berlin. 'The idea was simple', one of them explains: 'to create a level of expertise unparalleled in Germany by bringing together major research players' (Interview 7).[3] Subsequent talks with Vivendi led to the company agreeing to spend DM 10 million (ca. €5 million) a year for ten years on water research in Berlin as part of the consortium contract. Some commentators regard this commitment as instrumental in smoothing the passage of the whole privatization deal (e.g. see Interview 7).

It took another two years of protracted negotiations, however, before the Berlin Centre of Competence for Water (KWB) could be launched as a non-profit limited company (gGmbH) in December 2001. In its initial constellation, four partners held an equal 25 per cent share in the company: Veolia, the BWB group, the Technical University of Berlin and the Technology Foundation of Berlin (TSB) – an innovation network funded by the Senate Department for Economics and the Investitionsbank Berlin (TSB, 2004). The supervisory board of the KWB included, in addition, representatives from three Senate departments (for science, economics and urban development/environment), and a network of small and medium-sized businesses (SMEs) in the region active in water management: the *Verein zur Förderung des Wasserwesens e.V.* In late 2003, however, the proportion of publicly funded partners and board members had to be reduced in order to avoid having to advertise research bids across the EU. Since then, Veolia and the BWB have held together a 75 per cent share in the KWB and the TSB 25 per cent. The Technical University is associated via an agreement of cooperation and the Berlin Senate is represented by only one department (for economics and technology) on the supervisory board. Within the KWB a key role is played by the committee responsible for selecting the research projects to be funded, which is currently composed of representatives of OEWA (a 100 per cent subsidiary of Veolia), the TSB, the Senate Department for the Environment and BSU – an organization responsible inter alia for managing EU structural funds in the city. By 2008, following the successful acquisition of major research funding (see below), the number of staff employed by KWB had risen to 25. To help coordinate the growing number of projects, a steering and a technical committee comprising in-house staff and external experts has been created for each research area (groundwater, surface water, wastewater technologies) to provide advice on project development and future research priorities (KWB, 2008a, p2).

Expectations of the core actors

The task of the KWB was summarized in the organization's first annual report as follows: 'To combine expertise, to stimulate innovations, to create jobs' (KWB, 2002, p2). More specifically, KWB's purpose is to identify research and development (R&D) priorities, and initiate joint research projects on key issues of water management of relevance to Berlin and elsewhere. To this end it should seek to combine business and research expertise on water in a way which helps local researchers and businesses, especially SMEs, to gain access to international markets. Given the strategic importance attached to the KWB, it is surprising that the purpose of the organization was not further specified in the privatization contracts – 'a major deficit' in the words of one commentator (Interview 3).[4] Even on a more general level, 'it was never clearly defined what a centre of competence really could be' (Interview 7). This meant, firstly, that the purpose and mode of operation of the KWB were largely open to interpretation and definition by those involved; and, secondly, that, as a result, the development of the KWB was very much a product of an interactive process of negotiation between the key players. In analysing its workings, it makes sense, therefore, to explore first the expectations of the KWB held by the main actors and then to contrast these with the realities of the KWB as a new force for water governance in Berlin today.

For Veolia and the BWB the immediate interest lay in combining the research capacity of the largest water utilities in France and Germany. Both companies were looking to use the KWB as a network organization capable of linking research conducted by utilities and research organizations in the region, and of exploiting markets abroad and strengthening Berlin's international standing.[5] Within the Berlin government the idea of the KWB appealed to three separate state ministries – termed senate departments in the city-state of Berlin – though for very different reasons. The Senate Department for Science and Research (SenWiss) was keen to support an initiative that promised to provide substantial funding into water research it could no longer deliver under the beleaguered city budget (Interview 8).[6] The Senate Department for Urban Development and the Environment (SenStadt) viewed the KWB as a tool for using research to develop solutions to environmental problems of water management in the region (Interview 5).[7] The Senate Department for Economics and Public Utilities (SenWirt) was interested in the potential contribution of the KWB to Berlin's economic development and the creation of jobs, 'translating research expertise into concrete economic performance' (Interview 2).[8] Many of the water researchers involved, particularly in the early years, viewed the KWB primarily as a golden opportunity to finance their own research projects. Other researchers closely involved in the KWB's genesis – particularly from the Technical University of Berlin – were more aware of the strategic opportunities of the network and keen to develop practical, marketable applications for their research in close collaboration with two leading utilities (Interview 1;[9] Interview 7). The interests of the business community are reflected in a survey of 350 SMEs in the region conducted by the KWB. It revealed that the highest proportion (80.3 per cent) hoped the KWB would create new opportunities for cooperation, followed by opportunities for funding (63.2 per cent), support and advice on R&D projects (52.6 per cent), and assistance in gaining access to international markets (43.4 per cent) (KWB, 2003). Given the recent decline in public sector contracts, the KWB research budget appeared an attractive source of funding and collaboration with international players (Interviews 1 and 3).

The KWB in practice

To what extent has the KWB been able to meet these varied and far-reaching expectations in practice? How effective has it proved to date in delivering the anticipated benefits? These questions are now pursued with respect to three key aspects of water governance: networking the region's expertise in water management, mobilizing funding for water research and translating research into markets for the regional economy – all tasks demanding intermediary work.

Networking the city's expertise on water resource management

The KWB has certainly succeeded in providing a solid, formalized framework for advancing collaborative research activities in Berlin. The key actors – the BWB, Veolia, the Technical University, the Technology Foundation and three senate departments – are all involved, albeit with different positions and functions. The organization has – for the first ten years at least – been financially well endowed. Reaching agreement between research, business and administrative organizations, and between researchers of different disciplinary fields, has proved difficult at times. More recently, however, a culture of cooperation has begun to develop through collaboration on projects, not only between the different organizations, but also between university departments (Interview 1). The restructuring of the KWB's membership in 2003 has helped clarify the KWB's role, restricting the shareholders to the two utilities – Veolia and BWB – and the TSB.

Whereas the early research projects were largely bilateral between Veolia and the BWB, the more recent projects involve a greater variety of organizations. Particularly noteworthy is the project NASRI – Natural and Artificial Systems for Recharge and Infiltration – involving seven research organizations from the region, including the universities, the Federal Environment Agency and a publicly funded research institute, as well as Veolia and the BWB. With a budget of €6.8 million, this project, completed in early 2006, is claimed to be the largest research project on bank filtration in the world (Interview 7).

Other major projects address integrated sewage management to avoid over-loading sewage systems and sanitation concepts for separate treatment of wastewater.

According to some of those involved, the dominant role of a global player is, however, nurturing distrust amongst small companies in such a sensitive field as innovation and development (Interview 6).[10] This may help explain why relatively few of the region's SMEs play an active role in KWB projects (Interview 7). More serious is the criticism of undue private sector influence over the regional water research agenda. The degree to which the publicly funded Technical University is engaging in research projects of direct com-mercial interest, not only to the region's BWB but also to the multinational Veolia, raises issues about what public interest is being pursued here and whether public funding for research organizations should be used – albeit indi-rectly – to advance the business interests of individual companies. The recent shift in emphasis of the projects funded from a combination of basic and applied research to primarily technology development is indicative of this trend (Interviews 3 and 7).

Mobilizing funding for water research

The KWB has succeeded in mobilizing funding resources for water research at a crucial time, when Berlin's environment administration has stopped fund-ing environmental research. Beyond the annual grant supplied direct by Veolia, the KWB has been effective in acquiring considerable additional fund-ing from external sources on a project basis. Between 2001 and 2008 the KWB conducted more than 50 research projects, budgeted at €24.5 million in total. Of this sum, €14.2 million went on funding the KWB's own research and €10.3 million were allocated to external research partners, of which 71 per cent went to partners from the Berlin region (KWB, 2009). In 2008 the KWB boasted 19 ongoing projects, seven of which extend beyond 2010. The annual research budget that year totalled €3.3 million, of which 54 per cent came from Veolia, 30 per cent from the EU and the national research min-istry (BMBF), and 16 per cent from the BWB (KWB, 2009). The intended multiplier effect would appear to be working. As one senior researcher put it: 'In the past we didn't bring enough money from outside into Berlin and now it's running into the millions – really successful' (Interview 7). Beyond fund-ing the network organization, the staff and its own research projects, the KWB's budget is used to supplement university staff funding, financing for a five-year period a chair in water supply and wastewater disposal at the Technical University which had been left vacant for years. The KWB is thus covering a shortfall in the university budget.

At the same time it is clear that funding is selective. As one researcher puts it: 'Those that provide the money call the shots' (Interview 3). Proposals that 'simply don't fit into the philosophy of the funding bodies' stand little chance of selection (Interview 7). It is for this reason that the possibility of the Berlin authorities withdrawing all financial support from the KWB, owing to budget constraints, is cause for serious concern. It is unclear at present how long the TSB, funded by the city government, will be able to continue supporting the network activities of the KWB. If the city does cease contributing financially its influence over the kinds of research projects funded – whether out of environmental, economic or scientific interest – is likely to decline sharply. Put bluntly by another key actor:

> *The State of Berlin can only expect to shape the Centre actively if it makes a sizable financial contribution itself. If it doesn't, then – well – the projects will go in a different direction (Interview 1).*

The other financial uncertainty hanging over the KWB is the durability of the current funding model. No decision has been made to date, but, according to the head of the KWB and other participants, Veolia is likely to retain Berlin as a location for its water research, though in what form is unclear (Pawlowski, 2007; Interview 7). The shareholders would appear to be keen to renew the funding agreement for the KWB, not least in view of the success in acquiring external funding for water research projects. Whether the practice of Veolia providing large sums for water research is desirable in the longer term is a moot point. Critics warn of the risk of a subsidy culture in which recipient partners grow dependent on KWB funds and are reluctant to provide resources of their own. More important than the availability of research funding is, in their opinion, the leverage the KWB can potentially provide in getting SMEs from the region access into national and international markets for water expertise (Interviews 3 and 8).

Translating research into markets for the regional economy

This raises the question of how far business in the Berlin region is likely to benefit from these research activities – directly and indirectly. The region's water-related SMEs are keen to gain access to new (international) markets via the KWB. Some commentators even claim that integrating these businesses into the KWB's activities is essential for creating the critical mass of expertise necessary to make substantial inroads into international markets (Interviews 2, 3 and 8). So far, however, there are only limited signs that this is happening. The potential would appear to be there, in particular in the form of engineering and management expertise, but is currently not being exploited to the full. This is attributed partly to the reticence of many small businesses to come forward and bring their specialist knowledge into the KWB network. Apart from the handful of SMEs that have long cooperated closely with key actors in the KWB, others are suspicious of having their ideas exploited by the global player Veolia through too close a collaboration (Interview 7). The problem is partly also an expression of the lack of knowledge about relevant SMEs in the region – especially in the surrounding state of Brandenburg – and their potential contribution.

In response to this perceived deficit, the KWB developed a database of the profiles of businesses active in water management in the Berlin–Brandenburg region and conducted an initial appraisal of this market (KWB, 2003). In 2006 the KWB launched its networking project, WaterPN, as a platform to intensify these links to the business community and to the economics administration. In order to circumvent legal problems of operating within the KWB as a non-profit organization, the WaterPN network has since been formally separated from the KWB and is now able to promote business development itself. Following an initiative of the TSB, the KWB has recently conducted an extensive, systematic data survey of the region's water industry with co-funding from the TSB. On the basis of this sector profile, the prospects for integrating companies from the region into the research networks generated by the KWB have been strengthened.

A further reason given for the as yet limited benefits of the KWB for local business and the Berlin economy is the lack of coherence and direction of public policy towards innovation in the water sector in general, and the KWB in particular. Those closely involved complain that the KWB is widely perceived as a service provided by Veolia in accordance with the privatization contract. Notwithstanding the rhetoric at the time of privatization and in various policy documents since (SenWirt, 2003; TSB, 2004), the responsible senate departments have not used their positions to develop a strategy for the KWB with which to advance the city's policy objectives (Interview 4).[11] Members of the network criticize the city authorities for not formulating clear priorities for the KWB's development: 'You've got to have an agreed strategy, you've got to know where you want to go, what you want to achieve precisely' (Interview 3). They point to the diverse interests of the three senate departments involved, and the difficulty in reaching agreement across their economic, environmental and research agendas – 'a real balancing act' in the words of one KWB insider (Interview 7).

The intermediary work of the KWB

What does the case of the KWB tell us about processes of intermediation in the Berlin water sector? For our analysis, we draw on the conceptualization of intermediaries and the governance of socio-technical networks developed in Chapter 2 of this book. The study of intermediaries, it is argued there, is valuable for investigating the interfaces between different actors, between different policy fields and between different scales of governance. These three dimensions provide the structure for the following interpretation of the KWB's work as an intermediary.

Intermediating between actors

The KWB has proven highly successful, in the relatively short period of its existence, in bringing together a wide range of actors in the Berlin region around a common interest in water research. The network extends beyond the water utilities and public authorities to include research organizations, a state-funded technology agency (TSB) and regional SMEs, representing together the principal players of water management in the region. The KWB enjoys a solid organizational base, is financially well endowed at present, and has a reasonable prospect of having its core funding extended. For an emergent network organization it is institutionally in an enviably strong position. The KWB has used this position of strength to create new contexts of action for water research and open up new possibilities for collaboration between researchers which had not been possible to this degree in the past. In the process it has contributed to reconfiguring relations between participating actors, notably strengthening a collaborative axis between the utilities and researchers at the Technical University. It has also stimulated the establishment of a regional network of SMEs specializing in water management, which – under the new mantle of WaterPN – seems better placed than its predecessor to exploit new market opportunities and to take a significant step towards developing the Berlin–Brandenburg region into one known for its commercial, as well as its research, expertise in water management.

Within the KWB, the intermediation at work is – it should be noted – an exchange not between equals, but between member organizations of very different status, resources and connectivity. On the one hand, the asymmetries within the KWB are structurally determined, emanating, for instance, from the financial inputs and economic power of the utilities and the organizational isolation of many SMEs. On the other hand, we can observe how certain asymmetries have developed during the course of the KWB's existence. The failure of the city-state authorities to formulate and pursue a coherent strategy for KWB's contribution to policy delivery would appear to be one such example. In the absence of clear and practical proposals for the network's development, the public authorities have been unable to provide an adequate corrective to the commercial interests of the utilities. A second example is how the research funded and conducted has, under the leadership of the two utilities, focused on developing water technologies rather than on ways of exploiting them to the advantage of the region. This substantive orientation towards the research, rather than the development component of the original strategic orientation, has been a contributory factor behind the less successful enrolment of regional SMEs in the network's activities to date. From this we can conclude that the nature of intermediarity in a network such as the KWB does not evolve automatically from its organizational structure and the influence of its members. Intermediarity needs to be actively cultivated by the network members and can, consequently, take on unanticipated dimensions, opening up some channels for joint action and blocking others.

Intermediating between policy fields

The idea of translating water research into practical applications of benefit to the regional environment and economy is ambitious and especially novel in the context of German water management. The attraction of this strategic idea has lain in it being potentially beneficial to all parties: utilities, researchers, administration and business. The danger has been that it has nurtured diverse expectations of the KWB. How far the KWB has contributed to creating new markets and jobs for the Berlin region so far is hard to assess. Veolia and the BWB have strengthened their own expertise and international standing, but the economic advantages for water-related businesses in the region are far less obvious. Some of the more recent research projects of the KWB demonstrate real potential in this respect, but considerable additional effort will be required to develop a more coherent and concrete strategy for strengthening the development aspect of water research in and beyond the network. This will involve identifying firstly the areas of expertise of regional SMEs and their potential applications for water research funded by the KWB; secondly, their capacity to contribute to the international markets targeted by the KWB and; thirdly, the networking skills necessary for overcoming some of the problems of interaction between the utilities and the SMEs experienced in the past. The survey of the region's water sector conducted in 2008 (see above) represents an important first step in this direction (KWB, 2008b). Beyond this, the case of the KWB has demonstrated the limitations of intermediating between policy fields in the absence of strong strategic guidance from the policy-makers. As the responsible senate departments have gradually withdrawn from active involvement in the KWB, the policy agendas have been largely left open to interpretation by other network members, generally to the detriment of balanced policy delivery.

Intermediating between territorial scales

Water supply and sanitation services in Germany have traditionally been fairly parochial, typically characterized by a municipal utility operating a monopoly over the territory of one or more local authorities (Kluge and Libbe, 2006). Even prior to partial privatization in 1999, the BWB was expanding its commercial operations spatially, providing basic water and sanitation services to neighbouring communities in Brandenburg and exploring international markets. What the partial privatization has created is the opportunity to collaborate with a global player. The KWB is intended, in part at least, to pursue this opportunity, using water expertise and research as a nodal issue around which to explore and exploit common interests and complementarities between the Berlin actors on the one hand, and Veolia on the other. As such, the KWB is at the vanguard of attempts to span different scales of water management. In order to maximize its potential for cooperation, the KWB and its members need to work across scales of action ranging from locally rooted SMEs, territorially bound public authorities and the regional networks of the BWB to the international markets of Veolia. On current experience it would appear that some members of the KWB are adapting well to the internationalization of the city's water management; notably, the research community. Others, such as local SMEs (especially those not specializing in readily exportable technologies) and the city-state authorities, are having greater difficulty in devising a response and making their voices heard.

The KWB – a strategic intermediary?

We conclude this section by reflecting on the strategic nature of the intermediary functions performed by the KWB. The notion of a 'strategic intermediary' was coined by Simon Marvin and Will Medd to describe an organization that 'position[s itself] to have a particular role in ... intermediating between sets of different social interests, to produce an outcome that would not have been possible, or as effective, without their involvement' (Marvin and Medd, 2004, pp84–85). Central to this understanding is the deliberation implicit in this kind of intermediary activity.

Given the high degree of intentionality attached to the KWB and the multiple policy fields it spans – from water research and environmental protection to technological innovation and regional development – the case for terming the KWB a strategic intermediary would appear to be self-evident. The question is rather: strategic to what end? And for whom? Our research has established that beyond the initial rhetoric about the strategic functions of the KWB in advancing Berlin's development interests, little thought has so far gone into specifying exactly what the KWB can – and cannot – achieve. In particular there has been no attempt to define explicitly what public interests the KWB is expected to pursue and in what ways. As one key actor put it: 'What competence do we really want to sell?' (Interview 8). In the absence of a clear action plan, the considerable strategic potential of the KWB is being used selectively by those exerting most influence on the network – primarily Veolia, the BWB and the Technical University. As a result, the interests of others – notably of the city-state government and local SMEs – are receiving less attention than they anticipated. It could be argued that the strategic orientation of the KWB towards the interests of the two utilities is an inevitable consequence of their powerful position in the organization and that any expectation of them entertaining anything other than their own commercial motives is naive. However, the opportunity for the utilities to set the agenda of the KWB in collaboration with their research partners has been made considerably easier by the relatively low profile and uncoordinated position of the public agencies involved.

Conclusions

The privatization of water services in cities and countries across the globe is widely acknowledged to be having a major impact on the governance of water, reaching far beyond the immediate issue of utility ownership. Recent literature on this topic has drawn attention to the implications for issues of water quality, accessibility, affordability, employment and infrastructure investments. By contrast, we know comparatively little about how emergent forms of water governance are influencing – and are being influenced by – urban transitions and urban governance. This chapter has analysed the performance of a network intermediary organization, the KWB, to shed light on the shifting governance of water supply and sanitation in Berlin following the partial privatization of its water utility. Given the recent erosion of traditional modes of public sector influence over local water management, the central interest from a governance perspective has been in establishing how far the KWB has been able to compensate for this loss of public control by creating a new context for the pursuit of collective interests and urban policies, ranging from research expertise and environmental protection to technology development. To this end, the concept of intermediarity was applied to highlight the ways in which the KWB has – or has not – generated new modes of connectivity within and beyond water management, using research expertise as a vehicle.

The case for studying the KWB as an intermediary has proven compelling for providing illustration of three key dimensions of intermediarity: interaction between different actors, between different policy fields and between different scales of governance. Firstly, it represents an attempt by the city of Berlin to persuade a global player – Veolia – to combine its co-ownership of the local utility with a commitment to collaborate in advancing water expertise in the region. Secondly, the medium of an intermediary network of diverse public and private organizations operating across a variety of policy fields marks a novel experiment in a country where water governance is traditionally oriented around strong, sectorally-based regulation. Thirdly, the KWB uses water research as an issue to improve not only the region's environment, but also its R&D competitiveness in markets at home and abroad.

Our empirical analysis has shown that, perhaps inevitably, the realities of the KWB in action fall behind the multiple expectations at its inception. The KWB has proved remarkably successful in enrolling the key actors of water management in the region behind the idea of the network. It has created a solid financial and organizational base from which to fund a large number of innovative research projects, which, increasingly, involve a wide range of actors. Evidence suggests there is an international market for the research conducted and the technological applications developed. However, the considerable potential of the KWB has, in the eyes of many participants, not been tapped to the full. In particular, there is little evidence as yet that collaborative water research primarily between Veolia, the BWB and the Technical University has opened up new commercial opportunities for SMEs in the Berlin region – a principal motive behind the KWB's creation for many stakeholders. More generally, considerable lack of clarity surrounds the public interests and policies the KWB is meant to be pursuing. Opportunities for advancing specifically public – rather than merely collective – goals for the city's development by means of the KWB network have not been adequately exploited. There has been surprisingly little effort on the part of the city-state authorities or others to specify how the KWB is to contribute to the delivery of which policies. In the absence of a clear strategy of the public sector, those providing most of the funding and/or expertise – primarily the utilities and researchers – are interpreting the KWB's agenda to suit their own interests. There are signs that this problem has been recognized, in part at least, resulting in steps to strengthen the involvement of SMEs via a new platform – WaterPN – created to promote interaction between the research and business communities. The wider issue of defining the public interest to be served by the KWB and securing more effective means of policy delivery remains open, however, so long as the city-state authorities are reluctant or unable to engage more actively in the network's development.

From a governance perspective, the KWB has introduced innovative modes of collective action which the concept of intermediarity has helped reveal. Operating as an intermediary between highly diverse actors of water management in the region, the KWB marks a symbolic shift in the *style* of water governance, characterized by greater reliance on interaction and negotiation in the context of a formalized, issue-based network. Secondly, the KWB marks a bold attempt to extend the *scope* of water governance by cultivating better connectivity between water research, water protection, technology innovation and regional economic development. Here, success has been more mixed, with very limited progress, for instance, in promoting local SMEs to date. Thirdly, the KWB is distinctive in spanning various *scales* of water governance, ranging from the global markets of Veolia and the regional embeddedness of the BWB to the strictly urban remit of the responsible senate departments. On this issue, some member organizations – in particular the researchers – have demonstrated greater adaptability than others.

In terms of contributing to the pursuit of public – and, in particular, urban – policies, however, the case of the KWB is ultimately one of governance failure. The collective identity and action it has developed have been shaped by the search for commonality between the diverse interests of its members, rather than by any attempt to identify, let alone actively advance, a genuinely public interest, however defined. This failure to develop a strategic profile in the public interest for the KWB can be attributed to a number of factors: power asymmetries within the network organization; the limited engagement and multiple voices of the city-state representatives; and the selective interests of the utilities and researchers. The question today is whether the window of opportunity for developing such a profile has passed as the KWB's activities become routine, or whether timely recognition of this deficit – already identified by many of our interviewees – could yet effect a substantive modification in the strategic orientation of this pioneer of interactive governance in the organizational landscape of German water management.

Notes

1 Member of the Berlin state parliament Frank Steffel (CDU), in a speech to the parliament on 1 July 1999 (Abgeordnetenhaus-Drucksache 13/66, p4805).
2 Between 1990 and 1999 the debt of the city-state of Berlin had grown from €11 billion to almost €35 billion (SenFin, 2005).
3 Interview 7: Representative of the Technical University of Berlin, 13 April 2005.
4 Interview 3: Representative of the TSB, 12 October 2004.
5 Vivendi executive Christoph Hueg, in *Entsorga-Magazin* 4/2003, p40.
6 Interview 8: Representative of the Senate Department of Science, Research and Culture (SenWiss), unit for research/research infrastructure, 21 June 2005.
7 Interview 5: Representative of the Senate Department for Urban Development and the Environment (SenStadt), unit for comprehensive environmental protection, 21 October 2004.
8 Interview 2: Representative of the Senate Department for Economics, Labour and Women (SenWirt), unit for economic and technology policy, 26 August 2004.
9 Interview 1: Representative from the KWB, 25 May 2004.
10 Interview 6: Two representatives of the Senate Department for Economics, Labour and Women (SenWirt), unit for technology and innovation policy, 15 February 2005.
11 Interview 4: Representative of the BWB, department for coordination and strategic development, 14 October 2004.

References

Abgeordnetenhaus-Drucksache 13/66 (1999) 'Plenary minutes of 1 July 1999', Berlin House of Representatives, 13th legislative period

Bakker, K. (2001) 'Paying for water: Water pricing and equity in England and Wales', *Transactions of the Institute of British Geographers*, vol 26, pp143–164

Bakker, K. (2003) *An Uncooperative Commodity: Privatising Water in England and Wales*, Oxford University Press, Oxford

Beveridge, R. (2010) 'Translating neo-liberalism, privatising water services: Experts, elites and governance in 1990s Berlin', unpublished PhD thesis, University of Newcastle, UK

Beveridge, R. and Hüesker, F. (2008) 'Nichtöffentlichkeit als Prinzip. Die Teilprivatisierung der Berliner Wasserbetriebe', in Wasserkolloquium (ed) *Wasser: Die Kommerzialisierung eines öffentlichen Gutes*, Karl Dietz Verlag, Berlin, pp58–74

Finger, M. and Allouche, J. (2002) *Water Privatisation: Trans-national Corporations and the Re-regulation of the Water Industry*, Spon Press, London/New York

Frank, S. and Gandy, M. (eds) (2006) *Hydropolis. Wasser und die Stadt der Moderne*, Campus, Frankfurt/Main

Hecker, J. (2001) 'Privatisierung unternehmensstrategischer Anstalten öffentlichen Rechts. Anstaltsrechtliche, demokratiestaatliche und privatisierungstheoretische Überlegungen am Beispiel der Teilprivatisierung der Berliner Wasser-Betriebe (BWB)', *Verwaltungs-Archiv*, vol 2, pp261–291

Hüesker, F. (2010) 'Auswirkungen von Privatisierungen auf die Gemeinwohlfähigkeit des Daseinsvorsorgestaates – untersucht am Fall der Wasserbetriebe des Landes Berlin', unpublished PhD thesis, Free University of Berlin, Germany

Kluge, T. and Libbe, J. (eds) (2006) *Transformation netzgebundener Infrastruktur. Strategien für Kommunen am Beispiel Wasser*, Difu-Beiträge zur Stadtforschung, Band 45, Deutsches Institut für Urbanistik, Berlin

Kluge, T. and Scheele, U. (2008) 'Von dezentralen zu zentralen Systemen und wieder zurück? Räumliche Dimensionen des Transformationsprozesses in der Wasserwirtschaft', in T. Moss, M. Naumann and M. Wissen (eds) *Infrastrukturnetze und Raumentwicklung. Zwischen Universalisierung und Differenzierung*, Oekom Verlag, Munich, pp143–172

Kompetenzzentrum Wasser Berlin (KWB) (2002) *Tätigkeitsbericht 2001*, Kompetenzzentrum Wasser Berlin, Berlin

KWB (2003) *Tätigkeitsbericht 2002*, Kompetenzzentrum Wasser Berlin, Berlin, pp8, 19

KWB (2008a) *KWB Newsletter 1/08*, Kompetenzzentrum Wasser Berlin, Berlin

KWB (2008b) *Branchenreport Wasser Berlin-Brandenburg*, Kompetenzzentrum Wasser Berlin, Berlin

KWB (2009) *Tätigkeitsbericht 2008*, Kompetenzzentrum Wasser Berlin, Berlin, p5

Lanz, K. and Eitner, K. (2005) *D12: WaterTime Case Study – Berlin, Germany*, www.watertime.net, accessed 13 September 2010

Lobina, E. and Hall, D. (2000) 'Public sector alternatives to water supply and sewerage privatization: Case studies', *International Journal of Water Resources Development*, vol 16, no 1, pp35–55

Marvin, S. and Medd, W. (2004) 'Sustainable infrastructures by proxy? Intermediation beyond the production–consumption nexus', in D. Southerton, H. Chappells and B. van Vliet (eds) *Sustainable Consumption: The Implications of Changing Infrastructures of Provision*, Edward Elgar, London, pp81–94

Mohajeri, S. (2006) 'Die Privatisierung der Berliner Wasserbetriebe damals und heute – Eine kritische Betrachtung', in S. Frank and M. Gandy (eds) *Hydropolis. Wasser und die Stadt der Moderne*, Campus, Frankfurt/New York, pp169–187

Monstadt, J. and Schlippenbach, U. von (2005) *Privatisierung und Kommerzialisierung als Herausforderung regionaler Infrastrukturpolitik. Eine Untersuchung der Berliner Strom-, Gas- und Wasserversorgung sowie Abwasserentsorgung*, netWORKS-Paper 20, Deutsches Institut für Urbanistik, Berlin

Ochmann, D. (2005) *Rechtsformwahrende Privatisierung von öffentlich-rechtlichen Anstalten. Dargestellt am Holdingmodell zur Teilprivatisierung der Berliner Wasserbetriebe*, Schriften zum Wirtschaftsverwaltungs- und Vergaberecht, vol 4, Nomos, Baden-Baden

Pawlowski, L. (2007) 'Interview', *KWB-Newsletter*, no 16, p2

Senatsverwaltung für Finanzen (SenFin) (2005) 'Haushalt und Schulden von Berlin. Eine Übersicht, Mai 2005', unpublished document

Senatsverwaltung für Wirtschaft, Arbeit und Frauen (SenWirt) (2003) *Innovationsbericht des Landes Berlin*, Senatsverwaltung für Wirtschaft, Arbeit und Frauen, Berlin

Swyngedouw, E. (2004) *Social Power and the Urbanization of Water: Flows of Power*, Oxford Geographical and Environmental Studies Series, Oxford University Press, Oxford

Swyngedouw, E., Kaika, M. and Castro, E. (2002) 'Urban water: A political-ecology perspective', *Built Environment*, vol 28, no 2, pp124–137

Technologiestiftung Berlin (TSB) (2004) *Jahresbericht 2004*, Technologiestiftung Berlin, Berlin

Wasserkolloquium (ed) (2008) *Wasser. Die Kommerzialisierung eines öffentlichen Gutes*, Karl Dietz Verlag, Berlin

Wolfers, B. (2004) 'Privatization of the Berlin Water Works – a blueprint for balancing public and private interests?', *Journal of European Environmental and Planning Law*, vol 2, pp116–124

8
Mobility, Markets and 'Hidden' Intermediation: Aviation and Frequent Flying

Sally Randles and Sarah Mander

Introduction

This chapter contributes a distinctive perspective on processes of intermediation by focusing on a particular sub-category of intermediaries: intermediaries of the *market*. It considers the nature, characterization and affective powers of intermediaries as *market agents*, involved in processes of competitive *market construction* and *market reconstruction*, sitting within socio-technical systems, in relational terms 'in-between' processes of production (of goods and services) and their consumption. Importantly, we argue, market intermediaries exert affective powers as change agents on both sides of the production–consumption landscape, providing explanatory leverage on the construction and characterization of both, whilst paradoxically thus far being invisible, in analytical terms, to both the academic and the policy gaze.

The second setting which concerns this chapter is that of 'mobilities'. John Urry helpfully takes this term to mean much more than its technical dimension of transport, seeing mobility as both a social 'good' and an individual right (Urry, 2002, 2007; Sheller and Urry, 2004). We can appreciate this when we think about the social and individual consequences when, for any reason, we are stripped of our ability or freedom to be mobile; that is, our ability and freedom to move. It is also a concept which goes beyond the simple idea of corporeal mobility, as Urry calls it (2007), to incorporate the distinction between co-presence – meaning the physical body is present at a scene or with another person – and virtual mobility, when co-presence is not the case. Rather, virtual mobility is enabled through Internet- and screen-based technologies (travel programmes on television; Skype and conference calls through the Internet). This extended understanding of mobility enables us to think about how corporeal and virtual mobility interact.

Moreover, there is an equity dimension to the discussion, because evidence shows that the trend to fly more frequently per annum is skewed: the richest groups in society fly more frequently than do low-income strata (Randles and Mander, 2009a). This clearly has social equity implications, since it is these low-income and non-flying groups, particularly in urban societies, who are most vulnerable to the impacts of climate change, whilst its causes are exacerbated by the practices of the rich. Thus, for example, the urban low-income elderly suffer most as a result of heat-island effects, and low-income families living in high flood-risk areas are least likely to be insured against flood damage. Neither of these low-income groups have a propensity to fly frequently for leisure (where we define leisure frequent-flying as two or more return trips for leisure purposes in the previous 12 months).

The chapter therefore sheds light on the (hidden) contribution that market intermediaries of the tourism industry – such as travel agents and Internet sites, selling flights, hotels, car hire and excursions – make to the market-shaping and market-construction process. This network of market intermediaries allows us to access the different elements which together constitute an overseas trip. Further, this is a process where the individual traveller now exerts a high degree of autonomy, learning from others and deploying the requisite expertise to enable him/her to 'bundle' and customize a holiday as desired. The analysis provided in this chapter provides an early and incomplete commentary on how the activities of market intermediaries provide one of several factors which explain the growth of frequent flying – and thus the growth of flight-related carbon emissions – as a number of simultaneously operating 'ratchets' (Randles and Mander, 2009b).

We will proceed with a thumbnail sketch of the new and very broad-based literature on intermediation in the social sciences, whilst noting that Chapter 1 of this book provides a more comprehensive literature review. We note, in passing, some significant blind spots in the literature, in particular the tendency to see intermediaries as *benign*, thus missing nuances such as the notion of *gate-keeping* and also the parallel idea of *disintermediation*. Contributing to the theoretical analysis, we sketch a framework which we suggest can be fruitfully deployed in order to analyse, characterize, clarify and empirically interrogate the nuances and diversity of intermediaries, and to understand intermediation *processes*. In the framework we introduce three dimensions to analyse intermediaries, comprising: 1) a relational dimension (the intermediary sits between what and what?); 2) a functional dimension (it does what?); and 3) a dimension of affective power (what difference does it make to how the production–consumption system works and to processes of market transformation?). Ultimately, our key question is how do market intermediaries have the power to affect, re-shape and re-configure markets, and consequently transform socio-technical infrastructures?

We then apply this framework to the context of understanding market intermediaries of leisure flying. Our arguments are illustrated using quantitative material from secondary sources ('keynote' reports) and examples and quotations from our recent qualitative study of frequent flyers in South Manchester, UK, undertaken during 2008. Finally, we conclude by highlighting some policy implications which become visible when deploying the market intermediation lens to understand the recent emergence, growth and 'ratcheting-up' of what we might now see as a frequent-flying *phenomenon*.

Sketching a framework to analyse intermediaries

We can begin by noting two separate contexts within which the intermediation literature has emerged. The first is innovation studies, where intermediaries are held to play a role in innovation processes, through, for example, the transmission and circulation of new knowledge. In this vein we note the innovation intermediaries classification system and literature overview provided by Howells (2006). The second quite distinct literature is concerned with the environment, sustainability and the transformation of (primarily urban) socio-technical infrastructures. In this setting see, for example, Hodson and Marvin (2008), who provide a baseline summary and glossary of the sub-concepts of intermediation and sustainability.

Common to both literatures is an analytical and theoretical focus on social and technical *systems* and *networks*. On this, for example, see van Lente et al (2003) and Smedlund (2006), who look at the systemic and network aspects of transformative innovation, whilst Medd and Marvin (2007) are interested in illuminating the role intermediaries play in transformations of local, urban and regional, socio-technical systems, pointing out implications for sustainability. A conclusion emerging from both literatures is that intermediation remains theoretically and empirically underdeveloped, and as a consequence remains relatively invisible to the academic and the policy gaze; hence the notion of invisible and 'hidden' intermediaries is raised. An important objective of these authors is to draw the attention of *policy* to the contribution, which intermediaries make or could/should make towards bringing about sustainability objectives – for example, in the contexts of climate change and emissions reduction, or in the conservation of scarce resources such as water (Moss et al, 2009).

However, an important critique we would level at both strands of the emergent intermediation literature is that it tends to view intermediation and intermediaries as benign, approaching the topic with the intention of shaping systemic socio-technical change. In particular, in the innovation sub-literature, intermediaries take on a conceptual rosy glow. As a set of institutions within the system they are assumed to exert, always and everywhere, a positive influence on innovation and diffusion, by moving knowledge, expertise and know-how around the system, and connecting together its previously disconnected and fragmented parts.

Whilst that may be so, we mount two critiques of these underlying assumptions. Firstly we argue that the influence and impact that intermediaries have cannot be universally pre-assumed. On the contrary, it is context- and object-specific. Intermediaries might contribute positively to the realization of objectives concerned with facilitating the circulation and transformation of 'something' within a social system. Alternatively, they may not. It may, for example, be in the interest of some classes of intermediary to 'gate-keep' within the system. That is, to maintain a strategic position within which the flow of something from somewhere to somewhere else is blocked or interpreted in a particular way, because in so doing that class of intermediary can gain strategically from being the 'holder of the key' (to the gate they are gate-keeping). Often, in the case of market intermediaries, gate-keeping is a process which confers on the intermediary a power which can be used to extract economic rent from the system. This gate-keeping role can have the opposite effect to the idea of lubricating and facilitating the system. It can contribute to structural lock-in and resistance to change. For market intermediaries, competitive strategy to control customer interfaces and access points to products and services can be used to maintain existing market structure in the interest of incumbents. In this case, at the system level, change is resisted. Secondly, as this chapter demonstrates, intermediaries may contribute to the realization of certain outcomes, but in so doing they may precisely militate against the realization of others. For example, in this chapter, intermediaries are contributing to the transformation of aviation and tourism markets, but this very process is responsible for counter-effects of tourism intermediaries in militating against the realization of climate change objectives.

The third critique we would make is that the literature is all but blind to the existence and analysis of processes of *disintermediation*. That is, the emergence of a new class of intermediary, or the re-positioning of an existing one to take on the role and activities of disintermediation, by structurally moving around and 'behind', so to speak, an incumbent intermediary in order to gain access to a group which exists behind the back of the original intermediary. This process is both competitive and transformative. We therefore wish to recast the notion of intermediation as a *continuous duality* of intermediation and disintermediation processes; that is, as a dialectical process.

Our next step is to devise an analytical framework which makes possible the analysis of intermediation as it: a) is not always and everywhere benign; b) allows for the possibility that some intermediaries gate-keep the system and potentially bring about structural lock-in; c) allows for the possibility that in realizing one objective, others may be undermined if not directly contradicted; and d) interprets intermediation and disintermediation as constituted through a twinned and co-coupled dialectical process.

We therefore propose a generic framework through which to theoretically understand and analytically study processes of intermediation (and disintermediation). It comprises three parts, each focusing on a separate condition and analytical dimension. These are: 1) a relational dimension (The intermediation process sits between what and what?); 2) a functional dimension (What does it do? What happens in this space? What is done by whom on what?; and 3) a dimension of affective power (What difference does it make? What consequences and transformative potentials are brought into being at the system level?). We can represent this in a simple table (Table 8.1):

Table 8.1 *An analytical framework for the study of dual intermediation–disintermediation processes*

Three conditions of intermediation/disintermediation	Analytical questions
Relational	Situating between what and what?
Functional	Doing what?
Affective powers	With what effects and consequences?

Market intermediaries and mobility

There are a number of ways in which the study of market intermediaries raises different issues to those raised through the study of 'local' intermediaries within local socio-technical systems, whether they are addressing questions about sustainability or innovation. A first is that market intermediaries are closely bound up with processes of market competition and competitive advantage. And this is precisely one context within which disintermediation flourishes; that is, that market competition drives the quest for new models of intermediation and disintermediation. In fact, this offers cross-over points between the study of market intermediaries and the study of innovation, although the innovation literature has not yet addressed this cross-over potential.

Another significant departure can be offered when we look specifically at the mobilization of information and communication technologies into settings of competitive intermediation/disintermediation. We could argue, for example, that the Internet is an agent of disintermediation par excellence. One reason for this is that it has the capability to simultaneously engage all scales (local, national, international, global), whilst effectively collapsing all these scales into one. In terms of the relational dimension, it sits between the 'highly local' and the 'truly global'. From the comfort of the sitting room just about any tourist destination from across the world can be accessed and then studied in detail. In terms of a functional dimension, it brings places and people together, creating Urry's virtual presence, and in terms of affective powers it has a number of possibilities to make a difference.

One of these is that it 'scales for free' and therefore can offer many more holiday (hotels, flights) options from a single Internet site than does the traditional shop-front travel agent. It also has the capability to facilitate the making of direct comparisons of customer offerings (e.g. comparing flight times and costs). Finally, by publishing customer reviews, Internet tourism sites provide instant access to the 'independent customer voice', thus embedding legitimacy and credibility into the site, and effectively conjoining the provisioning side of the holiday, with the consumption side of it, in a way that local travel agents (or local branches of national travel agents) cannot do. In this case, the Internet 'disintermediates' the traditional shop-front travel agency or tour operator, by 'cutting out the middle man' and going directly to the decision-making customer.

There is also significance in terms of temporal scale. The Internet sits within a socio-temporal context, where market decisions can be made immediately because continuous availability makes access to researching options, booking and paying for holidays possible on a 24-hours-a-day basis. That is, the Internet facilitates immediacy and speed, and the holidaymakers themselves do the selecting, booking and paying for their holiday, independent of any assistance from knowledgeable sales personnel.

However, the traditional local travel agent does provide the advantage of direct customer contact. A knowledgeable, and importantly a trusted, person becomes the crucial interface intermediating between the customer and a range of holiday options. The resistance to the rise and rise of the Internet from some (in our group discussions, the older) customers provides some travel agents with a constituency that values the personal contact which the Internet does not yet provide. As we shall see in 'Hand-holding: Travel agents making it easy', this can make all the difference to those who prefer to select a holiday with the help of either a high-street travel agent, or from an agent with specialist knowledge provided to a 'niche' to specialist holiday markets, where, in both cases, face-to-face and telephone discussions are critical to decision processes (see quotes referring to the travel agent personnel Ron and Yvonne in our frequent flyers study below: 'Hand-holding: Travel agents making it easy'). This competitive struggle between the traditional travel agent and the Internet website provides a perfect example of the continuous duality and competitive intermediation/disintermediation dialectical process.

Indeed, Table 8.2 shows clearly that in the current period it is the Internet's disintermediation power that in general terms is winning out competitively against the incumbent travel agent option for booking holidays. And Table 8.3 shows that, increasingly, travel and accommodation arrangements are made independently by the holidaymaker(s), a trend which goes hand-in-hand with using the Internet to research and book holidays.

If we now conjoin the disintermediation power of the Internet with Urry's (2002) notion of mobility as a social good, where the encouragement and expansion of travel opportunities can be seen as a facilitator of both social (extending social networks internationally) and cultural (seeing far away places) capital, then we have a sense of the affective powers of the mobility-market

Table 8.2 *Main sources used to obtain information for last holiday taken in the past 12 months (percentage of adults)*

	2006	2007	2008
Internet (%)	16.1	23.0	24.9
Family/friends (%)	10.2	11.0	11.5
Been there before (%)	9.9	9.9	10.1
Travel agent (at shop) (%)	11.4	9.6	8.6
Brochures (%)	8.5	8.3	6.8
Tour operator/travel company (%)	4.5	4.5	4.1

Source: Keynote, 2009a

Table 8.3 *Selected methods of booking last holiday (percentage of adults)*

	1999	2003	2005	2008
Visited travel agent (shop) to book package (%)	15.9	14.4	13.2	9.7
Visited travel agent (shop) to book flight only (%)	3.9	4.1	5.6	3.8
Visited travel agent (shop) to book accommodation only (%)	2.1	2.2	4.1	2.9
Used tour operator to book package (%)	7.0	8.4	8.7	7.3
Used tour operator to book flight only (%)	1.1	1.4	3.0	1.8
Made independent travel/accommodation arrangements (%)	26.5	24.1	26.7	36.8

Source: Keynote, 2009b

intermediary nexus in creating a ratchet on aviation emissions. In contrast to the hidden good, avoiding the long-term climate change impacts of the trip, travel intermediaries allow the immediate good, the need to travel to be mobile, to be met.

Urry (2002) recognizes the social and mental health returns to society of enabling corporeal travel; that is, co-presence, involving physically being in a place, as opposed to virtual presence, mediated by information and other technologies. He argues moreover that a society which encourages mobility can be considered a 'good society'. He says:

> *Moreover, all other things being equal, then we could imagine that a 'good society' would not limit, prohibit or re-direct the desire for such co-presence. The good society would seek to extend possibilities of co-presence to every social group and regard infringements of this as involving undesirable social exclusion. This is partly because co-presence is desirable in its own right, but also ... there are other desirable consequences. It is, he says, 'good to talk' face-to-face since this minimizes privatization, expands highly desirable social capital and promotes economic activity, in mutually self-sustaining ways (Urry, 2002, p270).*

If we were to reprise the main point of this section, it is to interrogate the relationship between market intermediaries/disintermediaries and mobility. In so doing, we are left to find answers to the following questions: Does virtual mobility substitute for and therefore reduce corporeal mobility? Or conversely does the forming of social relations and social networks through the Internet, and the development of aspirations to travel mediated by the Internet, facilitate and *encourage* leisure flying? In other words, does virtual presence *increase* the propensity to seek face-to-face contact or to experience the 'destination' in order to give corporeal presence? To bring this full circle, does virtual mobility act as a *ratchet* on corporeal mobility, thus contributing more generally to increased energy use and carbon dioxide emissions associated with corporeal mobility? According to the evidence provided in this chapter the answer to this question would be yes. Virtual mobility (Internet facilitated) acts as a ratchet on corporeal mobility (the taking of overseas holidays) and in turn puts direct causal pressure on aviation emissions and thence climate change.

Market intermediaries as a 'ratchet' on frequent flying

Flying for leisure is on an upward trajectory in the UK. Between 1990 and 2008, flying passenger numbers in the UK have risen from 104 million to 238 million, an increase of 130 per cent (Civil Aviation Authority, 2009). Demand for leisure flying has been particularly notable, showing an increase of 185 per cent from 63 million passengers to 180 million passengers. The UK has seen a significant increase in both demand for long and short haul between 1990 and 2008, though the rate of increase in demand for long haul was significantly higher than for short haul between 2003 and 2008 (30 per cent compared with 15 per cent) (Committee on Climate Change, 2009).[1]

In our final section, we use material from qualitative group discussions and individual in-depth interviews, undertaken with approximately 30 frequent flyers in South Manchester conducted during 2008, where frequent flyers are defined as taking two or more round-trips by air during the last 12 months.

We present the material in such a way as to demonstrate the relational, functional and affective powers of the intermediaries and intermediation processes in question, referring both to Internet use and the traditional travel agent. The 'doing' of intermediation and the difference it makes is accessed via the voices of the flyers who engage with the market intermediaries in five examples. Thus we follow our flyers through processes of learning (about the Internet), socializing (whilst booking the trip), economizing (whilst researching and selecting a flight), coordinating (the trip with friends) and hand-holding (to make the holiday easier and stress-free). Four of these examples focus on the use of the Internet to enable flying overseas, demonstrating, as we have previously argued that virtual mobility, instead of substituting for the taking of a trip, can increase the number of trips taken. So next we introduce these five examples of market intermediary relations, functions and affective powers – the power to make a difference.

Learning: making it possible
The data presented in Table 8.2, illustrating the increasing importance of the Internet for researching and booking holidays, tallies with the experiences of many of our frequent flyers. People are increasingly familiar with computers and the Internet, using them at work, but doubt their ability to navigate the unfamiliar waters of both booking a holiday online and budget airlines. Friends and family tell of their travels, the cost, flexibility and ease of booking online, and eventually an unfamiliar user takes the plunge, as described by Gill below.

Gill's first experience of booking a flight online was ten years ago. As a first timer, she sat with her friend at the computer during a lunch hour at work. Her work colleague showed her how to do it, and she spent several lunch hours 'playing around', going through a process of learning the Internet. She has flown up to 12 times a year ever since. She goes to Expedia first and then checks the airline sites, noting that on the Internet you can quickly check various options. Seats can even be chosen from a diagram of the cabin. She could not believe it and has done it ever since.

Socializing: making it fun
Computers are no longer tools of the workplace and are common place in the home; 70 per cent of UK households now have Internet access at home (Office of National Statistics, 2010). For many, the year is structured around holidays and the planning is part of the fun, to be enjoyed with those going on the trip. In contrast to the coordination role described below, where one person takes charge of making the arrangements, others we spoke to turn the booking of a trip into a social occasion to be enjoyed with friends.

Stephen books his flights whilst sitting having beers at home with the friends he will be travelling with. He says he enjoys researching and booking the trip. He 'reads around, plans, coordinates, checks it out on the web, goes to see his GP about injections'. He used to use a travel agent and did so for his first big trip to Mexico. Sometimes he pre-books accommodation on the Internet, but not always.

For many people, like Stephen, who use the Internet extensively to research overseas trips, the virtual experience of far flung places is not a substitute for going there, but instead opens the door to more places for them to aspire to and plan to visit.

Economizing: monitoring through the web to catch the lowest price – re-appraising price expectations downwards

Researching the price of items online is one of the most common uses of the Internet, 60.4 per cent of respondents in a 2008 survey conducted on behalf of Keynote stating that they use the Internet for this purpose (Keynote/NEMS Market Research, December 2008). Holidays and trips abroad are no exception to this and the Internet enables the simultaneous comparison of prices between different agents using sites like Expedia, as well as those of holiday companies and airlines. Many consumers are familiar with the process of researching a holiday, but also understand the competitive nature of the market and the pricing strategy budget airlines use to ensure full planes. Thus, like Trevor, they use the Internet to monitor prices and book a trip only if the price hits a pre-determined level.

Trevor described how he 'checked out' availability and price for his annual spring trip to Italy to attend a series of Italian league football games. The flights to Milan were available for £120 return. He knew he could get cheaper ones if he waited, and therefore decided to wait and keep checking out the situation. He checked two or three times more and by January the cost was £75 return. He was happy with that, but left it a few days until he had the opportunity to book. When he came to book in February, the price was £45 return. He made the booking online and found that it showed up as 1p return. Surprised, he booked, not expecting it to be that price. Sure enough, the cost came up as taxes plus 1p and the total flying cost of flying was £45 per person. He was happy to commit immediately on behalf of himself and his friends, even though they did not at that point know what the football fixtures would be. He also noted that this experience 'raises the bar' on expectations of flight prices because 'having paid £40, next time you want to match that because you have a figure in your head'.

Selling flights online is a key element of the budget airline model, taking away the need to pay commission to travel agents and reducing operating costs. Increasing and lowering prices, depending on how full the flight is and the time till the day of departure, is used as a means to attract flyers, ensuring high load factors and increasing profit per flight. From an environmental perspective, this approach to achieving high load factors often encourages people who would not have flown otherwise to do so.

Coordinating: making it happen

Many trips described to us involved the mobilization and coordination of groups of friends or family travelling together. Frequently, this involved flying for special occasions to celebrate an event or a special date that previously would have been celebrated at home or locally (Randles and Mander, 2009b). Often these trips involved the use of the Internet and e-mail to facilitate organizing and scheduling. This process inevitably required a 'lead' organizer, who mobilized and directed the others so that group decisions could be made.

Hazel had previously been a social secretary where she worked, tasked with organizing events. She drew on these skills to organize trips away involving flying. Describing a recent trip to Prague with friends, she said she had been 'thinking of Prague from the beginning'. She wanted to go in January because she hates January and wanted something to look forward to. She started looking at the end of October/November, and sent an e-mail out to a group of friends to say she was thinking about it and asked: 'Who wants to go?' She had found out the approximate costs of a hostel plus flights and plus spending. The flights and hostel were found and chosen online. Her friends came from Leeds, Bradford, Blackpool and Manchester. The first priority was it had to be cheap, the next was to fly from the North (of England), anywhere in the North with convenient flights. She sent them the link to the flight and said to them all 'book now'. Hazel described booking the flights: 'It was stressful, the actual booking, making sure everyone had the correct flight, and it took a couple of hours of frantic phone calls. I had e-mailed a few days before and said, "On Friday night I'm going to call round everyone and tell you which flight to book". People booked themselves. A couple dropped out because of work; they had paid for the flight and could not fill places for a while.'

She described the on-line chatter that surrounded the trip from a long time before to a long time after the trip. 'We were all excited,' she said, 'we talked about it and people were asking about it – the hostel, people were talking about it. We were using e-mails to organize it and afterwards we all e-mailed photos around.'

A further interesting thing to note about the experiences of Hazel and her friends is that this was not one big group who all knew each other and decided to meet in Prague, but instead several separate groups all brought together for this trip abroad. Prior to the holiday, Hazel was the only person who knew everyone initially, but chatter via e-mail generated excitement. The speed and ease of virtual communication and the ability to book separately for the same flights, allowing everyone to pay their own costs, makes this type of trip increasingly possible. Without doubt, the Internet facilitated a trip abroad that this group would not have taken otherwise.

Hand-holding: travel agents making it easy

In the group of slightly older (retirement/pre-retirement lady golfers) there was a greater tendency for a close relationship to form between the frequent flyer and her favourite, often local, travel agent, built up over a number of years. For example, in Mary's case, Yvonne at XYZ Travel is charged with making the arrangements, getting a good price and in some cases coming up with ideas for the holiday. Mary said:

> *I just go in to Yvonne; I go back to her every time because it's local to home. I just pop in every time whether it's Madeira or Prague. I go in and say: 'Want some sunshine Yvonne, just want a bit of sunshine Yvonne'.*

Mary and her husband have been using Yvonne for a number of years, and she is also on hand as a trouble shooter to resolve problems, even during the time when the couple are away on holiday. When they had a poor experience in Paris with a hotel, Mary described how she rang home to Yvonne to sort it all out. Yvonne found them a new hotel. They moved hotel and Yvonne had the first one refunded.

Within this same group of lady golfers, several have booked their specialist golfing holiday through Ron for many years. Ron is a self-employed travel agent and a 'golf trip specialist'. He gets good deals through Monarch, an airline he usually uses because the golf clubs travel for free. By contrast, on a recent trip to Ireland, one of the group booked the flights and everyone had to pay £20 each way for the golf clubs. They described how Ron organized everything in the hotel and how good it was to be free of the pressure. Even when they went to Australia on a non-golf trip they turned to Ron. Mary also went to Ron to organize the cruises she takes; she had known him for several years but never met him. She talks to him on the phone and he always matches the trip you have already found and gets a better deal.

It is interesting to note, as we have illustrated above, that the organization of flying through the intermediation of the Internet (and travel agents) is an intensely social process, involving processes of learning, socializing, economizing, coordinating and hand-holding.

Conclusions and policy implications

We have proposed the thesis that competitive processes of market intermediation and disintermediation have affective powers, and operate in various ways to create a ratchet, driving the phenomenon of frequent flying upwards in ways that are largely 'hidden' from the policy gaze and underdeveloped in academic terms. The impact of the Internet cannot be overstated, effectively bringing the world into the home or workplace. Thus, for many, rather than virtual mobility providing a substitute for corporeal mobility, it opens the door into a new world and makes it easier to step through that door. Researching and booking an overseas trip becomes an opportunity to socialize with friends, sitting at home and booking a holiday over a few beers. Alternatively, groups are brought together through e-mail and meet in person for the first time in the departure lounge.

The Internet has proved effective at disintermediating travel agents in some circumstances, particularly where booking a trip becomes a social occasion. Thus, groups of friends are unlikely to enjoy a beer in a high-street travel agent, but instead from the comfort of their living room can choose hotel rooms, read reviews of beaches and compare prices, at their leisure. We have become skilled navigators of the Internet, and purchases that only take a click seem somehow more game-like.

For the uninitiated, friends can help them take the plunge and teach them the skills to arrange a trip; alternatively, travel agents still have a role to play, particularly in niche markets such as cruises or golfing trips. These agents effectively act as gate-keepers, maintaining their position by focusing on these niche markets and potentially on a type of customer who does not have the knowledge to bypass them. The nature of Internet travel sites and their focus on either flying or rail, but seldom both, presents another type of gate-keeper, one that effectively helps to maintain the strategic position of aviation within the system. Thus a consumer is not presented with alternative modes of travel on the same site, and thus may not realize that there is a lower-carbon way of making their journey.

Given the priority accorded to climate change legislation by the UK government, the importance of intermediaries as a ratchet upon demand is an important finding. We can witness this policy-push through the establishment of the Committee on Climate Change, and its recent focus on the tensions between climate change and aviation policy, highlighted in the report 'Meeting the UK aviation target – options for reducing emissions by 2050' (Committee on Climate Change, 2009). The report describes three scenarios for emission reduction, based on different levels of technological innovation, biofuels penetration, modal shift and video conferencing. The headline message is that unconstrained growth in aviation passenger numbers could be 200 per cent between 2005 and 2050; the climate change impact of this level of growth cannot be mitigated by technology alone. The report argues that only a lower growth rate of passengers of 60 per cent will enable the UK to remain within climate change targets; this will require demand side measures (e.g. a carbon tax and capacity limits at airports). However, we would note that given the growth of frequent flying facilitated in part by the increasing penetration of the Internet as market intermediary (disintermediating the travel agent), then the target of 60 per cent growth in passenger numbers will be very difficult to achieve.

In order to analyse processes of market intermediation, and in coming to the policy conclusion we have, we developed an analytical lens through which to interrogate intermediation processes. The framework comprises a relational dimension, a functional dimension and a dimension of affective powers, which enables us to pose and offer an answer to the question 'what difference do processes of market intermediation make?'. In answer, we find that in the context of mobilities and aviation, market intermediaries have the potential to exert affective powers, reshaping and restructuring markets, and exerting upward pressures on frequent flying. With this finding, we highlight that the impact of intermediaries is not always benign. Market intermediaries, travel agents and particularly the Internet represent the 'dark side' of intermediation, and appear to be contributing to the transformation of socio-technical systems and market infrastructures in adverse ways, if we take the criteria of compromising the ability to meet policy targets to reduce aviation emissions as one plank of climate change policy.

Acknowledgements

This chapter reports on research funded by the Tyndall Centre for Climate Change research, and we are very grateful for this support. The chapter has benefited from feedback from Simon Marvin and Tim Moss. We would like to thank SURF for giving us the opportunity to contribute to the book. Special thanks also to Kalle Nielson, Doctoral Researcher at the Manchester Institute of Innovation Research.

Note

1   Demand for aviation has fallen as a result of the recession, starting in the second half of 2008. However, demand is projected to increase with the return of gross domestic product (GDP) growth (Committee on Climate Change, 2009), and the market is predicted to recover from 2011 onwards (Keynote, 2009b).

References

Civil Aviation Authority (2009) 'Aviation trends, Quarter 2, 2009', http://www.caa.co.uk/docs/80/ERG_AviationTrends_Q2_2009.pdf, accessed 22 February 2010

Committee on Climate Change (2009) 'Meeting the UK aviation target – options for reducing emissions by 2050', London: The Committee on Climate Change, http://www.theccc.org.uk/reports/aviation-report, accessed 15 September 2010

Hodson, M. and Marvin, S. (2008) 'Glossary of intermediaries, Research note 1', www.energychange.info/downloads/doc_download/186-glossarydec2008, accessed 22 February 2010

Howells, J. (2006) 'Intermediation and the role of intermediaries in innovation', *Research Policy*, vol 35, pp715–728

Keynote (2009a) 'Holiday purchasing patterns', *Market Assessment Report*, June 2009

Keynote (2009b) 'Travel and tourism market', *Market Assessment Report*, September 2009

Lente, H. van, Hekkert, M., Smits, R. and Waveren, B. van (2003) 'Roles of systemic intermediaries in transition processes', *International Journal of Innovation Management*, vol 7, no 3, pp247–279

Medd, W. and Marvin, S. (2007) 'Strategic intermediation: Between regional strategy and local practice', *Sustainable Development*, vol 15, pp318–327

Moss, T., Medd, W., Guy, S. and Marvin, S. (2009) 'Organising water: The hidden role of intermediary work', *Water Alternatives*, vol 2, no 1, pp16–33

Office of National Statistics (2010) 'National statistics omnibus survey', www.statistics.gov.uk/cci/nugget.asp?ID=8, accessed 26 March 2010

Randles, S. and Mander, S. (2009a) 'Aviation, consumption and the climate change debate, "Are you going to tell me off for flying?"', *Technology Analysis & Strategic Management*, vol 21, no 1, pp93–113

Randles, S. and Mander, S. (2009b) 'Practice(s) and ratchet(s): A sociological examination of frequent flying', in S. Gössling and P. Upham (eds) *Climate Change and Aviation: Issues, Challenges and Solutions*, Earthscan, London

Sheller, M. and Urry, J. (2004) *Tourism Mobilities: Places to Stay and Places in Play*, Routledge, London

Smedlund, A. (2006) 'The roles of intermediaries in a regional knowledge system', *Journal of Intellectual Capital*, vol 7, no 2, pp204–220

Urry, J. (2002) 'Mobility and proximity', *Sociology*, vol 36, no 2, pp255–277

Urry, J. (2007) *Mobilities*, Polity Press, Cambridge, UK

PART III

INTERMEDIARIES AND SCALAR TRANSITIONS

Simon Guy

Introduction

Part III shifts the focus to look more explicitly at the intermediation of transitions at different scales that sit within and around the urban level. Parts I and II of the book have introduced various conceptualizations of the notion of intermediaries, explored how they act to bridge production and consumption interests in both overt and covert ways, acted to reconfigure governance structures, worked strategically to open up new spaces of innovation across sectors and place, and enabled, as well as hindered, new pathways of environmental development. In Part III of the book we focus further on these transformational qualities of intermediaries, in particular exploring processes and practices of intermediation between scales of action. In doing so, we foreground the ways in which intermediaries actively inhabit the 'in-betweenness' of sectors and spaces, in order to variously reconfigure and recombine structures, relationships, interests, visions, controversies, plans and so on, with the strategic aim of enabling innovation.

Each of the chapters in Part III explore these processes of intermediation in very different ways. In following the four case studies, we encounter very different types of intermediaries: individual citizens and professionals; public and private organizations; mundane and smart technologies; and local, regional and national planning systems. Each of the chapters also works across very different boundaries: between local and regional policies of water management; between the setting of national thermal regulations and local practices of building design; between electricity production and consumption; and between the resolution of crisis and recovery in the management of a local disaster. Moreover, as Medd and Marvin point out, these intermediaries always appear in hybrid forms, combining technology, organizations, texts, money, people and other networks. But across each case study, a similar set of questions are raised:

1   How are intermediary roles constituted and what roles do they perform?
2   What is the relational nature of the work undertaken by intermediaries?
3   How do intermediaries exploit 'in-between' spaces to promote innovation?

Part III begins with a study of the processes of translating regional strategies for sustainable water management to the local level in 'Strategic Intermediation: Between Regional Strategy and Local Practice', by Will Medd and Simon Marvin. Through a case study of North-west England, the chapter draws attention to the spatiality of socio-technical infrastructures and invites an understanding of the fluid space of intermediation between regional and network space. In particular, Medd and Marvin explore the role played by different types of intermediary organization in the pursuit of sustainable, integrated water resource management for the North West of England. Faced with a seemingly natural and integrated river basin, which Medd and Marvin reveal as socially and technically 'splintered' by multiple and competing social, institutional and regulatory interests and overlapping networks of energy, telecommunication and transportation infrastructures, they argue that the challenge for sustainable water management is to somehow reframe and reconnect the water course as a 'complex assemblage'. Here, intermediaries emerge to build multi-level partnerships between public and private enterprises, to act as 'go-betweens' providing advice and information to promote shared interests, and to 'facilitate' inter-company collaborations across scales, in order to enable the translation of sustainable water practices and technologies from strategic concerns into local contexts. This focus on boundary-spanning intermediation points policy-making away from a focus on structure and systemic integration towards an appreciation of the incomplete nature of network building, in which boundaries are open as much as defining, and in which relations between continuity and change, and between stability and instability, remain unresolved but productive.

Jan Fischer and Simon Guy's chapter, 'Re-interpreting Regulations: Architects as Intermediaries for Zero Carbon Buildings', draws attention to emerging spaces of intermediation between the design and regulation of buildings. In particular, the chapter investigates the impact of a changing regulatory regime on the working practices of architects, as they become 'interpretive intermediaries', situated between the textual and representative challenges of new forms of performance-based regulation. In particular, Fischer and Guy explore how the building regulations have grown in scope and complexity with regards to thermal and energy regulations, shifting the relationship between regulation and architecture from a dialectic of constraint and autonomy to one of interpretation of design pathways, with the work of architects focusing increasingly on interpretive intermediation between often competing priorities. More specifically, the design process requires the architect to have enough understanding of each professional discipline to translate between the various experts working on the project, as well as lay stakeholders. Translation in this sense is not merely an issue of specialist languages, but also one of interpretation, of transferring and displacing meaning, and of enrolling the various actors into the project. Seen this way, the growing maze of regulation around carbon reduction policies provides an opportunity for architects to work in a professional context that is potentially supportive of 'innovative' design that promotes forms of sustainability, in contrast to simply safe design that meets minimum regulatory requirements. In this way, architects could look beyond their traditional role as 'lone' designers and reinvent themselves as interpretive intermediaries who can help facilitate the effective transition to sustainability.

The following chapter, 'Smart Meters as Obligatory Intermediaries: Reconstructing Environmental Action', by Simon Marvin, Heather Chappells and Simon Guy, moves to a focus on the 'smart meter' as a technological intermediary that is able to re-order social relations and open up new spaces of innovation around energy production and consumption. The key to this socio-technical transformation is the way utility meters are being transformed from simple measurement devices to complex socio-technical systems, enhanced by the addition of new informational and communication capabilities. In this chapter, Marvin et al explore the multiple opportunities for the development of environmental applications within smarter metering systems, including improving the efficiency of generation and distribution networks by more imaginative and customer-specific load and tariff control packages, and providing customers with cost and environmental messages through user displays. Identifying four distinct metering technical development pathways (TDPs), the chapter shows how the insertion of environmental functionalities into different smart meters is only partly a technological issue, with the take-up of these potentials strongly framed by the competing commercial priorities established by privatization and liberalization. Within this context, each TDP is designed to intermediate between users and the utilities, and in doing so make energy use more visible, more responsive to the needs of users and more flexible in terms of demand management. Different types of environmental opportunities exist within each TDP, but these potentials are dependent upon new forms of relationship developing between producers and users of energy services. Smart meters provide the necessary intermediary space that has been previously limited to traditional telecommunication media, which has severely limited any form of active dialogue. However, implementing these environmental applications would require a powerful shift in regulatory and institutional frameworks within which utilities and manufacturers configure the functionalities of smart meters. To fully exploit the intermediation potential of smart meters would require a more flexible approach that looked beyond the need to maximize volume sales of energy, and instead recognize and reinstate environmental objectives into their design and development.

Finally in Part III, 'Bridging the Recovery Gap', by Beccy Whittle and Will Medd, examines the role of intermediaries in disaster recovery, exploring the forms of intermediation that emerge during the extended processes of urban flood recovery. Drawing on a case study of flooding in Hull in the summer of 2007, the chapter offers an account of the experience of intermediation 'on the front line', and a critical evaluation of the 'gap' between the lived experience of flood recovery and the policy 'lessons' learnt. In particular, Whittle and Medd point to a 'recovery gap' which emerges during the longer process of recovery at the point where the legally defined contingency arrangements provided to the affected community by its local authority diminish, and where the less well-defined services provided by the private sector (e.g. insurance, building repairs) start. It is the existence of this recovery gap, they argue, that makes the role played by intermediaries so vital in negotiating, providing essential information and resolving immediate conflicts. Seen this way, disasters may involve exceptional circumstances, but they can also tell us much about the everyday, 'hidden' work of intermediation that goes on behind the scenes in managing the urban environment, and how policy change at the local and national level has given rise to particular kinds of intermediation which translate these policies into practical change on the ground. Consequently, what seems to be the technical problem of managing flooding actually involves a reconfiguration of social relations and a renewed understanding of the roles that intermediaries play in urban governance on a daily basis.

9

Strategic Intermediation: Between Regional Strategy and Local Practice

Will Medd and Simon Marvin

Introduction

The European Union Water Framework Directive (WFD) (European Commission, 2000) is an attempt to provide a coherent and comprehensive framework for water management. It came into force in December 2000 and is the most substantial piece of European Commission (EC) water legislation ever produced (Woods, 2004). The demands of achieving 'good water status' for all water bodies by 2015 will necessitate a reformulation of the boundaries through which sustainable water management takes place. In particular, the governance of sustainable water management, under the WFD, is to be focused on spatial boundaries defined by hydrological zones; namely, designated river basins and river catchments. The aspiration of the WFD is that through a focus on hydrological boundaries, the development of integrated river basin management (IRBM) as a holistic approach to sustainable water management will be more feasible.

Developing holistic approaches to sustainable water management is an attractive response to overcoming the limitations of the previously fragmented directives relevant to water management. The extent to which established institutional boundaries and practices can, and are willing to, adapt to those defined by the hydrological zone remains to be seen (Moss, 2003; White and Howe, 2003). While current debate framed in this way focuses on how to integrate different institutional actors and stakeholders into strategy formation and practice, in this chapter we want to suggest there is a need to understand the hidden work of intermediaries that work in-between regional and network space, and in doing so work in-between regional strategy and local practice. For us, 'regional' space refers to territorially proximate and bounded clusters of activities, while 'network space' refers to the socio-technical networks that can simultaneously both enable the occupation of regional space and also cut across that space, 'bypassing' users and spaces.

While noting the neglected significance of networked space, the focus of this chapter is on illustrating the significant role that intermediary organizations, often absent in conventional analysis, play in governance processes. In particular, intermediaries are significant in translating sustainable water management from regional strategy to local practice, largely through their hidden work characterized by adaptability and transformation. We use three case study examples of intermediaries working in the North West of England to illustrate the importance of understanding their work in the practices of sustainable water management. Each example demonstrates different forms of intermediary work, while also revealing the need to understand the transformations involved in translating sustainable water management from strategy into practice.

The chapter is structured in three sections. In the first section, we argue that questions about institutional alignment around regional spaces defined in the WFD by 'hydrological zones' must also refer to the network spaces constituted by socio-technical infrastructures. In the second section, we examine the work of three intermediaries to ask how sustainable water management can be translated from strategy to practice. Finally, we conclude by examining the implications for understanding the challenges of the WFD and regional research agendas.

Regional and network spaces of water management

Using topological representation, regional space is determined by drawing boundaries around objects, practices or people clustered together (Mol and Law, 1994). The WFD is an attempt to define an appropriate regional boundary, and it does this through the 'natural' spaces of river basins. As such, IRBM is, in principle, defined by an eco-system boundary, a biophysical region rather than other institutional or infrastructural boundaries. In England, the challenges of orienting current institutional arrangements to these natural spaces are lessened because existing water management is oriented to boundaries established in 1973 that were determined by river basin areas (Kinnersely, 1994; Bakker, 2003). In the North West of England, where the case study for this chapter is located, the responsibilities of United Utilities, a private sector company who own the assets and operating rights for water in the North West, are drawn broadly around a river basin area (see Figure 9.1), with some overlapping boundaries in the south and north of the region. In addition to the utility companies, within this North-west water sector we also find the regulators with regional offices – for the environment, economic efficiency, customer services – as well as some private forms of operation; for example, supply water through private boreholes.

While for the utility company the region is presented as a 'seamless flow' (Chappells, 2003), the challenges of implementing the WFD are bringing to the fore questions about what the extent of integration really requires. The WFD is an attempt to achieve an appropriate spatial fit between institutional

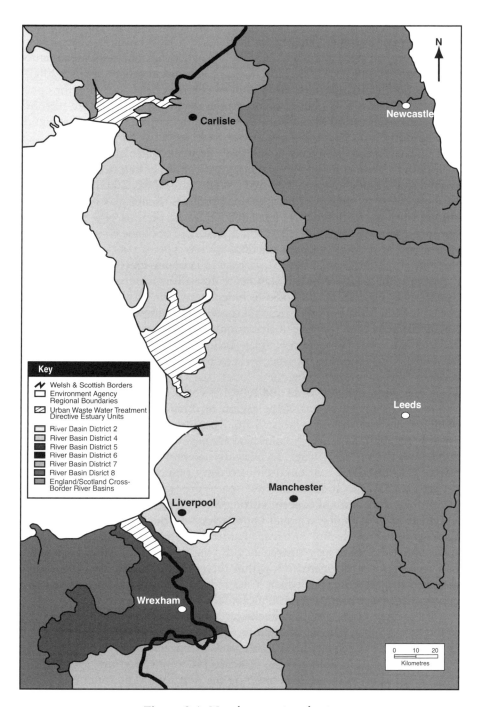

Key

⋀	Welsh & Scottish Borders
☐	Environment Agency Regional Boundaries
▨	Urban Waste Water Treatment Directive Estuary Units
☐	River Basin District 2
▨	River Basin District 4
■	River Basin District 5
■	River Basin District 6
▨	River Basin District 7
▨	River Basin District 8
▨	England/Scotland Cross-Border River Basins

Figure 9.1 *North-west river basin*

boundaries and resource management, by managing water resources according to the territorial unit of an ecosystem rather than political–administrative boundaries. River basin management is designed to address the interdependencies between, in particular, upstream and downstream effects, water quality and water quantity, and water and adjacent land-use resources (Moss, 2003). However, difficulties for integration soon emerge, not just concerning the interconnections across scale, but also concerning the multiple and nested regional spaces that overlap and are constituted by a multiplicity of interests (see Figure 9.2). As institutions adapt towards a river basin model as the territorial unit of water management, 'problems of interplay between water and other relevant institutions – such as for spatial planning, agriculture or nature conservation – may be exacerbated' (Moss, 2003, p86; White and Howe, 2003).

In addition to the risk of exacerbated problems of interplay between institutions working to differently defined boundaries, there is also the need to consider the significance of networked spaces. Topologically, difference is understood in network space, as defined by the type of relation between the elements (Mol and Law, 1994). Difference in network space is determined by the form of the relation, rather than being defined by membership of a spatial cluster, as in regional space. Socio-technical networks play an important part of enabling the constitution of regional spaces; for example, by enabling travel, communication and resource distribution (Graham and Marvin, 2001; see Barry, 2001, on the European Union – EU).

For the North-west water sector there are a multiplicity of networks that 'splinter' the apparently integrated zones (see Graham and Marvin, 2001). There is a wide array of loose and tight networks enabling people, resources and materials to travel across the region in different directions, while connecting otherwise distinct places. Moreover, just as there are different and overlapping regional spaces, so too there are networks among networks. There are networks of local water supply, for example, but also interlinkages between water supply and electricity (to drive pumps and treatment works), between wastewater and rivers. These spaces are significant, for they point to some of the difficulties of conceptualizing what 'integration' actually means in a context of overlapping regional boundaries, and the fragmentation of linkages across, through and in-between different networked spaces. While to some extent the WFD may emerge as a driving force for investment strategies that reconfigure water networks within the context of integrated river basin management, the extent to which a desired congruence can be achieved and how it will be achieved remains conceptually underdeveloped.

The people in the city of Manchester, in the south-east of the region, for example, use a large supply of drinking water supplied from the Lake District, in the north of the region. The water travels through large-scale pipelines running for over 160 miles, built through the innovation of 19th-century engineers. Importantly, while connecting the north with the south-east of the region, these pipelines also create new boundaries between different populations. The extent to which the water supply that runs through these pipes is available for people whom the pipeline runs nearby, or, indeed, the extent of accessibility to the land through which the pipeline cuts, becomes the site of

Figure 9.2 *Regional and sub-regional governance*

legal, political, economic and community contestation (see Graham and Marvin, 2001, on these 'bypass' issues). Importantly, then, the network space of the water infrastructure is one that denies access as much as it connects (see Figure 9.3). Networks can cut across regional spaces. They cut across the different scales of hydrological zones defined by the WFD and, in doing so, complexify the extent to which different practices that will impact on such zones can be managed through strategies of integration. The critical challenge for the WFD, in this context, is therefore how it will translate strategies designed at the regional, river basin, level into the context of local practices, where such practices are constituted through different socio-technical networks. At the level of a regional spatial framework, patterns of water consumption and wastewater production can of course be aggregated. Such aggregation can include some differentiation of types of user; for example, households, industrial users, small to medium-sized enterprises (SMEs) and public sector organizations. However, the practices of these different users are dispersed through the water region, connected through many types of network, not just those of the water infrastructure. The challenge of translating sustainable water practices across different types of consumer has been the subject of many different strategies; for example, from 'harder' legislative mechanisms such as licensing and fining to 'softer' strategies such as promotional campaigns. However, less attention has been given to those organizations that work in different ways in-between the spaces of regional strategy and local practice.

In particular, while the Water Framework Directive gives considerable weight to the role of stakeholder engagement (Carter and Howe, 2006), the analysis of the role of intermediary organizations is absent. Yet, across a range of sectors, increased attention is being given to the transformative role played by intermediary organizations; for example, in facilitating town planning (Paddison, 2003), creating contexts for innovation (van Lente et al, 2003) or shaping pathways for social care (Allen, 2003). In particular, there is a need to understand the emergence of organizations that act as strategic intermediaries in the water sector. These intermediaries always appear in hybrid forms, combining technology, organizations, texts, money, people and other networks (see Callon, 1997). They constitute new forms of interdependencies and socio-technical assemblages. Moreover, the legitimacy and expertise of intermediaries does not emerge within a space between distinct spheres of supply or consumption. Instead, they gain their legitimacy by working across the boundaries of a range of interests not normally considered as significant to strategies of sustainability. They are strategic because of their deliberate work in acting in-between different sets of interests in order to pursue their goals.

Strategic intermediaries

Critically, then, the challenge for sustainable water management is to somehow reconnect the multiple and diverse spatialities of ecological, institutional and network space at the regional scale with the practices that can more effectively and rapidly promote action at the local level. Significantly, we need to

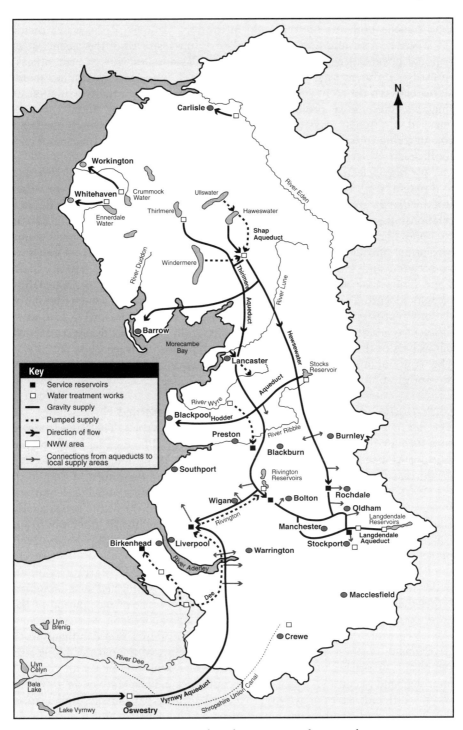

Figure 9.3 *United Utilities' regional network*

look outside both the conventional institutional frames of the water sector (production, consumption and regulatory interests) and the agencies of regional governance (development agencies, assemblies, government offices) towards a different class of actor-intermediaries, who actively position themselves between different social interests and spatialities. In the North West of England, there is a proliferation of intermediary organizations that are engaged in different ways with sustainable water management, each playing a role in trying to translate the strategies of sustainable water management into local practices across multiple spatialities.

We have selected three examples of intermediary activity that all illustrate a different way of translating from regional strategy into local practice. Intermediaries are distinctive because of the role they play in-between defined relationships, rather than their particular organizational form. Each of the examples highlights a particular characteristic of intermediation, namely intermediation through a multi-level partnership, intermediation through a go-between and intermediation through facilitation. In fact, they all share some similar characteristics; for example, multi-level funding arrangements, roles as educators and brokers, and so on. Together they give some insight into the different ways in which water is translated and transformed across quite different types of context. The examples draw on interviews that were carried out as part of the EU intermediaries research project between 2002 and 2005. The names of interviewees and their exact positions within their organizations are not given in order to ensure anonymity.

Intermediating through multi-level partnerships

The first example is the Mersey Basin Campaign (MBC). The River Mersey runs through the centre of England's urban industrial landscape, including the cities of Manchester and Liverpool (see Figure 9.4). Prolonged pollution had meant that the river had struggled to sustain life, and the return of salmon to the Mersey Basin in 2003 hit the headlines, provoking much celebration. Indeed, 'the water quality improvements within the industrial and urban heartland of the Mersey Basin are substantial and rank with the most improved waterways within the UK' (Burton et al, 2003, p446). Central to these developments has been the role played by the MBC.

The name 'Mersey Basin Campaign' is a significant starting point in understanding the work of the organization. It was established as a campaign rather than a government programme, precisely because of recognition of the need to engage a wide variety of organizations and people if it was to be a success. As a campaign, the MBC brings into partnership a rare combination of government, business and community. The structure of the partnership is also significant: firstly, because it brings together representation of a wide range of interests; and secondly, because it reconfigures representatives in different ways at different scales of activity, as a cross-sectoral partnership organization that would work 'embracing government, public agencies, local authorities, business and industry and local communities and individuals' (MBC, 2005, p8). The structure of the partnership consists of the council, which determines strategic guidance; advisory groups, which provide a focus on specific policy

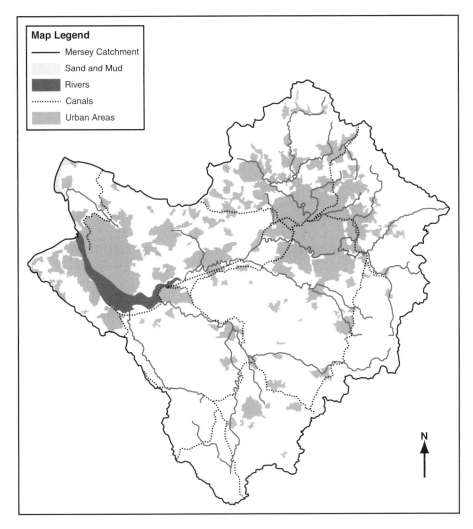

Figure 9.4 *Mersey Basin catchment*

development and guidance; the Mersey Basin Business Foundation, a mechanism for business and financial management, contracts and employment of
staff; and The Healthy Waterways Trust, the charitable arm of the campaign,
which also acts as a registered environmental body for the Landfill Tax Credit
Scheme. The chair of the campaign is a government appointee. Through these
different entities, different funding mechanisms can be accessed, different forms
of work undertaken and different sets of interests brought together. Core
funding for the campaign comes from the government, with additional funding through corporate, programme and project sponsorship, including grants
and European funding (MBC, 2005).

    As well as this complex partnership structure, the MCB is also innovative
in its internalization of multi-level governance. At the North-west regional

level, the MBC seeks to contribute to policy development, as well as to specific regional projects, through its partnership arrangements:

> We'll comment on the regional economic strategy and try and encourage more investment in the image of the region and the environment of the region, try and get more redevelopment and regeneration money into the regions (Interview with MBC manager).

For example, they are working with the NWDA on land reclamation and trying to encourage the regeneration of waterside areas. This regional concern also means working at the national level; for example, trying to influence the periodic review that determines investment in the water sector over a five-year period.

At the local level the practical work undertaken by MBC is through the river valley initiatives (RVIs), in which the MBC partnership is formed anew, though 'the objectives of all the river valley initiatives are the same as the overall campaign but on a smaller scale' (interview with MBC manager). The precise composition of the RVIs, however, will depend on local circumstances, and includes public, private and voluntary sector, including representation from the Environment Agency (EA) and United Utilities. RVIs are about getting the 'regional agenda operating through local activities', as one MBC representative put it:

> To plug the gap between local delivery and regional initiative, we've got a number of sub-regional programmes which are perhaps partly a mechanism for drawing in funding to do practical stuff. So we've got programmes going in each of the sub-regions, we really do follow NWDA's lead on this (Interview with MBC manager).

In the case of the Greater Manchester Waterways Action Programme, for example, by aggregating together three RVIs' concerns with litter and debris, different funding sources could be accessed: 'On the ground it will look like lots of bits of actions', but to the funders it will be presented as 'strategic and catchment wide' (interview with MBC manager).

The intermediary as a go-between

While the practices of SMEs might become visible to the EA when an infringement takes place – for example, when a company releases wastewater into a river this is reported by the public – regularly monitoring the activities of SMEs is a time-consuming and expensive business. Furthermore, the EA perceived reluctance by SMEs to approach the EA for advice because of the risk of subjecting their practices to investigation and risking high penalties or investment costs. A solution for the North Area office of the EA in the Northwest regions was to establish a project that would act as an advisory service for SMEs. However, such a service, if it was to be acceptable to SMEs, would need to link into SME networks, and to do this could not be based within the EA. A pilot project was established, called Sustainable Water in East Lancashire, which involved funding an environmental water advisor in the local Business Environment Association (BEA). In this way, the project could work through the existing local business networks offering free advice to business on sustainable water management issues. The project was successful and further funding was established to cover the wider Lancashire Authority district. Now Sustainable Water Environment in Lancashire (SWEL), the project continues to offer advice and support to SMEs in the Lancashire area; for example, offering services such as industrial water management, flood risk management and advice on sustainable drainage systems.

The work of the SWEL project highlights an important aspect of the boundary work of SMEs. The ability of SWEL to present itself in different forms is crucial. The water advisor at the time explained how she would respond to companies when she first met with them:

> As you talk to, [sic] the first time you meet someone or as you're talking to them you get a sense of which direction they're coming from, which is why the Agency gives us the money, because the Agency are only coming from the green side, purely coming from the environmental side. The business is coming from the business side and we tread the line to keep everybody happy, which is what I like and why the job works and why SWEL works because you choose where you're coming from. You're not a greeny. You're not Friends of the Earth, you're not WWF... If they need to be greener and they know they need to be greener I keep mentioning the Agency. If they need to make a business improvement because they're losing money we keep mentioning the BEA because it sounds more business[-like]. So you're sort of, you choose the slant to take with them (Interview with SWEL advisor).

While some SMEs are motivated by money saving, others might, however, be motivated by achieving ISO 14001 status. Hence SWEL might present to a company in relation to how it can avoid high fines for wastewater discharge; it may present to a company in terms of the potential costs savings of reduced water use or of reduced insurance through a sustainable drainage system (reducing flooding risk); or it may present to a company in terms of the symbolic value a company might gain by being seen to contribute to sustainability. In each of these, not only does SWEL present a different form (e.g. sometimes it makes explicit its work for the EA, sometimes it presents instead in relation to the local business network), but it also shows how the issues of sustainable water management become transformed into different contexts: as legal practice, a commercial practice, a symbolic practice. And in doing this, through its adaptability, SWEL is translating sustainable water practices and technologies into the localized regional space of the SME that is in turn connected to wider networks of water supply and wastewater disposal.

The intermediary facilitator

The North West has the UK's largest cluster of chemical industry companies, with around 450 manufacturers, 220 service providers, 110 sales offices and eight universities; it generates a turnover of around £10 billon (Chemicals Northwest, 2003). Yet it is threatened by fragmentation across the region, an aging workforce and the need to improve its environmental impact. As one of several industrial cluster groups in the North West, Chemicals Northwest (CNW) was established in March 2000 as a non-profit organization to support the sustainable development of the sector through the Northwest Regional Development Agency's economic growth strategy. CNW defined itself as 'an industry-led organization driving strategic and sustainable development for the chemical and related industries in England's Northwest' (interview with CNW Director).

An objective of CNW is the Mersey Banks Industrial Symbiosis (IS) project, which encourages companies to work together to achieve resource efficiency and develop the lessons from this experience for the North West as a whole. Within this project, water has emerged as a significant area for potential resource saving. Several areas of potential improved efficiency of water utilization have been identified: low-quality water from re-use of discharged water (e.g. condensate streams, wash-down water, cooling water or effluents); boreholes where the extraction rate is well below the licensed rate; high-purity water sources, such as reverse osmosis units, which are underutilized. Within the project there are some groups of companies in the same local area that have generated several of these utilization or supply issues. The possibility therefore exists to explore whether inter-company collaboration could reduce overall demand on water supply or sewerage systems. Though in fact the Mersey Banks project has not succeeded in changing any actual practice, CNW are now looking to develop the work at the regional level. The CNW then provides an interesting example of some of the challenges that facilitation involves and limits of the role that an intermediary can play. While the technical possibilities for water saving are there, the commercial and regulatory contexts have made this problematic.

The role of CNW was very much as a facilitator of the Mersey Banks IS project, aiming to raise the visibility of synergies between companies and identify possibilities for developing resource saving at the collective industrial cluster level. This work involved companies looking at their collective water usage in order to identify areas where shared resource use could be of benefit. This included, for example, increasing use of currently underutilized desalination plants, companies recycling other companies' discharged water and developing shared grey water recycling facilities. By exploiting synergies between companies, new relations are potentially formed that extend beyond the existing socio-technical network. Key here was that CNW was just the facilitator of the cluster; they would not actually do the work.

The risks that become visible through the process of facilitation are significant and expose the limits of what the intermediary can achieve. Firstly, there is the problem of the interdependencies that the IS project demands from companies in a context when they each operate in different markets subject to market risks and so on. During the context of the IS project, some of the possibilities for synergies came and went as company production increased and decreased. Secondly, the regulatory context could pose limits to what is possible:

> *I think there are some issues that a collaborative project does give rise to in relation to the way the Environment Agency operates. Their legislation is written very much with a focus on individual operations. They would look at an individual site and they would look for improvement within that site and they would look for improvement in the next site and improvement in the site just down the road. The idea that you might put a group of companies to collectively achieve a benefit, three or four of them individually will have a benefit that they can display, but the last one looks as though its performance is worse than it was before because it may be the site where a new treatment unit is located (Interview with CNW manager).*

The significance for the intermediary here is twofold. Firstly, it shows how intermediary work extends the normal frames of reference for understanding the producer, consumer and regulator relationships. Here, the configuration of a cluster of companies into a set of relations that recycle water collectively not only raised interest from the utility company, but also revealed limits in the regulator structure. Secondly, however, these problems also raised limits to what an intermediary can actually achieve. Here, a further process of negotiation with the EA in relation to national policies, as well as local enforcement, was required.

The focus of CNW is the chemical sector, and water itself became a particularly interesting boundary object that led to potential synergies between the companies, but that also drew into the local network representatives from regional organizations such as United Utilities and the EA.

The work of intermediaries

In summary, the MBC illustrates an example of an intermediary organization that translates sustainable water management through an adaptable multi-level partnership. The partnership's structure is constructed such that it maintains a core identity from the regional to the local level, while allowing flexibility in terms of accessing different forms of funding and enrolling different sets of actors across different levels. By contrast, the work of SWEL illustrates the boundary work undertaken by an intermediary that works as a go-between across the logics of environmental regulation and business practice, and across the problems of regional funding and local practices. The work of CNW demonstrates another significant intermediary role in reconfiguring the relations between utility companies, regulators and particular clusters of consumers, and how the move from principles and strategies into practice reveals problems that may not have otherwise been foreseen. Through their different ways of working, new technologies and changed social practices are introduced across different socio-technical networks and different geographical spaces.

Looking across these intermediaries, the significance of their work is in how they enable the translation of sustainable water practices and technologies from strategic concerns into local contexts. Through their different forms of working and organizational arrangements, they work across different scales and different regional spaces. This involves making connections between different social and technical networks. This is not about the processes of policy implementation from higher to lower levels of practice or the integration of ground level activities into policy frameworks. The work of intermediaries across different scales of practice involves a complex array of negotiation, (re)representation and translation of what 'sustainable water management' becomes in relation to different contexts. Critically in relation to water itself, it was not simply that the intermediaries would bridge already existing sets of interests, as if they were some neutral arbitrators. Intermediaries are strategic and have their own sets of interests, translating into strategies, programmes and practices. Their strength comes in their ability to adapt their relationship to water into different sets of interests and contexts without necessarily integrating these interests.

Conclusions

The WFD is an attempt to integrate spatial practices through integrated river basin management as a holistic approach to sustainable water management. Such aspirations are hard to resist, and the vision of integration and holism can be inspiring. Much of the energy currently invested in implementing the WFD, as well as evaluating it, looks at the extent to which core institutional actors will align their interests while engaging stakeholders effectively in decision-making processes. Incorporation of the role that intermediary organizations can play in these processes has been neglected. And yet intermediary organizations, of which we have explored three, demonstrate the intricacies involved in translating sustainable water management from strategy to practice. Institutional alignment at the river basin level, for example, will be of little significance per se for those actors undertaking different types of water practice, according to quite different sets of agendas. To understand the effectiveness of the governance strategies of the WFD, more consideration will need to be given to understanding the different forms of intermediation, through which sustainable water management can be translated across different scales of activity and across different socio-technical networks.

The current governance strategies of the WFD focus on different regional scales of action and integrating actors through various formal mechanisms. However, the work of intermediaries suggests that the translation of sustainable water management across different contexts requires sensitivity to the multiplicity of relations that differentiate as much as integrate the regional space. Indeed, in our examples, we find that the work undertaken by the intermediaries leads to improved water governance through complementarity with the strategies of organizations charged with delivering the WFD (namely the EA).

Until now this work, and the spatialities through which it is performed, has remained hidden to mainstream analysis and policy frameworks. Research needs to contribute to revealing such relations and the hidden work that intermediary organizations perform, and to developing recommendations for policy that move beyond the goals of integration towards open-ended and process-oriented approaches. Such approaches require appreciation of the incomplete nature of the work, of boundaries that are open as much as defining, and that the relations between continuity and change, and between stability and instability, are not resolved but can be used productively.

What then does this imply more generally for establishing where solutions to sustainability lie? One way to think about this is to look beyond 'top-down' or 'bottom-up' approaches. Top-down approaches, for example, might develop particular policy initiatives or technological solutions, which are then implemented from national to local level. The problem of such 'top-down approaches' is the compromise that the context of implementation inevitably demands and the externalities – as well as failures – this can create. An alternative approach is the focus on the consumer. Much attention has been given in recent years to raising awareness of water consumption, be this through promotional activities or financial disciplinary practices (i.e. metering). This we might talk of as a more bottom-up approach to sustainability. Tensions between bottom-up and top-down approaches will always prevail. This is the case whether discussing the solutions (politics) to issues of sustainability (does responsibility lie with the state or the consumer?), or trying to understand the emergence of sustainable social practices and technological innovations (does explanation focus on local decision or wider structural constraints?). In other words, the ways in which debates about sustainable consumption have focused on issues of production (e.g. more effective ways of recycling waste water) or on consumption (e.g. shifting consumption practices towards using less water) can be understood in terms of tensions between a top-down (production/supply) and a bottom-up (consumption/demand) approach.

Focusing either on bottom up (demand) or top down (supply) for understanding the emergence of intermediaries would be misleading. The emergence of the intermediaries takes place in relation to specific actors, logics, populations, practices and so on. They constitute new contexts, enabling and making visible possibilities that would otherwise not have been present. The question this raises is what the implications of new intermediaries, emerging within the context of changing infrastructures, are for understanding sustainability. Firstly, understanding infrastructural transition needs to take account of the emergence of new intermediaries that act in-between the traditional divides between the consumer and the utility. These emerging actors generate novel and interesting ways of developing sustainable practice. Secondly, to distinguish separate spheres of consumption and production can be misleading. These new intermediaries suggest we need to work towards the ways in which sustainable practice combines moments of production and consumption to generate new circuits of sustainability. Finally, the rise of new intermediaries means thinking beyond the capacity of the state, public agencies, social movements and commercial companies to explore how it is that the interrelationships between them, within particular contexts, can generate added value that contributes to sustainable practice.

Acknowledgements

This is a revised and shortened version of Medd, W. and Marvin, S. 'Making water work: Intermediating between regional strategy and local practice', *Environment and Planning D: Society and Space*, vol 26, no 2, pp280–299. We are grateful for permission to publish the paper in revised form.

References

Allen, C. (2003) 'On the logic of "new" welfare practice: An ethnographic case study of the "new welfare intermediaries"', *Sociological Research Online*, vol 8, no 1, <http://www.socresonline.org.uk/8/1/allen.html>, accessed 31 August 2010

Bakker, K. (2003) *An Uncooperative Commodity: Privatizing Water in England and Wales*, Oxford University Press, Oxford

Barry, A. (2001) *Political Machines: Governing a Technological Society*, Athlone, London

Burton, L.R., Howard, A. and Goodall, B. (2003) 'Construction of a historical Water Pollution Index for the Mersey Basin', *Area*, vol 35, no 4, pp438–448

Callon, M. (1997) 'Techno-economic networks and irreversibility', in J. Law (ed) *A Sociology of Monsters: Essays on Power, Technology and Domination, Sociological Review Monograph*, Routledge, London, pp132–161

Carter, J.G. and Howe, J. (2006) 'Stakeholder participation during river basin planning in England and Wales: The case of the Ribble Pilot', *Local Environment*, vol 11, no 2, pp217–233

Chappells, H. (2003) *Reconceptualising Electricity and Water: Institutions, Infrastructures and the Constitution of Demand*, Lancaster University Department of Sociology, Lancaster

Chemicals Northwest (2003) 'Mersey Banks Industrial Symbiosis Project: A Study into Opportunities for Sustainable Development through Inter-Company Collaboration', http://www.chemicalsnorthwest.org.uk/doxuploaded/MBIS_Final_Report.pdf, accessed 9 August 2010

European Commission (2000) 'Directive 2000/60/EC of the European Parliament and of the Council of 23 October 2000 Establishing a Framework for Community Action in the Field of Water Policy', *Official Journal of the European Communities L*, vol 327, no 1, pp1–72

Graham, S. and Marvin, S. (2001) *Splintering Urbanism: Networked Infrastructures, Technological Mobilities and the Urban Condition*, Routledge, London

Kinnersley, D. (1994) *Troubled Waters*, Penguin, London

Lente, H. van, Hekkert, M., Smits, R. and Waveren, B. van (2003) 'Roles of systemic intermediaries in transition processes', *International Journal of Innovation Management*, vol 73, pp247–279

Mersey Basin Campaign (MBC) (2005) 'Corporate plan, 2005/2006', Mersey Basin Campaign, Manchester

Mol, A. and Law, J. (1994) 'Regions, networks and fluids: Anaemia and social topology', *Social Studies of Science*, vol 24, pp641–671

Moss, T. (2003) 'Solving problems of "fit" at the expense of problems of "interplay"? The spatial reorganization of water management following the EU Water Framework Directive', in H. Breit, E. Engels, T. Moss and M. Troja (eds) *How Institutions Change: Perspectives on Social Learning in Global and Local Environmental Concerns*, Leske and Budrich, Opladen, pp86–87

Paddison, A. (2003) 'Town centre management (TCM): A case study of Achmore', *International Journal of Retail and Distribution Management*, vol 31, no 12, pp618–627

White, I. and Howe, J. (2003) 'Planning and the European Union Water Framework Directive', *Environment Planning and Management*, vol 46, no 4, pp621–631

Woods, D. (2004) *The EC Water Framework Directive: An Introductory Guide*, Foundation for Water Research, Marlow

10
Reinterpreting Regulations: Architects as Intermediaries for Zero Carbon Buildings

Jan Fischer and Simon Guy

Introduction

In recent debates, codes and regulations have been identified as highly influential in shaping urban places and architectural form (Ben-Joseph, 2005). But while there is some existing work on the impact of regulation on the work of architects in terms of stifling or encouraging design creativity (Gann et al, 1998; Imrie, 2007) and about the processes surrounding the setting of regulations (Raman and Shove, 2000), there is still a surprising neglect of the wider impact of changing regulation on the working practices of design professionals. As has been often noted, architects appear to have little influence on the setting of building regulations (Raman and Shove, 2000; Imrie, 2007), and 'most commentators' highlight a tendency of architects to view regulations as a burden on creativity or professional licence (Hunt and Raman, 2000). However, with global climate change increasingly linked to the release of carbon dioxide into the atmosphere caused by the use of fossil fuels (McMichael et al, 2006; Metz et al, 2006; Stern, 2006), the built environment has become a key focus of regulatory intervention aimed at cutting carbon emissions.

The UK Department for Communities and Local Government (DCLG) estimates that 27 per cent of the UK's carbon dioxide emissions come from the use of homes and a further 17 per cent from the use of non-domestic buildings (DCLG, 2008b). Scholars have estimated CO_2 emissions from buildings to be as high as 50 per cent (Henderson and Shorrock, 1992; Guy and Osborn, 2001; Campbell, 2007). In response, the UK government aims to achieve a significant reduction in CO_2 emissions by requiring that new-built homes are to be 'zero carbon' from 2016 onwards (DCLG, 2006, 2007). A key mechanism to achieve these reductions will be the use of building regulations. Rating new dwellings against the 'Code for Sustainable Homes' is a legal requirement, and performing up to certain levels of the code was scheduled to become legally binding over time when the research for this chapter was carried out. By 2016 the highest level of the code is planned to become mandatory for all new residential dwellings (DCLG, 2006, 2007). Similarly, the Government has announced ambitions that all new non-residential buildings are to be zero carbon by 2019 (DCLG, 2008a). Both advances will entail extensive changes in the regulation of energy consumption in buildings.

This tighter disciplining of design to meet more onerous regulatory targets is leading to a new challenge for architects, who are responding either defensively, as guardians of aesthetic autonomy in the face of regulatory intervention, or more positively, as the new intermediaries in the struggle to interpret and respond to the new regulatory regime. Seen this way, the regulatory process is moving away from being conceived and experienced as an external constraint, towards being viewed as a space of intermediation in which the meanings and methods of zero carbon buildings are being negotiated. As Stephen Fineman has suggested: 'regulating the environment is plainly more than reading off legal prescriptions. It is a process of technical and social ritual embedded in particular political contexts, where personal and professional reputations are on the line' (Fineman, 2000, p108). This raises the question of how architects identify themselves in relation to this emerging space of intermediation, in particular as they are not alone in attempting to position themselves as guides through the growing regulatory maze. Engineers and other consultants are emerging as alternative intermediaries, creating new forms of professional competition, and potentially shifting power away from architects towards new energy and environmental consultants. For many architects this sits uncomfortably with the widespread – but perhaps professionally biased – belief that they should be the chief designers of buildings. As a result, a key question for architects, we argue, is whether, how and with which effects new forms of interpretive practice are becoming central to architectural work, in a context of enhanced regulatory pressures and competition from other professional stakeholders.

Looking ahead to the likely further unfolding of this process, the chapter will argue that this regulatory offensive in the pursuit of zero carbon buildings will powerfully affect the influence of architects on building design and potentially reshape patterns of collaboration with other built environment professionals. If they are to retain their status as leaders of design innovation, this shift may require architects to take a greater role as intermediaries between the regulatory requirements and regulators on the one hand, and the design process and its actors on the other hand, while also accepting that others control some design decisions that have historically been an architectural prerogative. The chapter will explore the emergent logic of architectural intermediation from an empirical perspective, while highlighting how various engineering consultants gain greater importance in the web of regulatory enforcement. Focusing on the new Code for Sustainable Homes, we will explore the emerging implications of this new regulatory push on the role, identity and influence of architects as they pursue the goal of zero carbon buildings.

The chapter is in three sections. Firstly, 'The regulatory push: disciplining buildings' outlines how recent changes to the regulatory regime are reframing contexts of design. Secondly, 'The challenge of enforcement: the interpretative turn' explores how the relationship of regulation and design is shifting from a dialectic of constraint and autonomy to one of multiple, dynamic and flexible interpretations of appropriate pathways to zero carbon buildings. Finally, 'Architects as intermediaries' identifies the response of architects to this newly emerging mode of design, their anxieties over their loss of autonomy and the emergence of new design practices.

This chapter draws on data from 21 in-depth, semi-structured face-to-face interviews with architects. Respondents were recruited by writing to, e-mailing and phoning architects across England, but predominantly in the North West. While there is no claim that interviewees were by any means representative, the sample ranked from very junior staff to principals. The practices they worked for ranged from some of the UK's largest to sole practitioner practices; they varied in their portfolios, design philosophies and economic success. However, there was a distinct predominance of men in the sample, with only four women interviewed. All interviewees gave written informed consent. The interviews were audio recorded, transcribed and coded with the aid of the software package MAXqda2. Codes from the interviews relating to regulation, enforcement, design team relations and energy-efficient design practices were analysed thematically using Framework (Ritchie and Spencer, 1994).

The regulatory push: disciplining buildings

To explore the impact of regulations on the work of architects, we will briefly sketch out relevant recent changes and expansions to the regulatory regime framing building design, and illustrate a growing maze of regulations that has emerged as a result. Throughout the building industry there is a perception that regulations are becoming more complex. In its recent consultation paper, the Building Control Working Group of the Department for Communities and Local Government recognized that expansion of the building regulations may confuse stakeholders, and that there 'there remains a need for these issues to be better understood by building professionals and members of the public if we are to achieve increased compliance with the standards' (DCLG, 2008a, p12).

Regulating for climate change

The most substantial recent developments in regulatory policy have taken place with regards to carbon dioxide emissions from buildings and particularly homes, which will here serve as a case study reflecting on the regulatory regime in general. Energy efficiency of buildings is currently regulated by Part L (Consumption of Fuel and Power) of the Building Code, which has undergone regular revision, including further strengthening in 2006 to make new homes more thermally efficient, raising standards by 40 per cent compared with 2002. Only limited research has been undertaken in this area. For example,

Raman and Shove (2000) followed the processes of revising Part L of the building regulations, observing an increasing blurring of boundaries between business practice and regulation, both due to the Government's decision to open up the process to private regulators and to the building industry's ability to influence the policy-making process (Raman and Shove, 2000). Critically, they also argued that the recent shift towards a performance-based building code paved the way towards new forms of government and industry interaction. The prescriptive code set specific minimum efficiency values for specific parts of the building. For example, insulation in walls and roofs had to achieve a certain heat transfer coefficient in each element, measured in U-values. By contrast, the new performance-based code uses a simple model of the performance of the whole building, assuming certain standardized occupant consumption patterns. Requiring performance levels for the overall building, it thus allows designers to off-set weak performance in one element of the building with better performance elsewhere (Raman and Shove, 2000).

A new regulatory tool in energy-efficiency regulation is the 'Code for Sustainable Homes' (here also abbreviated as the 'Code'), which is also a performance-based assessment tool. It addresses a number of issues other than energy consumption, such as waste and water, and while the general approach is overall performance scoring, the Code also requires minimum performance levels in each concern that is addressed. It is a key plank to current government policy aims that all residential buildings built from 2016 onwards should be 'zero carbon', a stage that should be reached in a three-step process (DCLG, 2006, 2007). The Code has been implemented as a mandatory rating scheme for new homes since 1 May 2008. It uses a 1- to 6-star rating system to assess the overall sustainability performance of a new home, and it also sets minimum standards for energy and water use. It is intended to replace the Building Research Establishment's EcoHomes scheme. Policy planning currently is that by 2010 all new homes are to meet Code level 3, which is estimated to be a 25 per cent improvement in energy efficiency on the current Part L requirements. By 2013 this is to rise to level 4, which is a 44 per cent improvement on the current Part L, and by 2016 to level 6, which is meant to be 'zero carbon' (DCLG, 2006).

However, the definition of 'zero carbon' remained unclear to commentators for years after it entered the policy debate (Planning, 2007a,b; Davis and Harvey, 2008). For example, the Government hinted that a zero carbon home could rely on on-site micro-generation of electricity through technologies such as wind turbines and photovoltaic cells. This suggestion faced criticism as to the efficiency of such an arrangement, as these technologies are often best deployed outside of urban centres (Banfill and Peacock, 2007). The Government conducted a consultation on the meaning of zero carbon, which concluded after the interviews for this chapter were conducted (DCLG, 2008b). Even as the consultation results were published, there were still a number of unresolved questions as to the exact definition of a zero carbon building (DCLG, 2009). Uncertainties over the detail of planned legislation contribute to the perception that regulation is an increasing maze for the designers who work with them.

One might question the need for the tightening of Part L on British designs, given that 'sustainability' and 'zero carbon' have already become such buzz words in the industry. In fact, a number of interviewees remarked that they already specified buildings to higher energy-efficiency standards than regulations require as a matter of routine, in order to foster the practice's green or sustainable credentials, as designing to minimum requirements was seen as insufficient. However, interviews show that the significance of Part L in its current form depends on the nature of the design project, and that it is highest in very cost-conscious and commercially speculative projects. Also, while highly energy-efficient homes are seen by some as a growth sector, it is widely acknowledged that many or even most clients are still reluctant to afford the costs associated with energy-efficiency technology, whether it is more insulation, greener materials, controlled ventilation systems or renewable energy sources. In particular, speculative housing developers were still seen to favour bare-minimum solutions with regards to environmental performance. This was typically explained by the fact that developers expect to sell their houses or flats to individuals who will be unaware of or unconcerned with the energy performance of their new property. Once the sale has taken place, the higher costs of an inefficient building are born by the customer.

In sum, it seems likely that regulatory requirements (Part L and the Code) will continue to define the energy efficiency of a substantial share of the new housing stock in the near future. Current regulations are less stringent than plans for the future, and yet architects have many concerns about the challenges of implementing existing legislation. This raises critical issues for future regulatory change and the role of built environment professionals in its implementation.

Accelerating regulatory change

Reflecting on changes since the 1990s, almost all interviewees confirmed that Part L has become more complex both in its actual text and in its implementation. Part L was often described as a regulatory exercise which had turned from meeting a simple set of technical requirements to a much more time- and effort-consuming task, which is much more influential in the eventual design.

Architects generally felt that it was simple to ensure adequate U-values in the building envelope by specifying material details, as it was required by earlier versions of Part L. However, it was seen as less simple to work out the requirements of the performance-based code. Although performance-based codes could theoretically contain less detail than prescriptive regulations, the emerging energy regulations, alongside tightening standards on other parts of the building code, were seen as a complex maze that architects struggled to work out. The perception that building regulations are decreasingly comprehensible to architects is furthered by the apparent contradiction of segments of the regulations and particularly of the guidance in approved documents. Architects spoke about the difficulty of compliance with Part L when refurbishing a listed or conservation-area building. The new requirements for noise insulation imply at times undesired temperature insulation between rooms of the same house. In a heating strategy that centrally warms the whole house, this can hamper heat transfer between rooms and thereby increase fuel consumption. For some designers the building regulations represent a maze that they cannot comprehend without outside assistance. The Building Control Working group recognizes that these concerns have been raised by some in the building industry (DCLG, 2008a).

Finally, there was concern that building regulations are something of a maze to architects not just because of their inherent complexity, but also because of the frequency of change. Interviewees remarked that it required a lot of resources in training to keep up with the changes to Part L in particular. Several architects still had some design projects which had already passed under the old Part L, while already working on some under the new Part L. It was far from unheard of that design specifications had to be changed because of an update to the regulatory requirements, and although this was often thought to benefit the design, it seemed to cause both work and stress to the designers. This was also recognized as a concern by the Government's working group (DCLG, 2008a).

The increasing complexity of the building regulations does not only impact on the design professions, but also the building inspectors who are in charge of enforcing regulations. Moreover, a performance-based code also opens regulations up to a wider scope of interpretation and raises issues of enforcement, which will be discussed in the next section.

The challenge of enforcement: the interpretative turn

Commentators on the regulatory process have pointed to the difference between the wording and the practice of regulation, and in particular the 'fragility' of the process of enforcement (Lipsky, 1980; Fineman, 2000). Some argue that building control is becoming overstretched and under-resourced to an extent that renders it ineffective in interpreting regulatory requirements, thereby shifting the task to design professionals. Raman and Shove (2000), for example, have made the case that enlarging the UK's building regulations might overtax the inspection regime, reporting that 'several respondents argued that building control was already stretched to the limit and that efforts to extend the scope, or change the mode of regulation would founder if attempted within the present framework of inspection' (Raman and Shove, 2000, p146).

Already there are reports that building regulations, 'compliance is not being enforced for energy conservation: only fire safety and structural safety are seen as worthy of enforcement by Building Control inspectors' (Boardman, 2007, p369). A study conducted by the Building Research Establishment found that about one-third of a random – possibly unrepresentative – sample of new dwellings did not meet the air permeability standards of Part L, and several dwellings did not meet other specifications from plans submitted to inspectors (Grigg and Slater, 2004). These findings were followed up in a study by a think tank, which interviewed 59 Building Control Officers and found that Part L was seen as a matter of low priority by many of these officers (Cox and McCubbin, 2006). Non-compliance was often described as a triviality and officers' training in how to enforce Part L appeared to be lacking (Cox and McCubbin, 2006).

Furthermore, there are also concerns that a performance-based regulation regime offers fewer mechanisms to confirm compliance than a prescriptive regime. In a prescriptive regime, the building inspector can confirm whether all measures prescribed by the regulations have been implemented at any given stage of the design and construction process. However, in a performance-based regulation regime, it is left up to the designer to choose how to meet requirements and often compliance can only be tested when the building is complete (Meacham et al, 2005).

Interviewees confirmed some of these published findings pointing towards a weak inspection and enforcement regime. Architects suggested that this growing regulatory maze is part of the explanation for low regulatory compliance, as it strains an already under-resourced enforcement service. Lack of training and skills among enforcement officers, and a regulatory culture that attributes a low priority to energy efficiency, were described by architects. In addition to information deficits, interviewees also stated that some Building Control Officers are suffering from a too large workload to effectively enforce Part L. Problems with compliance and enforcement of energy-efficiency regulations have been indirectly acknowledged by the Government, when it included them in the summary of stakeholder opinions in its consultation report on regulations (DCLG, 2008a).

One response to the over-stretch of the building control regime has been the privatization of regulation. There are now approved inspectors operating on a business model and regulating buildings in return for regulatory fees. However, generally there was no evidence from the interviews that approved inspectors are more knowledgeable with regards to Part L than building inspectors from the council.

Generally, there appears to be a belief within the industry that private regulators are more likely to be lenient in their decision-making than council staff. Statements from several interviewees agree that neither should be expected to be outright corrupt, but that private companies are more accommodating to their fee-paying clients than councils currently are. With councils increasingly competing with the private market for regulatory customers, this picture is shifting towards councils behaving in a similar profit-driven manner. Hence, privatization has transformed the role of the regulator to that of just another service supplier within the market system.

Yet most architects expressed a wish for more buildings to be designed to high energy-efficiency standards and explained this with their own environmental concerns. Several interviewees felt that the limited surveillance and weak enforcement exercised by Building Control Officers or approved inspectors shifted responsibility for compliance into the remit of architects. While this was seen less as a legal and more as a moral obligation, the interviewee's views on the desirability of this outcome varied. For some it was a welcome challenge that enabled creative architectural response, while others were concerned that architects might not rise to the challenge without pressure from the state. Nobody counted inspectors out altogether, but their significance with respect to Part L was seen as limited, as this architect explained:

> *Some of [the inspectors] may be more concerned with the kind of life safety aspects of building regulations and the environmental energy efficiency and what-have-you is of secondary importance to that... A lot of it is probably down to just the designers and contractors making sure that they can self-regulate that side of it. And I am not sure how well it is regulated (Interviewee).*

Weak enforcement by inspectors lowers the incentive for regulatory compliance, as there is a smaller risk of facing state coercion or punishment due to non-compliance. Designers often have to have their own motivations or objectives that require conformity with regulation, whether these are a feeling of duty due to professional commitments, moral considerations or financial advantages; for example, by charging for time spent on compliance issues. This is compounding the interpretive challenge signalled by the growing regulatory maze that surrounds design practice, as architects will consider other factors than regulatory requirements in their compliance decisions. The potential consequences for the architectural profession are explored in the following section.

Architects as intermediaries

As this book demonstrates, the term 'intermediary' is a diverse one with many applications. Drawing on the definition developed in the other chapters of this book, we understand an intermediary to be an in-between agent working deliberately towards achieving an objective (also see Medd and Marvin, 2006; Moss et al, 2009). It is worth noting that there are a number of actors and groups involved in design who can be described as intermediaries, and architects rarely have a hegemonic right to the role of intermediation. Instead, they are situated in a network of engineers, quantity surveyors, building contractors, the client and sometimes other stakeholders; all of whom can at times function as intermediaries. We will, however, argue that the incentives are currently high for architects to take on the intermediary role.

Architects often view themselves as bridging the interests of and between key stakeholders and professions in a project. In fact, architects who fail to bring varied interests together may receive blame for consequential project problems. One interviewee described how this led him repeatedly to help architect colleagues when they struggled to intermediate:

> *You have got client, builder, architect, local authority. Sometimes you know somebody steps out of line and quite often the poor architect is blamed and I used to step in as an*

> *intermediary... You know, kind of get people to see the way for-*
> *ward instead of just arguing, just see how they can get out of it*
> *(Interviewee).*

Architects act as facilitators between many stakeholders involved in building design. This facilitation is not divorced from the design process, including when the architect is drawing, writing reports and so on. Instead, much of the architect's work is to unite and reconcile different actors' positions and translate between those involved in design. Not all of this translation is in direct interaction with those other actors, but compromises can also be found in their absence (also see Callon, 1996). The design process requires the architect to have enough understanding of each specialty to translate between the various experts working on the project, as well as lay stakeholders. Translation in this sense is not merely an issue of specialist languages, but also one of interpretation, of transferring and displacing meaning, and of enlisting the various actors into the project (for a short definition of 'translation' in this sense, see Latour, 1988). One interviewee highlighted the necessity to coordinate by bringing together the other professionals' different work in the building design:

> *I think one of the things that differ in architects from other*
> *members of construction teams, maybe less so builders, but cer-*
> *tainly where architects differ from the structural engineer and*
> *the M&E engineer, quantity surveyor is that part of our role is*
> *to coordinate the whole building. In a similar way that a con-*
> *tractor or a constructor does as well, you know, he has to*
> *understand the sub-contracts that he is letting and the different*
> *trades that he is contracting (Interviewee).*

As the interviewee observes, the architect's intermediation is limited to a phase of the overall construction process and it is mostly limited to the process of design. Once the building design has been completed, drawings have been drawn and reports been written, much of the task of intermediation passes to the contractor or head builder, who then engages in a similar intermediation process between the different building trades.

However, for some architects, intermediation takes a new form through the rise of regulations, as their role also embraces that of the 'interpretive intermediary', situated between the textual and representative challenges of performance-based regulation. The extent to which architects take on textual interpretation alone, and how they draw on the network of actors which they intermediate, varies between practices and individual architects. While some architects interviewed still did Part L calculations in-house, others reported that they relied on the assistance of mechanical and electrical engineers or specialist consultants to show compliance with the regulation. Initially, many aspects with profound influence on energy efficiency, such as heating strategy, use of daylight and cooling strategy, are suggested by the architect, but design details can then to varying degrees be taken on by consultants. Furthermore, many interviewees confessed that the exact details of the consultants' work were unknown to them:

> They do some sort of modelling and things like that. It is a little bit like black magic. We don't know what happens... We still sort of work on the elemental idea; on the elemental basis of trying to improve the U-values of the elements. And then we send it to them and just hope. 'Tell us, is that going to work?' So they will come back and, you know, we are actually waiting there for an SBEM [Simplified Building Energy Model] to come back and say 'yes', 'no'. And then we just sort of fiddle the numbers again. It is very difficult to design that way, because you can't sort of go 'that is a no, that is a yes' (Interviewee).

As many architects pass the actual calculations to show Part L compliance to specialist consultants, their efforts to 'self-regulate' are mostly in coordinating between the different design team members. There was no unified approach among interviewees in how to design with specialist consultants, and practices varied between firms and also between projects. In some firms and particularly for low-budget projects, contact with consultants often was by e-mail and telephone and focused on receiving the least amount of input necessary from the consultant. Larger and high-end projects more often resulted in consultants attending design team meetings and having a greater say on the final design. Success in reducing energy consumption was often attributed to bringing engineering consultants into the design process early, as this allows consultants to have an influence on fundamental design decisions such as building form and orientation. Bringing consultants into the process earlier also generates fees earlier, which this architect found difficult to explain to her clients:

> And we find we need [mechanical and electrical engineering (M&E) consultants] earlier and earlier, so we can meet all these requirements. But of course the client is used to just having us for planning and then getting an M&E consultant later on. Or even, if it is design and build, the contractor would do that (Interviewee).

Trying to achieve better energy-efficiency performance than currently required also often resulted in closer cooperation with engineers. Most interviewees felt that the new requirements of Part L and the increasing focus on energy in client briefs necessitate that engineers have a greater say on the development of a project. Thus, engineering consultants were seen to gain a greater amount of control over the building project than they historically had. There was also a greater amount of specialization and fragmentation of the design professions observed, as some specialize as assessors (for BRE EcoHomes or the Code), consultants for a specialist aspect of design (sustainability consultants instead of mechanical and electrical or building services engineers) or even consultants for particular design features (such as green roofs). The new division of labour can result in struggles within the design team over control, as engineering consultants try to meet the new performance-based Part L requirements cost-effectively by changing design elements such as building form and orientation. Both impact substantially on energy efficiency, but are historically seen as the remit of the architect. However, the increasing workload can also impact negatively on the work of the engineers:

> [Mechanical and electrical engineers] are on a very, very cut-rate fee... but they will sometimes work on a very, very cut-rate fee and not have enough time built into their ... or just not have the ability to spend time to come up with the right answers. So you get a very off-the-shelf solution: 'Right, this is what we are going to do', rather than spending time and thinking of something a bit more intelligent. I think that is often quite a big issue (Interviewee).

Hence, conflict about professional remit was often hidden within apparent conflict over technical issues. For example, highly standardized responses by consultants can fuel conflict as architects resist solutions that they view as an insufficient answer to a bespoke problem. Although interviewees still felt that these developments in labour division are too new to predict certain effects, they saw their role increasingly as one of intermediation. This is further facilitated by the emergence of other professions around building design, such as quantity surveyors and project managers. These contributed to the architect's role change that increasingly sees her as driving a design agenda by bringing together the requirements of different 'other professionals', reinterpreting the brief and related regulations accordingly and reconciling the varying interests that may impact on a design project (Callon, 1996). For while the underlying struggle between architects and engineering consultants is partly about the remit of each profession, there is also a mutual dependency between various designers, which is commonly reinforced by the need for repeated interaction over the duration of several design projects. It is precisely through these iterative interactions that we can identify and explore what Fineman terms the 'enactment of regulation', in which the architect may become the 'creator of the regulation-rules in practice' (Fineman, 1998, p953).

Conclusion

Towards the end of 2008 we saw further consultations on changes to building energy regulations for 2010 and amendments that are to come into force in 2013 (DCLG, 2008a,b). These consultations were also intended to outline issues that will serve to focus the draft Forward Plan for the whole set of regulations. The trend towards greater disciplining of building design with the changes to design practice outlined in this chapter will probably continue, possibly even accelerate. Our findings point towards a number of emerging challenges and opportunities for the architectural profession as a result of these changes. On the face of it, the expansion of scope and complexity of the building regulations in England and Wales entails a higher burden of compliance for the design professions. This necessity is welcomed by many architects as a tool to get clients to fund better buildings; better in this case, for example, meaning more energy efficient. Seen this way, regulation could be an opportunity for architects to work in a professional context that is increasingly supportive of 'innovative' design that promotes forms of sustainability, as opposed to simply safe design that meets minimum regulatory requirements (Guy and Moore, 2005).

However, because of the complexities of the building code, the almost piece-meal method of developing it, the inadequate dissemination of information about changes, the rapid nature of recent transformations and finally the difficulties in defining performance targets, the building regulations appear as something of a maze to practitioners. This is not inherent to regulations per se, but particularly in the manner in which the building code developed. Understanding, interpreting and conveying this maze has become a crucial challenge to the architect. While the Government is consulting and deliberating on a future strategy for the building regulations (DCLG, 2008a) and a clearer definition of 'zero carbon' (DCLG, 2008b), architects can expect to need to accommodate changes to regulations in an on going, even escalating, process.

For those architects who are able to adapt quickly, the new regulations may well prove a good fortune, as they can successfully reposition themselves as intermediaries in the design process as we have described. Moreover, the evidence suggests that the enforcement regime is at risk of crumbling under the weight of increasing responsibilities and systemic failures. While one might describe this as an opportunity for preserving the architect's autonomy, it also imposes the need to enforce the building regulations without support from the state. As a result, the disciplining of design that the building regulations strives for will not, in effect, leave the drawing board of the architect and consulting engineers, unless the British enforcement regime catches up. This, as well as the privatization of inspections, increases the risk of capture of the regulatory process by the building industry. The possibility is not limited to private inspectors, as councils now also compete in a 'market place' for inspections. Architects are as hired consultants less independent than state regulators and also in greater supply than private inspectors. Close proximity between regulator and regulatee has been described to contribute to the emergence of capture (Baldwin and Cave, 1999), and architects usually have to work closely with their clients. Thus, resisting 'capture' is also a formidable challenge for architects.

These processes of regulation and weak enforcement impact on the division of labour within the design team. To economically achieve energy efficiency and to demonstrate that designs meet targets, architects rely on engineers. Their consultation is required earlier in the project and architects understand less and less of their activities. Especially when projects are hurried and built on a tight budget, the engineers deliver their 'black magic' without the architects' understanding. Projects with more funding for design consultants, in contrast, allow engineers to impart more explanations for their actions. In either case, shifting design responsibility from architects to engineers can be a source of tension. This tension is rarely resolved openly and instead may contribute to conflicts over design issues. Such tensions become acute when time-pressured engineers provide standardized responses, while architects strive for bespoke solutions. In this way, the practice of interpreting and translating regulations into design can become highly contested. Moreover, while conflict may mostly be about professional remit, the resulting working relationships might also limit the ability of designers to push for more energy-efficient design. The design task becomes fragmented, with each consultant seeing only a small aspect of the whole project. Architects can only facilitate within this framework, as they have less overall control. Clients will continue to limit budgets and then expect architects to make them feasible.

As regulatory efforts to encourage and/or require zero carbon buildings are stepped up, architects are having to become both more self-regulatory and regulators of other built-environment professionals. Certainly, with respect to energy efficiency, architects often perceive themselves to be 'doing the best they can'. They would like to design more efficient buildings, but often believe they are constrained by factors beyond their control. To readers of publications on architecture, this may not be an entirely new lament. Historically, it is sung with regards to architects' inability to design both aesthetically pleasing and environmentally innovative buildings. However, taken the growing importance of energy efficiency in public opinion, architects routinely feel they have acquired responsibility for yet another task that will be difficult for them to achieve.

The challenge then is for architects to look beyond their traditional role and reinvent themselves as interpretive intermediaries, thereby escaping their perceived inability to act within existing constraints. In taking on this role of interpretive intermediation, architects might wrest back overall control of projects from engineers and environmental consultants to offer a more integrated vision, which incorporates aesthetics, techniques and ecological issues in the design framework. Critically, this would position the architect 'in-between' regulations and design practices, between texts and technologies, and therefore in a strategic position to set the collaborative agenda. Certainly this suggests a very different view of the architect than as a visionary who designs buildings almost single-handedly (Cuff, 1991), or that of celebrating successful 'starchitects' as idols, heroes and prophets (Lewis, 1998; Guy and Moore, 2005). Further research is needed to investigate whether other professionals share this perspective, or indeed on how representative it is among architects. We also believe that a more thorough mapping of the effects of building regulations on society is long overdue. Bearing this in mind, our research suggests that the recent regulatory push in England and Wales will change the way architects practice, shifting design work even further from the romantic image of the lone genius towards that of the systemic intermediary.

Acknowledgements

This chapter was developed from a paper first published in *Urban Studies*, vol 46, no 12, pp2577–2594, November 2009, by Sage Publications. It is available at http://usj.sagepub.com/cgi/content/abstract/46/12/2577, accessed 15 August 2010. We are grateful for permission to publish the paper in revised form. The authors thank Rob Imrie and Emma Street for organizing the 'Regulating Design' research workshop; the participants of the workshop; Albena Yaneva and the Urban Studies anonymous reviewers for feedback; and the interviewees for making their time and knowledge available.

References

Baldwin, R. and Cave, M. (1999) *Understanding Regulation: Theory, Strategy and Practice*, Oxford University Press, Oxford, p36

Banfill, P.F.G. and Peacock, A.D. (2007) 'Energy-efficient new housing – the UK reaches for sustainability', *Building Research & Information*, vol 35, no 4, pp426–436

Ben-Joseph, E. (2005) *The Code of the City: Standards and the Hidden Language of Place Making*, MIT Press, Cambridge, MA

Boardman, B. (2007) 'Examining the carbon agenda via the 40% House scenario', *Building Research & Information*, vol 35, no 4, pp363–378

Callon, M. (1996) 'Le travail de la conception en architecture', *Situations, les Cahiers de la Recherche Architecturale*, vol 31, no 1, pp25–35

Campbell, K. (2007) 'Energy performance and building regulations', *Journal of Building Appraisal*, vol 3, pp231–235

Cox, C. and McCubbin, I. (2006) *Compliance with Part L1 of the 2002 Building Regulations (An Investigation into the Reasons For Poor Compliance)*, The Energy Efficiency Partnership for Homes/Future Energy Solutions, Didcot, UK

Cuff, D. (1991) *Architecture: The Story of Practice*, MIT Press, Cambridge, MA, pp72ff

Davis, I. and Harvey, V. (2008) *Zero Carbon: What Does It Mean To Homeowners And Housebuilders?*, National House Building Council Foundation/IHS BRE Press, Amersham

Department of Communities and Local Government (DCLG) (2006) *Code for Sustainable Homes: A Step-Change In Sustainable Home Building Practice*, DCLG, London

DCLG (2007) *Building a Greener Future: Policy Statement*, DCLG, London

DCLG (2008a) *The Future of Building Control: Consultation*, DCLG, London, pp6–31

DCLG (2008b) *Definition of Zero Carbon Homes and Non-domestic Buildings: Consultation*, DCLG, London, p9

DCLG (2009) *Summary of Responses to Consultation on Definition of Zero Carbon Homes and Non-domestic Buildings*, DCLG, London

Department of the Environment, Transport and the Regions (DETR) (2000) *Our Towns and Cities: The Future*, The Stationery Office, London

Fineman, S. (1998) 'Street-level bureaucrats and the social construction of environmental control', *Organisation Studies*, vol 19, no 6, pp953–974

Fineman, S. (2000) *The Business of Greening*, Routledge, London

Gann, D.M., Wang, Y. and Hawkins, R. (1998) 'Do regulations encourage innovation? – The case of energy efficiency in housing', *Building Research & Information*, vol 26, no 4, pp280–296

Grigg, P. and Slater, A. (2004) *Assessment of Energy Efficiency Impact Of Building Regulations Compliance*, Building Research Establishment, Watford, UK

Guy, S. and Moore, S.A. (eds) (2005) *Sustainable Architecture: Cultures and Natures in Europe and North America*, Spon Press, New York

Guy, S. and Osborn, S. (2001) 'Contesting Environmental Design: The Hybrid Green Building', in S. Guy, S. Marvin and T. Moss (eds) *Urban Infrastructure in Transition: Networks, Buildings, Plans*, Earthscan, London, pp87–102

Henderson, G. and Shorrock, L.D. (1992) 'Energy use in dwellings and carbon dioxide emissions', *International Journal of Energy-Environment-Economics*, vol 2, pp15–21

Hunt, J. and Raman, S. (2000) 'Regulation matters: Global environmental discourse and business response', in S. Fineman (ed) *The Business of Greening*, Routledge, London, pp114–133

Imrie, R. (2004) The role of building regulations in achieving housing quality, *Environment and Planning B: Planning and Design*, vol 31, no 3, pp419–437

Imrie, R. (2007) 'The interrelationships between building regulations and architects' practices', *Environment and Planning B: Planning and Design*, vol 34, no 5, pp925–943

Latour, B. (1988) *The Pasteurization of France*, Harvard University Press, Cambridge, MA, p253

Lewis, R.K. (1998) *Architect? A Candid Guide to the Profession*, MIT Press, Cambridge, MA, pp262–263

Lipsky, M. (1980) *Street-Level Bureaucracy: Dilemmas of the Individual In Public Services*, Russell Sage Foundation, New York

McMichael, A.J., Campbell-Lendrum, D.H., Corvalán, C.F., Ebi, K.L., Githeko, A.K., Scheraga, J.D. and Woodward, A. (eds) (2003) *Climate Change And Human Health: Risks and Responses*, World Health Organization, Geneva

Meacham, B., Bowen, R., Traw, J. and Moore, A. (2005) 'Performance-based building regulation: Current situation and future needs', *Building Research & Information*, vol 33, no 2, pp91–106

Medd, W. and Marvin, S. (2006) 'Ecology of intermediation', in K. Green and S. Randles (eds) *Industrial Ecology and Spaces of Innovation*, Edward Elgar, Cheltenham, pp238–251

Metz, B., Davidson, O., Coninck, H. de, Loos, M. and Meyer, L. (eds) (2006) *IPCC Special Report: Special Report on Carbon Dioxide Capture and Storage*, Cambridge University Press/Intergovernmental Panel on Climate Change (IPCC), Cambridge

Moss, T., Medd, W., Guy, S. and Marvin, S. (2009) 'Organising water: The hidden role of intermediary work', *Water Alternatives*, vol 2, no 1, pp16–33

Planning (2007a) 'Diary', *Planning*, vol 1713, p48

Planning (2007b) 'Code triggers rise in cost of housing', *Planning*, vol 1714, p1

Raman, S. and Shove, E. (2000) 'The business of building regulations', in S. Fineman (ed) *The Business of Greening*, Routledge, London, pp134–150

Ritchie, J. and Spencer, L. (1994) 'Qualitative data analysis for applied policy research', in A. Bryman and R.G. Burgess (eds) *Analysing Qualitative Data*, Routledge, London, pp172–194

Stern, N. (2006) *The Stern Review: The Economics of Climate Change*, Cambridge University Press, Cambridge

11
Smart Meters as Obligatory Intermediaries: Reconstructing Environmental Action

Simon Marvin, Heather Chappells and Simon Guy

Introduction

Utility meters represent what Bruno Latour and other sociologists of science and technology term an 'obligatory passage point' (Latour, 1992, p234). That is, domestic gas, electricity and water meters are the 'gateway' technology around which the most significant transactions between utilities and their customers are based. Energy and water resources pass through the meter, which records consumption, providing the information for the billing of utility services. Moreover, the meter acts as the referee of legitimate access to the infrastructure network, potentially signalling the application of the ultimate sanction for non-payment and indebtedness – disconnection from the network. As Madeleine Akrich (1992) suggests:

> *The way in which the individual/consumer relates to the network, and via the network to the electricity company, is codified and quantified by means of a basic technical tool, the electricity meter. This formulates the initial contact between the producer and consumer. If one or the other fails to meet its obligations, the meter becomes invalid or inactive. Meters have a symmetrical effect on the producer/consumer relationship. The agreement of both is required if they are to tick over. Accordingly, the set of meters is a powerful instrument of social control.*

Consequently, meters are critical intermediaries, and changes in the functionality, control and purpose of metering systems has key implications for the social relations between users and the suppliers of essential resources (Marvin and Guy, 1997). Driven by the commercial priorities of a liberalized marketplace, utility companies are reconfiguring the varying contexts of utility consumption by commodifying essential resources through the introduction of new tariffs, products and styles of service, which vary across space, time and customer classification (Guy and Marvin, 1995). A shift in the role of the utility meter is central to this process. So-called smart metering technologies are creating new opportunities for efficient use of resources which have profound implications for our understanding of the role of information, interactive control and resource use in shaping the social, economic and environmental profile of contemporary cities. There are now growing calls for:

> gas and electricity meters to be dusted off, brought out from the cupboard underneath the stairs, and given pride of place in people's living rooms and kitchens. Advocates of so-called smart meters say the information provided by the devices can revolutionize the way households consume energy, and can reduce demand by up to 10% (BBC News Channel, 18 May 2006, http://news.bbc.co.uk/1/hi/sci/tech/4754109.stm, quoted in Darby, 2008).

Recent research into the energy savings that could be achieved by smarter meters or real-time displays suggests a 5–10 per cent reduction in consumer energy demand, which equates to a reduction of about 2.5–3.5 million tonnes of carbon dioxide per year for the UK and an overall saving of about 2 per cent of UK energy use (DTI, 2001). A more comprehensive review of several different feedback programmes indicates that the highest savings, of around 20 per cent in some cases, were achieved through smart metering technology (Darby, 2006). Smarter meters using two-way communication capabilities offer the potential to combine feedback with other demand-side interventions such as on- and off-peak tariffs. Estimated carbon savings from such interactive demand-side measures are in the region of 2.5–3.5 million tonnes per year and a 2.5 per cent reduction in peak demand for electricity and gas (Burgess and Nye, 2008).

These potential savings mean that UK central government is now committed to the development of smart meters and smart energy grids to reduce carbon emissions. The Energy Review (DTI, 2006) and the Energy White Paper (DTI, 2007) both emphasized the potential of 'smart metering' for reducing domestic energy demand, and encouraged the installation of smart meters within the next ten years for homes despite important technological hurdles and institutional constraints (Burgess and Nye, 2008). Consequently, a two-year, £20 million Ofgem/BERR trial for smarter energy meters in the UK, begun in autumn 2007, was designed to provide evidence about the benefits and disbenefits of smart metering (see Ofgem, 2007, for more details). Conclusive results were not expected until sometime in 2010 (Darby, 2008), yet in October 2008 the Government announced its intention to mandate a roll-out of electricity and gas smart meters to all homes in Great Britain (House of Lords Hansard, 28 October 2008, Column 1516). However, the estimated £8 billion investment required to deliver this network is intended to come from the private sector. The Department of Energy and Climate Change (DECC) published a 'Consultation on Smart Metering for Electricity and Gas' in May 2009, in order to confirm the development options and high-level requirements for the domestic roll-out, with the assumption that smart meters would have transformative implications:

> *Smart meters will pave the way for a transformation in the way that energy is supplied and consumed, contributing to our goals of energy security and carbon reduction. They will provide energy consumers with real-time information about their energy use, enabling them to monitor and reduce their energy consumption and carbon emissions. Smart meters will support improved energy efficiency advice and facilitate smoother, faster switching between suppliers. And they are an important step towards the future development of a smarter grid delivering improved network efficiency and responsiveness, which will in turn help facilitate the introduction and increased use of renewable energy and ultra low carbon vehicles (electric and plug-in hybrids) (DECC, December 2009, p4).*

Then, in summer 2009, the Low Carbon Transition Plan was published, in which the Government has 'committed to mandating smart meters and has set out an indicative timetable for getting smart meters in all homes by the end of 2020' (DECC, July 2009, p86).

The changing design of meters is being powerfully shaped by a wide range of socio-technical factors. In particular, the emergence of new metering technologies is taking place against a background of commercial restructuring of the government priorities and energy regulation, utilities marketplace, rapid technological innovation in the fields of metering and communications, and competing institutional structures of technical codes and standards (Sioshansi et al, 1990). Furthermore, fast-changing regulatory frameworks, complex choices over levels of commercial functionality, and the ebb and flow of social and political pressure, all have powerful implications for meter design and, by extension, the restructuring of customer and utility social relations. Each of these groups is pursuing their own technical agenda, driven by specific aims and priorities, each seeking to shape the social, economic and environmental benefits of new metering technologies in relation to competing and often conflicting factors: technological choices, economic costs, social acceptability, health concerns and access to information.

Consequently, the rest of this chapter is structured in five sections: firstly, we briefly review new information and communication technologies that have transformed metering systems and the environmental applications that can be developed; secondly, we examine the role of competing social interests in shaping the development of smart metering systems; thirdly, we identify four different smart metering development pathways and the way each uniquely structures social relations between utilities and users; fourthly, the emergence of technology development pathways (TDPs) and the blurring of boundaries between them are examined; finally, the conclusion argues that the social interest shaping the functionality of smart meters needs to be widened to ensure that practices of intermediation around environmental action is developed.

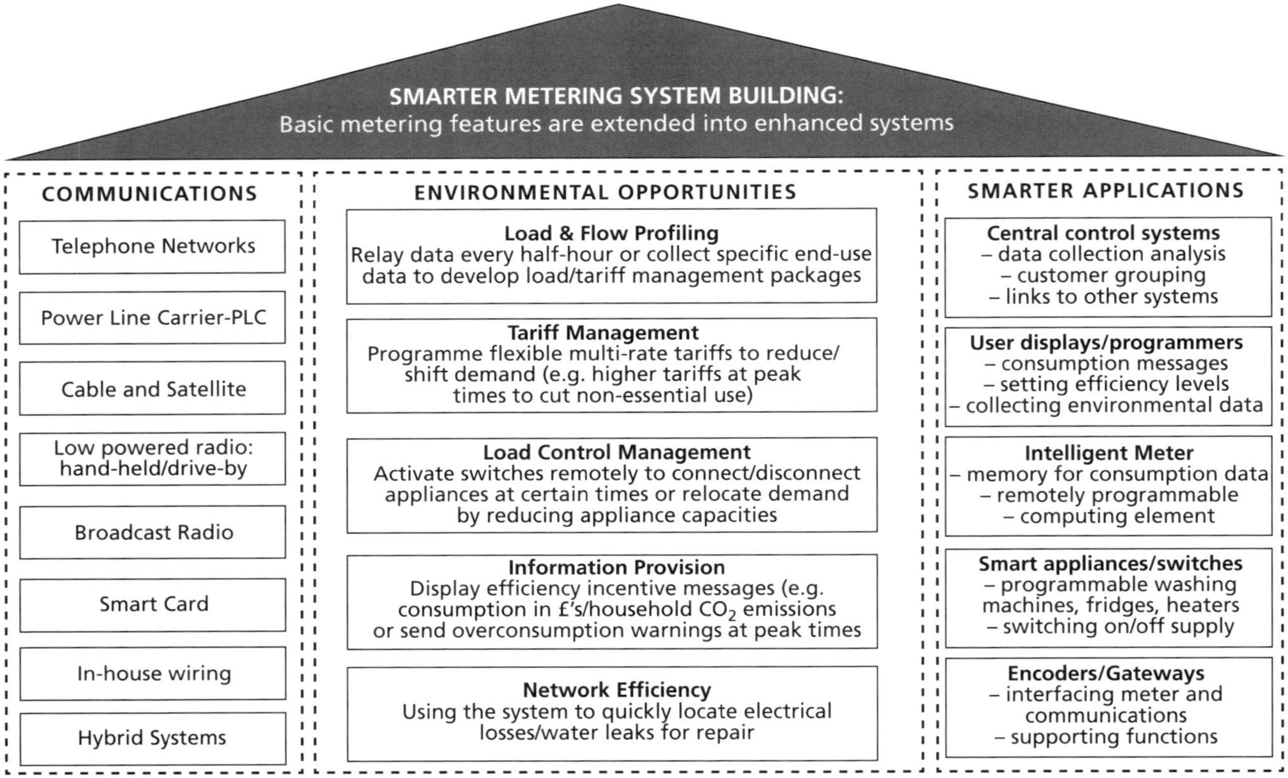

SMARTER METERING SYSTEM BUILDING:
Basic metering features are extended into enhanced systems

COMMUNICATIONS

Telephone Networks

Power Line Carrier-PLC

Cable and Satellite

Low powered radio: hand-held/drive-by

Broadcast Radio

Smart Card

In-house wiring

Hybrid Systems

ENVIRONMENTAL OPPORTUNITIES

Load & Flow Profiling
Relay data every half-hour or collect specific end-use data to develop load/tariff management packages

Tariff Management
Programme flexible multi-rate tariffs to reduce/ shift demand (e.g. higher tariffs at peak times to cut non-essential use)

Load Control Management
Activate switches remotely to connect/disconnect appliances at certain times or relocate demand by reducing appliance capacities

Information Provision
Display efficiency incentive messages (e.g. consumption in £'s/household CO_2 emissions or send overconsumption warnings at peak times

Network Efficiency
Using the system to quickly locate electrical losses/water leaks for repair

SMARTER APPLICATIONS

Central control systems
– data collection analysis
– customer grouping
– links to other systems

User displays/programmers
– consumption messages
– setting efficiency levels
– collecting environmental data

Intelligent Meter
– memory for consumption data
– remotely programmable
– computing element

Smart appliances/switches
– programmable washing machines, fridges, heaters
– switching on/off supply

Encoders/Gateways
– interfacing meter and communications
– supporting functions

Figure 11.1 *Alternative technological options for building metering systems*

Technological configurations of smart meters

Radical changes in information and communications technologies have revolutionized the potential of utility meters. The new systems have come to be known as 'smart' meters, as a reaction to their enhanced functional and communication capacities when compared with their 'simpler' predecessors, which merely measured consumption and required manual reading. Meter manufacturers and communications providers have been competing to provide utilities with their new smart metering systems. The metering industry now uses buzzwords such as 'interoperable', 'interfacing', 'multi-media' and 'multi-functional' when describing the design frameworks for new meters.

Figure 11.1 shows a menu of the design building blocks that are currently available to transform the meter from a simple measurement device to an extended system, highlighting the range of environmental opportunities that are open to selection. Over 50 different metering systems were identified through interviews and manufacturers' promotional material. A variety of integrated and modular remote metering systems (RMS) have been developed in the electricity and water sectors. Across both utility sectors, smart card and other prepayment systems were widely implemented, especially in the electricity sector, whereas others (such as integrated and modular meters) are being selectively trialled by utilities. The choice of communications supporting such systems is also extensive, with over 20 specific media competing to link utility operations with their customers.

Technological choices are now significantly enlarged, with each of the metering and communication systems having differential capabilities to support particular environmental applications. Systems designed for load and flow-switching applications can be configured with one-way radio teleswitch communications, which enable utilities to send messages to the meter to switch off appliances at peak load times or cut off non-essential water supply in times of shortage. Alternatively, high data capacity two-way communications networks linked into a meter enable the transfer of information on half-hourly consumption to utility central computer systems. Such information could be used to develop multiple tariff rates, allowing utilities to shape demand profiles by shifting consumption in real time. A study of 140 households in Bath showed how energy-efficient feedback relayed via information technologies reduced energy consumption by 25 per cent more than manual forms of feedback (Brandon and Day, 1997). However, the precise technical configuration of the meter is strongly shaped by the often conflicting objectives of agencies involved in developing and implementing the systems. The ways in which these different groups envisage the social organization of relations between the utility and the household, and their strength in influencing metering developments, frame the systems which emerge.

Social interests shaping utility meters

The actual choice of metering configurations emerging into UK homes is not as extensive as the technological diversity suggests because of the competing objectives of a wide range of social interest groups who are involved in the development of smart meters, including manufacturers, utilities, regulators, environmental interests, consumer groups and users. Figure 11.2 shows how each of these interest groups has particular institutional roles and diverse objectives, including economic and environmental efficiency, commercial competitiveness, technical competence and social welfare. These interests create the distinct contexts that frame the metering systems which emerge.

The shaping of the functionalities of metering systems, that themselves mediate household-utility relationships, reflect a complex interplay of social interests. Utility privatization has helped create a market for up to 20 million metering units in the electricity sector, with a total value approaching £1 billion (McNicholas, 1997). New commercial opportunities have accelerated the emergence of smarter metering, encouraging manufacturers to design systems which improve network efficiency and extend new value-added services, such as controlling security devices, home energy services and account management systems (Moran, 1994). All the electricity utilities have actively participated in trials of smart metering systems.

At the same time, the metering industry is operating within an uncertain economic context characterized by mergers, new international entrants and restructuring of the utilities sector (Barnett, 1996; Clarke, 1997). Although there has been commercial roll-out of some new systems, utilities have been reluctant to commit themselves to larger-scale smart metering programmes, citing market and regulatory uncertainty. Utilities have also questioned the value of adding-in environmental applications to different types of smart metering initiatives. For instance, one regional electricity company claimed

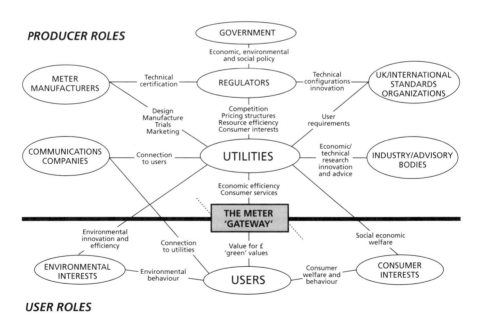

Figure 11.2 *Shaping metering – roles of key interest groups*

that people 'would not respond to complex tariffing' or 'move their consumption for relatively small economies'. In voicing such claims, utilities attempt to 'represent the user' in this case as universally inflexible consumers of electricity (Summerton, 1995). However, utilities often failed to produce evidence to support these claims across the diverse social groups that consume electricity in the UK. User interests represented through community or environmental organizations have remained largely silent about the possibility of exploiting environmental applications in new metering technologies. Across this unsettled landscape, there have been calls for stronger guidance from the regulators to provide guarantees of financial and administrative support, whilst utilities roll out their new metering networks.

While meter manufacturers spoke of the 'unlimited potential' of smart meters, environmental applications were often not exploited, because utilities were largely responsible for design selection. Decisions about the functionality of the meter were made on the basis of limited trial evidence, and generalizations about user requirements were not challenged by other interests such as environmental groups. An environmental design gap emerged, located not in the absence of key technological components, but rather in the under-utilization of existing technical capacity and the limited recognition of user-led environmental action. In order to understand how opportunities for environmental action could be created in smart metering systems, we need to focus on the diverse contexts for producer and user action which could be inscribed into the distinct metering system configurations.

Tracing technical development pathways

Despite the technical flexibility and social complexities surrounding the development of smart metering, four main TDPs along which smart metering systems are emerging can be identified in the UK. These are summarized in Figure 11.3. Each TDP represents a number of metering systems that do not necessarily share the same precise technical components and applications, but nevertheless are socially configured in ways which inscribe similar forms of producer/user relationships. An individual TDP produces a distinctive social context that simultaneously creates and delimits particular types of opportunities for utilities and users to participate in resource-saving action. Whilst systems representative of producer-led and user-led pathways may use some identical metering components, these will be arranged in very different ways to create a different social outcome. The producer-led meter transfers the relative balance of control over consumption to the utility, while the user-led meter leans towards the user. These characteristics of TDPs will be explained in further detail through case studies of systems representative of the smarter metering models. The monitoring TDP offers little in the way of extended 'smartness', but helps contextualize the range of opportunities being explored by utilities. Systems representing the gatekeeper and producer-led TDPs offer distinct new variations on the conventional meter, and are currently being trialled and implemented by utilities throughout the UK. The user-led example explores a system developed on a smaller scale by a research team based at Bath University.

TECHNICAL DEVELOPMENT PATHWAY (TDP)	*MONITORING*	*GATEKEEPER*	*PRODUCER-LED*	*USER-LED*
FORMATION P=PRODUCER U=USER	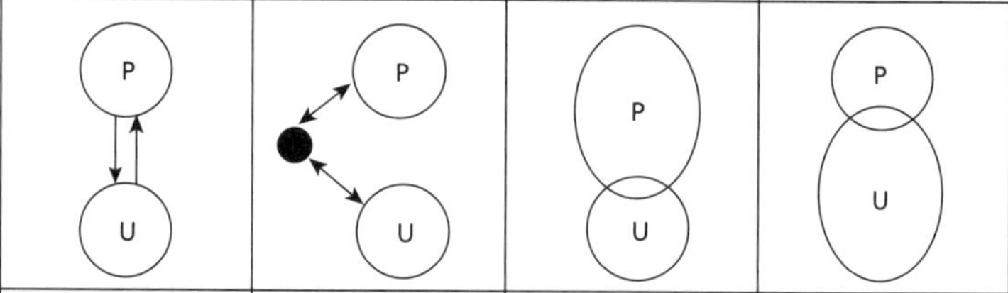			
TECHNICAL CONFIGURATIONS	CONVENTIONAL METER WITH SIMPLE FUNCTIONS	SMART CARD MEDIATES FUNCTIONS	PRODUCER CONFIGURES FUNCTIONS	USER CONFIGURES FUNCTIONS
PRODUCER/USER RELATIONSHIPS	LIMITED RELATIONSHIP	DISTANT RELATIONSHIP	AUTHORITATIVE RELATIONSHIP	DEVELOPED RELATIONSHIP

Figure 11.3 *Smart metering technical development pathways*

Monitoring TDP – conventional-type meters

Systems representative of the monitoring TDP are basic meters which measure resource consumption for the billing of users. The development of cheap, reliable meters at the turn of the century allowed electricity utilities to rapidly extend their networks into the domestic sector (Guy and Marvin, 1995). Experiments have also taken place to convert such conventional meters to allow meter readings to be taken automatically, through a hand-held unit; this speeds up door-to-door operations, but offers little extended functionality. In the water sector, households were not usually metered to ensure that there were no interruptions to consumption so that the public health of the users and the city was protected. In the context of debates about the role of water meters in demand management, a growing number now have basic volumetric meters, usually in boundary boxes outside the home. Current developments include encoder devices being retrofitted to the water meter, which allow the meter readings to be taken via a hand-held unit using low-power radio to relay measurements quickly and easily.

Conventional meters, and their more recent adaptations, set up relatively simple, symmetrical social relations between producers and users. The meter acts as an agent in the home, recording consumption on behalf of the utility, and its relations with users are transacted through the reading, billing and credit control systems. With manual or limited frequency communications and infrequent readings, utilities have relatively little information on users behaviour beyond the boundary of the meter. Consequently, the meter only has a limited role in shaping users' resource-saving action, which largely depends on the motivations of households. This monitoring TDP orientation is reflected in the way new technologies are being applied to conventional meters. Utilities are designing them to reduce costs, increase accuracy and solve meter-reading problems, rather than provide enhanced functions to promote environmental action, which remains firmly the householders' responsibility.

Gatekeeper TDP – prepayment meters

The gatekeeper TDP has a distinct technical configuration, highlighted in systems of prepayment meters in the electricity, gas and water sectors. These systems use a transportable medium such as a token, key or smart card to control access to utility services. The meters are configured to remove regular direct contact between utilities and users, and are a direct consequence of the move by utilities to develop a response to theft, non-payment and safety problems associated with traditional coin meters (Cowburn, 1996). Utilities can still retain control of the system, their energy and water resources, and the customer, by renegotiating relations through the medium. Our first case study focuses on one such system and illustrates the configuration of applications in a typical smart card system implemented in the UK.

Midlands Electricity collaborated with the meter manufacturer Landis and Gyr to produce the 'Smart Power' system (Kirby, 1996; Simpson, M.C.S., 1996); 40,000 meters have been fitted, with 4000 new meters installed each month. The customer 'charges' a smart card, which contains a microchip for data storage of credit and meter readings, at a point-of-sale (POS) terminal in a local retail outlet, and 'recharges' their domestic meter with purchased credit. The POS terminal is connected via two-way telephone communications to the utility central controller, from where tariffing and messaging data can also be downloaded and transferred to the card. Installed systems predominantly support improved cash flow and debt recovery operations. Key features and applications of the system are as follows: registers which could support up to eight tariff rates, but are presently configured to offer only two; displays designed for ease of use by the customer, which are currently configured by the utility to show credit remaining and emergency credit available for use when recharging terminals are shut; and a completely programmable card which can be used for transferring extensive consumption and pricing information, but which is restricted to sending only command messages to individual meters, such as amount of arrears to recover or new tariff rate changes for the generic customer base. The manufacturer of the system claimed that another major application area is 'resource management', but these applications relied largely on the interpretation by different users, with the utility reporting that some customers are receptive to the display of consumption in credit terms, which allows them to budget and use electricity more efficiently.

The potential functionality of such gatekeeper-type systems far supersedes the limited applications exploited hitherto. For instance, space exists on the card to programme a number of environmental applications, including the collection and analysis of more detailed consumption data, the use of differential tariff rates to modify demand, the transfer of resource-saving tips to users and the addition of shared savings schemes, where loans for the retrofit of homes with energy efficiency and conservation measures can be repaid in a similar way to debt recovery. Utilities have focused on a relatively narrow set of functionalities centred around revenue collection, while environmental applications remain unexploited. The gatekeeper TDP represents a new utility imperative which distances utilities from prepayment users and the high costs of debt and disconnection.

Producer-led TDP – 'cutting-edge' systems

An alternative range of producer-led metering systems have also been implemented by utilities in trials with selected users. Innovation has thrived in the electricity sector, where meter manufacturers have developed a wide range of innovative new metering technologies. These include 'modular meters', where enhanced applications can be added to basic communication units over time, and intelligent meters, which can be remotely programmed by the utility, adding or modifying functions over real-time communication networks. The quarterly visit from the meter reader is replaced by a remote interrogation from a central computer every 30 minutes. Sophisticated metering opens the way to different tariffs at different times of the day and give electricity companies the potential to manage demand by controlling appliances. This means they could have an agreement with the householder to, say, switch on the dishwasher overnight, when consumption is low, or to directly control storage heaters.

Meter manufacturers argue that these systems have potentially unlimited levels of functionality, which leaves utilities grappling with the difficulties of deciding what type of services to offer to different groups of customers. In the context of the liberalization of domestic electricity markets, utilities are particularly interested in using these systems to capture and retain lucrative users. In this sense, the producer-led TDP is about utilities extending their control 'beyond the meter' and into the home by offering value-added services, extracting new information about users and targeting new packages of services. The applications chosen will strongly frame the context within which different users can interact with the system. The second case study illustrates the way in which utilities are beginning to select 'appropriate' applications, to develop new customer service packages from the 'unlimited potential' which is seemingly on offer in advanced technologies.

The Remote Metering Systems (RMS) company was formed to exploit the capabilities of power-line carrier communications for utility and non-utility applications (Remote Metering Systems, 1993). The RMS system uses electricity power lines for the two-way transfer of data between users and the utility facilitating automatic meter reading, demand-side management and network automation. The technical configuration of the system offers a range of potential environmental applications, including the reading of a user's electricity consumption every 7.5 minutes, programming differential tariffs, controlling intelligent appliances, remote load-switching, and add-on options such as enhanced customer displays and customer-programmed controllers for energy management. Scottish Hydro-Electric undertook user trials and attempted to implement the system more widely, with the roll out of 2000 meters (Craig et al, 1996). However, the utility is having considerable difficulty in selecting applications from the extensive menu of functions available. Functions are restricted to meter reading and the automatic collection of profile information, with only 300 meters having been installed. This reflected a number of uncertainties, including lack of knowledge about how users will respond to new service options, the threat of competition from new entrants, the economic costs of rolling out the system and technical delays. The utility is now undertaking a more detailed and sophisticated round of market analyses to create new service packages. Initial findings indicate that load management will be given priority, with profile data being used to develop tariff packages for a number of customer groups who are each offered a 'total-heating-with-total-control tariff', enabling the utility to switch storage and water heating loads at different times, and even-out the load curve. User display trials are also being undertaken, with the eventual possibility of having an optional enhanced display unit. The utility hope to interrogate the meter, feedback load data and formulate consumption messages to send back to the user. The types of household information this will provide is unclear, but the utility has not ruled out those messages encouraging consumers to use electricity more efficiently. The case study shows how one utility is choosing to configure the meter with packages to help shape the timing and level of demand, which could keep a downward pressure on resource consumption.

In trials of systems identified as producer-led TDPs, utilities are most interested in developing applications which will allow them to have more centralized control over their customers' consumption. In contrast, the implementation of environmental applications such as customer-programmable controllers, offering users a more active role in demand modification, are notably absent from emerging configurations. This configuration also reflects the much narrower range of social interests shaping producer-led TDPs. When contrasted with the wider range of social interests involved in shaping both the environmental and community implications of other TDPs, there is very little critical debate over the functionality and redistribution of responsibilities implied in producer-led models. As such, the producer-led pathway can be described as one in which the utility seeks to develop a more authoritative relationship with their preferred customers.

User-led TDP – the Bath system

The user-led TDP is the most weakly developed in the UK. Although the technical components of such systems are similar to the producer-led model, they are organized in quite a different way. Instead of extracting information from the home and externally controlling tariff levels, the technical configuration re-orientates information flows and programming capabilities towards users. This is illustrated in the third case study of smarter system developments.

A research group based at Bath University has been funded by the Engineering and Physical Sciences Research Council to develop a new type of metering system which places more emphasis on giving customers information in the home (Brandon and Day, 1997; Oldroyd, 1997). Stimulated by research interests in environmental efficiency, energy invisibility, consumer feedback and new home information technologies, the project has developed a smart meter which enables people to learn about and monitor their energy consumption to see whether such a device will prove successful as a medium for promoting reductions in domestic energy use. The metering system is arranged so that the flow of information in the home is directed towards the energy/environmental information display unit, which is in a convenient location agreed by the customer. The small touch-screen computer consists of two screens: the main screen, which is always on-line, shows the date and time, readings in kilowatt-hours and pounds sterling, a reset option to monitor individual appliance consumption and inside/outside temperature; the optional screen shows tips of the day, consumption comparisons, a directory of environmentally efficient products and suppliers, bill predictions and a bonus points scheme, which aims to try and encourage cuts in peak demand by awarding points which can be traded in for cash or energy-efficient devices such as light bulbs. The system generates information from local temperature gateways to ask for readings and collects half-hourly consumption data from the meters. This information can then be combined with the individual household information manually collected by the team to create individually attuned efficiency applications. The system was installed in 20 households, each of which were closely monitored.

In the Bath system, the customer display is given much more attention in system design than in other metering pathways. It is a permanent and visible feature in the customer's home, and helps users make more informed choices about their consumption by relaying information about financial costs or energy savings, resulting from consumption activities. Essentially, the Bath project aimed to show how metering systems could be configured within the home, such that the utility delegates decision-making to the user and the home network. Such devolved and decentralized systems offer a contrast to producer-led systems, where centralized control of applications keeps a tighter grip on user activity. As shown in Figure 11.3, the user-led TDP raised the possibility of new producer–user relationships, in which the user exerts more of an influence over the services they receive, and can use the informational capacities of the smart meter to devise their own home energy efficiency and conservation regimes.

The emergence and blurring of TDPs

There is considerable diversity in the rates at which TDPs are emerging across different utility sectors in the UK. Gatekeeper TDPs are being rapidly implemented in the electricity sector, although water prepayment has been banned on health and safety grounds. Producer-led TDPs are the subject of multiple demonstration projects by utilities. Although trials have proven the value of these systems for some energy management applications, such as utility load control, the precise configurations of environmental applications and their target groups are still unclear. Utilities are concentrating on those applications that create the most commercial value. User-led TDPs are the most poorly developed. However, this may change, as more organizations are becoming involved in smart metering developments, including local authorities and housing associations, who have contracted with manufacturers to install systems for more integrated energy management at a local level; for example, the use of heatcards to regulate and control individual household consumption in district-heated flats, and the uptake of the RMS system by a housing association in Newcastle to manage tenants' needs more efficiently.

Across all the pathways, new market opportunities are undoubtedly stimulating the development of extended service opportunities. This dynamic context also means that boundaries between TDPs should be seen as transitionary and may begin to blur as different systems are reconfigured, and new relationships are negotiated between producers and users for the most appropriate exploitation of applications. For example, the recent development of 'tokenless' prepayment systems is currently reshaping the boundaries between gatekeeper and producer-led TDPs, by adding direct communications to customers' meters, but still retaining prepayment characteristics such as payment in advance of use (Clay and McEntee, 1996; Simpson, J.C., 1996). Such systems might herald a new form of interaction between utilities and users, or simply reinforce utility control over 'unreliable' customers. Similarly, the CELECT (Control Electric) system being developed by the electricity industry research company EA Technology could be configured to obscure the boundaries between producer and user-led models. The system passes broadcast signals from the meter via mains wiring to 'smart' optimizing controllers within storage heating appliances, which have the 'intelligence' to decide whether to use direct heating or thermal storage capacities. The user is involved in the system by a central control unit which enables them to set their own comfort levels, information which is used by the smart controllers to optimize energy use. The new producer–user roles in this system become blurred as users are reported as having greater control over their heating, but only within the context of the frameworks set by the utility.

Cross-sectoral issues are also important, with TDPs emerging at different rates across utility sectors. Smart metering developments are much more advanced in the electricity sector, with network management issues in the water sector more focused on 'leaky' distribution systems and smart metering still at an early stage. However, contrary to popular perceptions of the water industry as the 'laggard' for the introduction of remote metering, new systems may leapfrog those of the electricity sector because there is no 'legacy of either meters or meter readers to replace' Utility Week (1997, p15). Although this may be the case for monitoring-type pathways, where water companies are rapidly developing radio-read communications, these systems are directed towards basic applications such as more accurate reading and billing, and do not have the extensive functional capabilities of the producer-led systems in the electricity sector. Multi-utility metering is also being considered by utilities; for instance, trials of smart card meters, combining water, electricity and gas infrastructures through single point-of-sale terminals, can be configured to deal with all resource payments, saving customers time and effort and utilities money. Mergers, acquisitions and take-overs between utility companies and other service providers may make the development of smarter metering networks more economically feasible. Yet, more integration is raising community and user groups' concerns that consumers will have their lives 'run by one computer, owned by one private monopoly' (Tooher, 1996, p10). At the same time, the dominant role of producer interests mean that more innovative, diversified and user-led metering options may well be marginalized.

Conclusions – the 'meter' as new space of intermediation

There are, undoubtedly, opportunities for the development of environmental applications within each of the TDPs we have identified. It is not, therefore, the purpose of this chapter to identify a single communications or metering system that optimizes environmental opportunities. Instead, in the context of diverse new customer and utility requirements, attention should focus on the development of flexible configurations of environmental applications which can be embedded within each TDP. For example, gatekeeper systems could be configured to support the purchase of energy- or water-efficient appliances in shared savings schemes, providing revenue for the utility, but also meeting social and environmental needs, by assisting low-income households in the management of their consumption. In producer-led systems the utility could improve the efficiency of its distribution network through active demand-side management measures, reducing costs for customers, gaining their loyalty, and deferring generation needs to commercial and environmental ends. Furthermore, previously unexplored opportunities to promote environmental action might emerge from user-led systems of metering, providing more visible energy and water consumption information, or control panels for those customers interested in devising their own home resource conservation and efficiency programmes. Undoubtedly, the emerging TDPs do contain new opportunities for promoting environmental action amongst an increasingly diverse and segmented customer base across the water and electricity sectors. Yet the potential significance of these applications to contribute to environmental objectives in energy and water management needs to be more closely explored.

Environmental applications are, however, often 'squeezed out' of smart-metering configurations. Utilities are more interested in implementing those applications they consider most appropriate in the context of the commercial priorities set by privatization and liberalization. The emergence of competition, the fear of becoming locked into expensive or unnecessary metering programmes, and the lack of regulatory guidance, powerfully frame the utilities selection of TDPs and their specific functionalities. For instance, in the gatekeeper case study, the prepayment meter is strongly supported as a means of securing utility income, with chosen functionalities limited to those which reflect these commercial interests. The utility effectively searches for the most profitable 'killer applications', to justify its investment in the metering network, and, consequently, squeezes out other less-favoured functions (Froroth, 1996). Further evidence of this trend can be found in utilities' arguments that some applications of producer-led systems, such as home security services delivered through the metering network, would justify the costs of smarter metering installations, whilst home energy management applications are perceived as less commercially attractive.

Despite the marginalization of environmental applications, some new communities of interest have sought to exploit these unrealized functions of TDPs. In Scotland, environmental and community groups have utilized spare capacity on smart cards to establish shared-energy savings schemes, while a number of utilities used 'eco-tariffs' to promote conservation that may require more sophisticated metering equipment, and an electricity company has considered setting up an energy efficiency information service to reformulate detailed consumption information from households with half-hourly meters and turn it into household-specific environmental advice. Customers would have to choose to buy back such information. Such energy management services are already used by many industrial customers who can make major cost savings by optimizing their consumption profiles. However, the utility had decided that this was unlikely to prove popular or profitable for domestic customers.

In conclusion, the challenge of re-asserting environmental functionalities into TDPs is only partly a technological issue. Support for the installation of environmental applications across TDPs also requires a powerful shift in the regulatory and institutional frameworks within which utilities and manufacturers are configuring the functionalities of smart meters. The challenge for public policy is to create a context in which 'dominant social interests', such as utilities, manufacturers and communications companies, can be supplemented with the 'missing voices' of regulators and user groups, such as environmental and community organizations. This would allow more open debate and investigate the diversity of environmental applications which could realistically be built into each TDP.

The result would be to open new spaces of intermediation in which the relationships between suppliers and users of energy and water are potentially transformed. Critically, this is not 'hidden' intermediary work, unlike in some of the other case studies in this book. Instead, intermediation depends upon the meter becoming more visible, by being brought out from the cupboard under the stairs to become a central part of the home, factory or office. As the meter becomes more visible, it enables relations to be developed from information sharing to more strategic forms of intermediation around the provision and use of essential resources. Hence, the technical, the economic, the legislative and the culture (of use) must come together as an 'assembladge' that transforms the simple utility meter into an intermediary capable of promoting innovative practice.

Acknowledgements

This chapter is a revised and updated version of 'Pathways of smart metering development: shaping environmental innovation' in *Computers, Environment and Urban Systems*, vol 23 (1999), pp109–126. We are grateful for the publisher's permission to reproduce it in revised form.

References

Akrich, M. (1992) 'The de-scription of technical objects', in W. Bijker and J. Law (eds) *Shaping Technology/Building Society*, MIT Press, London, pp205–224
Barnett, A. (1996) 'Only connect...', *The Observer*, 2 June, p6
Brandon, G.R. and Day, A.K. (1997) 'The impact of feedback on domestic energy consumption', in *Sustainable Buildings*, Proceedings of a BEPAC/EPSRC mini-conference, 5–6 February, London, pp26–31

Burgess, J. and Nye, M. (2008) 'Re-materialising energy use through transparent monitoring systems', *Energy Policy*, vol 36, pp4454–4459

Clarke, C. (1997) 'War games', *Utility Week*, 25 April, pp16–18

Clay, M.R.J. and McEntee, A.J. (1996) 'Advanced meter reading (AMR): Tokenless prepayment', in *Proceedings of the Eighth International Conference on Metering Apparatus and Tariffs for Electricity Supply*, Institution of Electrical Engineers, Conference Publication 426, July, London, pp103–107

Cowburn, J. (1996) 'Electricity prepayment systems', *Power Engineering Journal*, vol 10, p96

Craig, A.D., Moore, P.M. and Long, C.D. (1996) 'Experience with a high speed MV/LV power line communications system for remote metering, load control and network automation', in *Proceedings of the Eighth International Conference on Metering Apparatus and Tariffs for Electricity Supply*, Institution of Electrical Engineers, Conference Publication 426, July, pp165–169

Darby, S. (2006) 'The effectiveness of feedback on energy consumption, A review for DEFRA of the literature on metering, billing and direct displays', Environmental Change Institute, University of Oxford, http://www.eci.ox.ac.uk/research/energy/electric-metering.php, accessed 7th September 2010

Darby, S. (2008) 'When, how, where and who? – Developing UK policy on metering, billing and energy display devices', 2008 ACEEE Summer Study on Energy Efficiency in Buildings 7, pp700–781, http://www.vaasaett.com:81/xmlui/bitstream/handle/123456789/131/darby08-aceee.pdf?sequence=1, accessed 22 February 2010

DECC (2009) 'A consultation on smart metering for electricity and gas', Letter, 11 May, http://www.decc.gov.uk/assets/decc/consultations, accessed 10 August 2010

DECC JULY 2009 'The UK low carbon transition plan, national strategy for climate and energy', July, http://www.decc.gov.uk/assets/decc/white%20papers/uk%20low%20carbon%20transition%20plan%20wp09/1_20090724153238_e_@@_lowcarbontransitionplan.pdf, accessed 7 September 2010

DECC DECEMBER 2009 'Towards a smarter future: governments response to the consultation on smart metering for electricity and gas', December, http://www.decc.gov.uk/assets/decc/consultations/smart%20metering%20for%20electricity%20and%20gas/1_20091202094543_e_@@_responseelectricitygasconsultation.pdf, accessed 7th September 2010.

DTI (2001) 'Smart metering working group report, Department of Trade and Industry', London

DTI (2006) 'The energy challenge: Energy review, Department of Trade and Industry', London

DTI (2007) 'Meeting the energy challenge', Energy White Paper, Department of Trade and Industry, London

Froroth, I. (1996) 'Home communications supporting energy interactivity', Proceedings of DA/DSM 96, vol III, pp335–350

Guy, S. and Marvin, S. (1995) 'Pathways to "smarter" utility meters: The socio-technical shaping of new metering technologies', Working Paper No. 56, Department of Town and Country Planning, University of Newcastle, Newcastle, UK, pp1–37

Kirby, R.J. (1996) 'The introduction of smart power into Midlands Electricity', in *Proceedings of the Eighth International Conference on Metering Apparatus and Tariffs for Electricity Supply*, Institution of Electrical Engineers, Conference Publication 426, July, pp113–118

Latour, B. (1992) 'Where are the missing masses? The sociology of a few mundane artefacts', in W. Bijker and J. Law (eds) *Shaping Technology/Building Society*, MIT Press, London

Marvin, S. and Guy, S. (1997) 'Smart metering technologies and privatised utilities', *Local Economy*, August, pp119–132

McNicholas, M. (1997) 'Remote control', *Utility Week*, 27 June, pp14–15

Moran, N. (1994) 'Keeping it current: Information and power may be on tap from mains sockets', *The Independent on Sunday*, 27 November, p7

Ofgem (2007) 'First trials for smart energy meters in Britain are to begin', Press release, 12 July, http://www.ofgem.gov.uk/Media/PressRel/Documents1/ofgem31%20_2_.pdf, accessed 10 August 2010

Oldroyd, R. (1997) 'Turn off the kettle now, says the computer', *The Times Interface*, 24 September, p2

Remote Metering Systems (1993) 'RMS power line carrier communications technology', Publicity brochure, Remote Metering Systems

Simpson, J.C. (1996) 'Paying as we go ... ahead', in Proceedings of a colloquium on UK electricity pre-payment systems, *Institution of Electrical Engineers Digest* No. 1996/047, pp2/1–2/5

Simpson, M.C.S. (1996) 'Smart power: A smart card electricity payment system', in Proceedings of a colloquium on UK electricity prepayment systems, *Institution of Electrical Engineers Digest* No. 1996/047, pp3/1–3/4

Sioshansi, F.P., Baran, P. and Carlisle, S.T. (1990) 'Bypassing the local telephone company: the case for electric utility industry', *Telecommunication Policy*, vol 14, no 1 (February), pp.71–77

Summerton, J. (2001) 'Brand name electricity: Shaping new identities for utilities and users in the 1990s', in S. Silviera (ed) *Building sustainable energy systems-Swedish experiences*, Stockholm, Sweden: Svensk byggtjanst

Tooher, P. (1996) 'Will we soon be paying bills to Big Brother? Centralised water, energy and council charges are causing alarm', *Independent*, 31 March, p10

Utility Week (1997) 'Remote chances', *Utility Week*, 5 September, pp14–17

12
Bridging the Recovery Gap

Rebecca Whittle and Will Medd

Introduction

This chapter examines the complex but pivotal role played by intermediaries in the 'messy' process of flood recovery. Central to our argument is the notion that flood risk management in the UK is a socio-technical system in transition. While policy is placing an increasing emphasis on the need to live with (rather than prevent) floods, there is very little understanding of how communities should actually go about doing this in practice. This is because, while emergency response procedures are well documented, there is a lack of clarity about how residents are to be helped and supported during the longer-term recovery process that follows, as people go about the difficult task of trying to get their lives and homes back on track. The result is a reshaping of the flood risk management system in ways that involve not only a shift from 'hard' to 'soft' engineering solutions, but also a reordering of social relations which reaches well beyond the immediate flooding event. Key to this reordering is a new role for intermediaries which emerge to deal with the challenges of flood recovery.

In this chapter, we identify four kinds of intermediaries, and illustrate the ways in which they step in to try and fill what we describe as the flood-recovery gap. The chapter is structured as follows: we begin by illustrating how recent changes to flood risk management approaches can be understood as a socio-technical network in transition; we then go on to describe the context of the Hull floods and the methodology on which this study is based; this is followed by an examination of the four kinds of intermediary work which we have identified as taking place during flood recovery; and the chapter concludes with some reflections on the role that intermediaries play in urban governance and socio-technical change more generally.

Learning to live with floods?

The flood risk management system in the UK is changing. Recent years have seen a shift from an approach which was based upon the extensive provision of large-scale structural defences in a bid to prevent flooding, to recognition that floods cannot be prevented entirely and, as a result, we must learn to live with them better. A key document in this respect has been Defra's flood and coastal erosion risk management strategy, Making Space for Water (Defra, 2005), which over the past few years has been reflected in an increasing number of policy documents that promote adaptation and resilience – rather than just prevention – as the way forward when dealing with floods. Key examples here include the Pitt Review (Cabinet Office, 2008), as well as Defra consultations on the National Flood Emergency Framework (Defra, 2008b), property-level flood resistance and resilience measures (Defra, 2008a), and the forthcoming Flood and Water Management Bill (Defra, 2009).

This emphasis on resilience-building is particularly important for and discussed in the context of climate change (Berkes et al, 2003; Brooks, 2003; Few et al, 2005; Yohe and Tolb, 2002), and suggests that processes of adaptation are required rather than a return to the 'original condition' (a goal which has itself been contentious, for example, in the aftermath of Hurricane Katrina in New Orleans; Daniels et al, 2006; see also Tobin, 1999). The theory is that, by exploring different experiences of – and perspectives on – the recovery process, we can begin to identify where the opportunities and constraints for institutional and engineering responses may lie.

However, this new emphasis on adaptation and resilience is about more than just engineering. Crucially, it also involves a reordering of social relations, which necessitates a new role for intermediaries, thus affecting the ways in which flood risk management policies are translated and played out on the ground (compare Medd and Marvin, Chapter 9 in this book). Documents such as the National Flood Emergency Framework (Defra, 2008b) and the Draft Flood and Water Management Bill (Defra, 2009) attempt to spell out which organizations should do what in the periods immediately before and immediately after a flood. However, once people have been appropriately warned and rescued from immediate danger, the picture becomes much less clear, and there is no mention of who should support people or what help they should get over the following months and years. There is therefore a 'recovery gap' which emerges during the longer process of recovery, at the point where the legally defined contingency arrangements provided to the affected community by its local authority diminish and where the less well-defined services provided by the private sector (insurance, builders and so on) start (Whittle et al, 2010, p1). It is the existence of this recovery gap that makes the role played by intermediaries so vital.

In this chapter, we identify intermediaries as those people and organizations who step in to fill the recovery gap that we have described above. Tracking their work is important because, as outlined by Medd and Marvin in Chapter 9 of this book, the roles played by intermediaries are often hidden. Indeed, as we will argue, many of the intermediation processes made visible by the flood are also involved in the more general urban governance processes that take place on a day-to-day basis. The following section provides some context by describing the Hull flood and the methodology on which the study was based. We then begin the analysis by outlining the four key types of intermediaries involved in the floods, and exploring the implications of their work for understanding flood recovery and urban transitions more generally.

The Hull flood study

On 25 June 2007 the city of Kingston-upon-Hull, in the North East of England, experienced severe flooding when heavy rainfall led to the city's drainage system becoming overwhelmed. The ensuing disaster directly affected more than 8600 households, incorporating around 20,000 people across the city (Coulthard et al, 2007), and set in motion a long and difficult recovery process that continues to this day. It was not only private households that were affected – key aspects of the city's social and economic infrastructure were also severely challenged by the floods, with, for example, 91 of Hull's 99 schools affected and 1300 businesses disrupted (Coulthard et al, 2007).

The research on which this chapter is based emerges from a desire to address this gap in our understanding. Using a tried and tested methodology that was employed to investigate people's recovery from the 2001 foot and mouth disease disaster in Cumbria (Convery et al, 2008), we recruited a panel of 43 people in Hull to keep weekly diaries of their thoughts and experiences over an 18-month period, which began in early November 2007. In addition to contributing diaries to the research, the participants also took part in individual interviews and quarterly group-work sessions, where they came together with other diarists to discuss their experiences. We also conducted interviews with an additional eight frontline workers[1] (ten of the residents are also frontline workers). The following statistics provide a profile of participants by age, tenure type and additional considerations:

- Tenure: Of the 43 diarists interviewed – 31 owner-occupiers, seven council tenants, two private rented, three housing association
- Age:

Table 12.1 *Age profile of the 43 interviewees*

Age (years)	20–29	30–39	40–49	50–59	60–69	70–79	80–89	90–99
Interviewees (n)	3	11	9	7	7	3	2	1

- Disability: Number of interviewees with a disability in the family – 11
- Gender: 32 women, 11 men
- Young families: 14 participants have children under ten
- Insurance: Seven participants were uninsured.

The chief advantage of using diaries for research is that they provide a regular, personal and contemporaneous record of people's experiences (Meth,

2003; Alaszewski, 2006). By giving participants the freedom to choose what to write about using their own 'natural language' (Coxon, 1996), the researcher can gain 'privileged access to the diarists' perceptions and world' (Alaszewski, 1996, p42; see also Zimmerman and Wieder, 1977; Verbrugge, 1980; Elliot, 1997). Crucially for the purposes of this study, the diaries also offered a real-time record of events and experiences, which made it possible to study change over time (Hayes, 2000). This meant that we were able to track the flood recovery process as it was experienced by the participants on a week-by-week basis.

Building on the design used by the foot and mouth disease (FMD) study (Mort et al, 2004), the weekly diary booklet began with a few 'warm-up' exercises, where we asked participants to rate their quality of life, relationships with family and friends, and health, using a simple scale ranging from 'very poor' to 'very good'. There was also a section where they could enter details of what they had done on particular days during the week. The main purpose of these sections was to get the participants used to writing in readiness for the main, unstructured part of the diary, where they were encouraged to write whatever they liked about their lives that week.

The final component of the methodology consisted of the use of six discussion sessions during the course of the project, where we brought the diarists together to talk about their experiences as a group. The use of standing panels in different forms as a consultative mechanism is well known (Coote and Lenaghan, 1997; Kashefi and Mort, 2000; Kashefi, 2006) and, by combining this approach with the diary study, we were able to delve deeper into the issues that were important to the participants, while also giving them the opportunity to feed in to the research design process.

When the diary-keeping finished in April 2009, we also conducted further telephone interviews with frontline workers to find out more about the recovery process, and the support arrangements available to residents and workers.

Filling the recovery gap: the four kinds of intermediaries who were prominent in Hull

'Traditional' intermediary roles

The most obvious kind of intermediary work which emerged during flood recovery consisted of a heightened role for well-known intermediaries who exist to bridge the gap between individual residents, and the various companies and agencies, that they need to deal with after a flood. The clearest example of this is the loss adjuster, who is sent to visit a homeowner after a major claim in order to record the details of the loss and agree a suitable settlement with the insurance company. Getting the home repaired is the primary task for flooded residents and, for those with insurance policies, the loss adjuster is a vital intermediary in this process. Following from Moss et al (2009), we can see how both information dissemination and conflict resolution skills are important here: in an ideal world, the loss adjuster exists to provide a point of contact with the insurance company where the resident can get information and support for his or her claim, while the insurance company gets some protection against fraud and grossly exaggerated claims.

In some cases, this system worked very well. Caroline's[2] loss adjuster advised her that, due to the volume of work involved in Hull, her repairs might progress faster if she hired her own builders (in contrast to using those appointed by the insurance company). Throughout the repairs process, Caroline contacted her loss adjuster with queries, and found her to be a 'smashing lady' who was very 'understanding' of her circumstances. The following extract is taken from Caroline's diary, where she was worried about having to pay extra for the very inefficient boiler in her rented house while her own home was being repaired:

> *Contacted loss adjuster to enquire if she could authorize any help for us re the enormous gas bill we received last Sat… Also told her the electricity bill for the driers comes to much more than the drying company estimated (£240) as we took our own reading and are awaiting a revised bill. I've been very anxious about all this money recently but she was very reassuring and told me to put all this in a letter with photocopies of our previous gas bills and she would help with payments.*

This example shows how the intermediary function of the loss adjuster helped the claims process to run more smoothly, to the benefit of both the resident and the insurer. In our study, however, such experiences were the exception and not the rule. For the majority of residents, the intermediary role of the loss adjuster was a hindrance to recovery for a variety of reasons. One of the most common complaints cited by residents was a lack of communication, whereby it proved difficult or impossible to get information to or from the loss adjuster, thereby delaying other aspects of the claims and recovery process. This problem was exacerbated by the scale of the disaster: the demand for loss adjusters was so great that they had to be brought in from other parts of the UK, as well as from abroad, in order to cope with the volume of work. However, residents also questioned the positioning of the loss adjuster. They argued that, far from being an independent intermediary, the loss adjuster's function was to save the insurance company money – a role which they saw as being at cross-purposes to the goal of helping them recover. Andy described these frustrations during an interview:

> *The biggest nightmare came about ten days afterwards when we thought we'd been assigned somebody at the loss adjusters firm, to be told that 'no, you weren't assigned to them ever'. And we spent the next, what seemed like ages, trying to find somebody that was assigned our case. When we eventually got a loss adjuster to come round, they'd drafted a few in from various places, we got one from Spain who didn't actually know what a gas fire was. And you know, you are sort of feeling as though you are not getting anywhere, he wasn't convinced that the*

> *water had got into our kitchen cabinets although you could see*
> *all the warping and so on.*

Equally, Nigel complained to his loss adjuster because his next door neighbour, who had the same circumstances and the same insurer, was given an allowance that was £100 more per month than he was getting:

> *'You negotiated your deal', that was the loss adjuster. I said 'I*
> *didn't realize I was negotiating'.*

Nigel's story shows that, in order to have a successful flood recovery experience, residents must recognize that the intermediary position of the loss adjuster requires them to enter into a process of negotiation. Those residents who were able to recognize this, and who had the skills to be able to negotiate, therefore did a lot better than those who did not. Nigel lost out because he thought the loss adjuster's role was just to provide him with information about his claim and to apply the same rules to everybody. By contrast, Bruce recognized the need for negotiation early in the process because he used to work in insurance and, consequently, when he felt he was getting nowhere with his loss adjuster, he bypassed them and approached his insurers directly. By taking a very active part in the negotiations, Bruce was able to get his family home for Christmas 2007: 'If you are not on the ball and you are not chasing it through and you are not hounding people, it sounds awful but due to the magnitude of it all, you are just lost within the system.'

Such examples show how the intermediary space occupied by the loss adjuster is complex because of the different circumstances and expectations that people bring to the table. Caroline was lucky enough to have a loss adjuster who was easily contactable and amenable to her requests. However, she still had to be quite proactive in her dealings with her, as evidenced by the fact that she had to make the first enquiry about reimbursement for her heating costs, instead of waiting to see if her loss adjuster would suggest this. By contrast, Nigel did not realize that he would have to take an active part in negotiating with his loss adjuster and, as a result, he did not get the deal that he wanted. Bruce and Andy also found the loss adjuster's intermediary function to be obstructive – so much so, in Bruce's case, that he bypassed him and approached his insurers directly.

Their examples illustrate why this intermediary relationship does not function as it should. In the first instance, the volume of work that is involved after a major disaster is too great for the insurance system to be able to cope with – the recovery gap is therefore too wide and too deep, resulting in the need for loss adjusters to be drafted in from other places. Too often, this resulted in mistakes, poor communication and a lack of understanding of the particular circumstances involved – a situation which is stressful for residents and loss adjusters alike. Equally, although the loss adjuster is positioned as an intermediary who exists to resolve conflicts between residents and insurers, this is an asymmetrical relationship as the loss adjuster is employed by the insurance company to keep claims to a minimum – the resident is therefore approached with an attitude of 'guilty until proven innocent', which is upsetting and unhelpful in the aftermath of a disaster. This point supports the conclusions of Medd and Marvin (Chapter 9 in this book), who show that, far from being neutral actors, intermediaries may also have their own strategic goals.

When the relationship with the loss adjuster breaks down, other traditional intermediaries such as the Citizens Advice Bureau (CAB) can also come into play. Within Hull, the CAB played a vital role by becoming another link in the chain between builders, insurers, loss adjusters and residents. Their primary role was one of conflict resolution, as residents would generally only approach them when they felt they could not cope any more. Consequently, CAB staff would take over on their behalf to try and resolve matters by making phone calls, writing letters and providing advice for residents. Typical situations included cases where insurers had refused to pay out, where the building work completed on a property had been dangerous and substandard, or where landlords had been negligent and left tenants living in flood-damaged properties.

The service offered by the CAB was vital in bridging the gap for residents, because it provided access to the classic kinds of intermediary skills of negotiation, conflict resolution and advocacy which were necessary for dealing with uncooperative companies. This was especially true for more vulnerable residents, such as some elderly people, who lacked the skills or confidence necessary to tackle disputes on their own. Crucially, getting the CAB involved also helped to address the power imbalance that exists between the resident and the companies that they were dealing with. However, there were also limitations to the service offered by the CAB. Firstly, it was generally considered to be a 'last resort' that was only consulted by those experiencing serious problems with the recovery process. However, in reality, the kinds of advice and advocacy services provided by the CAB could have been helpful to a wide range of residents right from the beginning of the recovery process.

The loss adjuster/CAB examples are important ones because they illustrate the kinds of hidden intermediation that occur on a regular basis in urban environments. The sheer number of residents experiencing problems in Hull gave rise to a debate about the technical problems of managing flood recovery. However, although the scale of the disaster made these problems more visible, it is important to remember that the kinds of issues experienced by residents are not unique to a disaster context. Rather, they are symptomatic of the more general urban governance issues that must be managed in the course of daily life in the city. For example, 'everyday' events such as burglaries, accidents, planning disputes or conflicts with neighbours all require access to the kinds of routine intermediation services provided by loss adjusters and the CAB. What we learn about these services and the ways in which they work after a disaster can therefore offer an important insight into how intermediaries shape 'business as usual' within urban environments. This is a theme that we return to throughout the chapter and in the conclusion.

'Responsive' intermediaries

In contrast to loss adjusters and CAB workers, for whom the floods represented a continuation of their usual job roles (albeit in more intense circumstances), other intermediary positions were created specifically with a view to filling the recovery gap. The classic example of this in Hull was the creation of the Flood Advice Service (FAS) – a dedicated team of city council staff and community wardens who were seconded from their usual jobs to offer a dedicated advice service to residents. The kinds of services offered by the FAS were very similar to those offered by the CAB, although in practice the FAS tended to deal with council tenants' problems more than homeowners and private tenants, who were dealt with by the CAB. Once again, the interviews and diaries of FAS workers illustrate how important this intermediary service was in bridging the recovery gap, especially for those who were particularly vulnerable:

> Have been dealing with a lady this week that had been living in appalling conditions. Unfortunately it is certainly not a one-off case. She had no floorboards downstairs and her floor space was still full of water. The whole of her upstairs was wet to the touch and everything in it. She is registered disabled and has severe epilepsy so felt the house was especially unsafe for her to be in. She appeared to have been overlooked and ignored by her insurance company. Emily and I managed to find her alternative accommodation and push her insurance company into dealing with her claim as a priority. We were so pleased to have been able to help her (Charlotte, diary).

In addition to dealing with insurance problems, the FAS were also able to help residents apply for assistance funding by filling in the forms for them, and advising them of where they were eligible for additional help and support. The FAS was originally scheduled to run for just five months (until November 2007). However, in reality, the demand for the service was so great that it was continued until summer 2008. This was partly due to the volume of residents needing help and the length of time needed for repairs to council properties. However, as the months went by, the FAS staff found themselves dealing with new kinds of problems, such as the phenomenon of 'secondary flooding'. This refers to the problems caused when water enters into the void beneath a household without the knowledge of the householder, and causes structural damage months, if not years, after the original event in the form of rising damp and rotting floorboards. Residents experiencing such problems in their homes needed special help and advice because many surveyors class secondary flooding as a damp problem that is not covered by insurance, and, as a result, making a successful claim for the damage could prove very difficult for residents.

The FAS was able to provide help and support for those experiencing such problems until it was closed down in summer 2008. However, at this time, new cases of secondary flooding were still coming to light. Writing in her diary, Charlotte expressed concern about what would happen to those who needed help after the service had closed down:

> *Still taking calls on secondary flooding – people want advice and to know for their insurance companies what the council are doing to prevent this happening in the city again. Because of the many insurance requests we have drafted a standard letter directing the insurance companies to the appropriate literature. We have directed the council call centre to take the majority of the calls coming in now – but we still get most of them because they do not know where to direct them or what advice to give. Because nothing like the floods has happened before I guess we are their first point of call. We are trying to get the different service areas to deal with the calls – but as soon as anyone mentions the word 'flood' they just get put through to us. It worries me that people will not get help to deal with the problems still arising after we have closed down (Charlotte, diary).*

This example shows how important it is to recognize that not all of the impacts of a disaster will be apparent immediately – other kinds of support may therefore need to be provided in the longer term in ways that are different to people's immediate emergency response needs. Again, urban governance issues are important here, as we can see that particular policies result in particular kinds of intermediation arrangements and new kinds of social networks developing. Having created such new tiers of intermediation, it can be very difficult to remove them, as other actors have come to rely upon the social networks that they initiate. The decision to withdraw the FAS was also based upon the assumption that things would 'go back to normal' after the flood when this was not, in fact, the case.

'Informal' intermediaries

In Hull, some of the most effective intermediary work came from 'informal' sources in the shape of various community groups across the city. In many ways, these sources bore a resemblance to the kinds of intermediaries described in the previous section in that their work emerged as a direct response to the disaster. However, unlike the FAS, these informal intermediaries were not the result of strategic intervention or funding. Instead, they developed spontaneously in response to what they perceived to be the needs of the community around them. A good example of this kind of intermediary work is the role played by Priory Baptist Church, in West Hull, as described in the box opposite.

It was not just churches offering this kind of support – other community and voluntary groups from across the city held coffee mornings and organized day trips out for flooded families. However, our study shows that such informal kinds of intermediation can be very helpful in filling the recovery gap because of their flexibility. Unlike more formal sources of help, where excessive bureaucracy or rules about funding can delay or constrain the kinds of

---

Box 12.1 *Priory Baptist Church, West Hull*

Priory Baptist Church was located in the centre of an area that was badly flooded. The church building was, itself, affected by the incident and, as members were cleaning up in the days following the flood, they realized the difficulties that residents were confronted with, and began to think about how they could help with this. They started by opening the church building as a space where residents could escape their flooded homes and meet each other for tea and coffee. However, within days, donations of furniture, clothing and money began to arrive from other churches and members of the public that could then be passed on to flooded families in the area. Residents were having trouble getting cleaning products for their homes as everywhere in Hull had sold out of these items, so church members went up to Beverley to buy a big stock of materials which they then brought back and distributed to residents. The church also organized free day trips for flooded families and created a play area for children who had nowhere to play at the church building. Many families coming to the church for help were struggling to get information about the repair of their homes, and so volunteers also made phone calls and enquiries on behalf of those who were having difficulties.

---

assistance available to residents, informal intermediaries are often quicker to mobilize and can shape themselves to the exact nature of the problems encountered. Priory Baptist Church began by addressing people's immediate needs for cleaning products, food and clothing, before moving on to provide other forms of support – such as advice and help with insurance claims – as people's needs changed. During an interview, Abby explained why this combination of flexible support was so helpful:

> *The only place I heard about was a little church, which really helped actually ... it was a bit out of my district but I still went and they did like a coffee day so you could go. There was other people that was going through the same thing, there wasn't just the little old ladies that didn't have nowhere to go, there was other families and young people there and they actually, they had a fund and they'd give you like, you know like they'd got the caravan and they didn't have a toaster or kettle ... and that was really helpful actually... They didn't like turn me away, even though they were doing it for their own district. They were still happy, even knowing where I lived, to help, which was really nice.*

Abby's example shows how the church building itself became important as an intermediary space. Here, people could escape their damaged homes, meet, have coffee and chat, while the church hall also became a much needed space where children could play. Crucially, Priory Baptist Church also continued to offer support to families long after more formal sources of help (e.g. the FAS) had closed down. This was because they realized that people were still having problems and that new cases of secondary flooding were emerging, for which people needed help and advice.

Of course, there are also problems with this kind of intermediation. Firstly, they are voluntary, which means that they are reliant on people coming forward with sufficient time, willingness and basic resources to help others. This means that their coverage across the affected population is sporadic: although the church was able to help people like Abby who arrived from outside the area, it couldn't reach everyone across the city. Secondly, the volunteers helping to run such services can feel overwhelmed by the volume of work involved. Emma was a church member who was passionate about the need to help. However, she admitted that her own family life became strained because she was so busy helping others:

> Obviously we weren't flooded but I have a family of my own and I think they suffered that summer because both myself and my husband were very involved in what was going on at the church. And when we weren't at the church … we were running around picking up donations and sorting out things like the cleaning fluid and on the telephone. And so it did put a strain on us as well although we weren't affected.

There can also be problems with funding for voluntary groups. Priory Baptist Church was able to get sufficient resources for its work in the form of donations from the public and from other Baptist churches across the country. However, many of the other groups who wanted to provide support for flooded families had to apply for funding from the disaster relief money that a charity had allocated to Hull. This became problematic when an early deadline was set for the money to be spent. Charlotte and Karen had both been flooded themselves, but had also worked to help and support residents after the floods. At a group discussion, they explained that they were furious about what they saw as a premature deadline for the funding:

> [Karen] The problem that we've got now with the [charity funding]… I am absolutely livid… They've sent all this money to the City, £720,000… So we were all like, 'Woo ooh, we are going to be able to do some really positive things in this city and really help people. Great.' And when the money came and we'd been applying for money, I've been setting up community groups, and getting people working together and doing different things and being really good. A few weeks ago, it was like… 'Deadline, all the money needs to be spent by the end of June because the donor is frightened of the anniversary.' I said, 'Excuse me, we've just got people moving out of their houses now and people moving back, the psychological effects, and where people have been

like that for a long time, where is that support going to be? It's
not just going to disappear on the 25th June, that is not going
to happen.' But what the [charity] are fearful of is the...

[Charlotte]...the anniversary and what they are saying is
their position is to come into a disaster area, basically bucket out
the water, dry it all out, spruce it all up, put plasters on, go. The
money has been around here too long they are saying ... but you
need the time to spend it wisely (Group discussion, 1 May
2008).

There are two issues here. Firstly, as we saw in the earlier example about
the closure of the FAS, this illustrates the problems that can arise when political pressures for the recovery process to be finished conflict with the much
longer-term timescales involved on the ground. From the perspective of the
organizations involved in recovery, things need to be seen to be 'back to normal' as quickly as possible, in order for their actions to be deemed a success.
However, from the workers' and residents' perspective, effective intermediation can take time and, for many residents, support may not be needed until
much later in the process. Here, the concern is that the various informal intermediaries who are emerging to fill the recovery gap from the community and
voluntary sector will be closed down before residents have had a chance to
benefit from them.

Secondly, however, it is important to realize that, once again, the floods
have made visible some of the hidden intermediation work that was already
taking place in the city. Particularly in cities like Hull, which have a history
of economic and social deprivation, the voluntary sector plays an important
role in caring for more vulnerable members of society and helping them with
some of the everyday problems that they face. The fact that so many community and voluntary groups were able to respond quickly and efficiently to
the floods was therefore largely a result of the work that they were already
doing in the city, and the social networks that had developed around this.
Consequently, there are important urban governance questions around how
the role of the voluntary sector can be supported, not just with emergency
funding during disasters, but also during times of 'business as usual'. This
point is developed further in the next section and the conclusion which
follows it.

'Modified' intermediaries

The final type of intermediary involved in flood recovery in Hull describes
those pre-existing intermediaries who transformed their role in order to deal
with flood-related issues within the city. The best example of this in Hull was
the work of the community wardens. Hull's community wardens are managed
by a third-sector organization, but funded by the city council. They work in
neighbourhood teams across the city to help residents with issues of concern
to them, such as anti-social behaviour, vandalism and environmental problems. As a result of performing this kind of work, the wardens already had an
in-depth knowledge of their local communities – including a good idea of

where vulnerable residents might be located – as well as typical intermediary skills of negotiation, advocacy and conflict resolution (Moss et al, 2009). The combination of these factors made them well placed to take on a role in the recovery effort and, as a result, the wardens got involved in a range of activities, from evacuating schools and care homes on the day of the floods, through to helping residents fill out assistance forms and performing caravan safety checks during the longer-term recovery process. Yet again, therefore, we have an example of how specific urban governance policies – notably the creation of the community wardens – introduced particular processes of intermediation that were already playing an important role in the community prior to the flood.[3]

After the floods, Hull City Council devised a gold, silver and bronze system, which was designed to ensure that the most vulnerable residents got the most help. Part of this system involved the wardens acting as caseworkers for 'gold' category residents. Being a caseworker required the wardens to exercise a variety of intermediary roles, from dealing with insurance companies on behalf of residents, through to helping those without insurance access flood relief assistance money and second-hand donations of furniture. For many residents, this system was a valuable source of support. For example, Cecil was a widower in his 70s who lived on his own and had a mobility problem. He also had no insurance and lost all his possessions, because living in a bungalow meant that there was nowhere dry to put anything. After trying unsuccessfully to resolve the issues with his repairs, he was given a community warden as a caseworker. Ted, the caseworker, visited him on a daily basis and was able to provide help with a variety of issues, including new carpets and furniture:

> *When it came to flooring he said, 'How about your carpeting?' So I said, 'Well it wants carpeting, I've got the money put by for that.' So he said, 'Well you'll be due to something.' I mean this was at the beginning as they were getting the information, what's going to happen. So he said, 'Don't do it yet, well you can't anyway until it's all done. Leave that with me.' And then another young lady came down and spoke to me and ... had various helpers coming round, I mean a van was just pulling up outside and two ladies got out and rang my doorbell and came in carrying boxes, kept bringing allsorts in, in big boxes.*

This system was not perfect: within Hull, the community wardens are much more active in some areas than others, and this, combined with the scale of the flood damage, meant that not everyone got a caseworker who needed one. Equally, although the wardens knew their communities and were used to certain types of intermediary roles, they were unprepared for the particular challenges of flood intermediation: in particular, the fact that so many people were really upset and angry proved quite tough for some of the younger team members to deal with. However, as James, who worked with the wardens, described during an interview, the positive side to this was that the wardens received external recognition for their intermediary role. They also developed a new confidence in doing their work, despite the difficulties that it caused them at first:

> *I think recognition for the wardens from people like the Council because I think they've not only recognized the flexibility, how quickly they can respond, but I think they've also recognized that they have skills and one of those skills is to talk to the public because a lot of people you know, can sit in an office and talk to the public across the table but to go out and talk to them in their homes and be understanding. And we've seen some wardens, especially some of the younger ones, who didn't want to go out and do it, who were getting very upset when they were at somebody's house and they were all weeping and they do this eight times a day. And they found that very demoralizing and emotional, but they've done a super job. So I think yes, there have been positive things coming out of it.*

Discussion and conclusion

We started this chapter from the premise that flood risk management is a socio-technical network in transition, with consequences not just for the management of the built environment in urban areas, but also involving a more fundamental reshaping of social relations during flood recovery. As Medd and Marvin argue in Chapter 9, intermediaries play a vital role in reshaping these social networks, as it is through their work that policy change at both the national and local level (e.g. the messages of adaptation and resilience contained in Making Space for Water; Defra, 2005) is translated into actions on the ground, with real consequences for everyday life in urban areas.

The case study of the Hull floods included in this chapter does three things. Firstly, it teaches us about the role of intermediaries in disaster recovery. We have shown that intermediaries are vital during disaster recovery because they come in to fill the recovery gap where residents are left to project-manage their own recovery, and negotiate the maze of different public and private sector agencies involved. One of the most common complaints made by the diarists in our study was that they had to deal with so many different agencies during the recovery process, from insurers and loss adjusters through to the city council, utilities companies, builders and decorators. (Indeed, for one diarist, we counted 15 different agencies that were involved.) This made the recovery process stressful and difficult for the householder who had to take responsibility for coordinating all these agencies. It is therefore as if the residents themselves are being forced to take on an intermediary role, characterized by well-known facets of intermediary work such as negotiation and conflict resolution (Moss et al, 2009). Many people – in particular the most vulnerable – do not have the skills or resources needed to step into this kind of role. This is why genuine intermediaries, such as the CAB or the FAS, were so important in supporting residents throughout their recovery.

However, we would argue that the kinds of negotiating, information provision and conflict resolution skills provided by helpful intermediaries were needed, not only to deal with the extreme problem cases of the kind dealt with by the CAB, but also with the general everyday issues experienced by residents. In other words, rather than being considered as a 'last resort', these kinds of intermediary services should be offered to support the wider population in the aftermath of a disaster.

Secondly, we can learn more about the ways in which intermediaries work, and how this has consequences for our understanding of more general processes of urban governance and transition. There are two key points to mention here: firstly, we have seen how large-scale disasters such as flooding can reveal much of the hidden intermediation work which is already taking place in the city; secondly, what at first appears to be the largely technical problem of managing the flood is, in fact, connected to the much wider issue of managing urban environments.

In particular, we have seen how the kinds of activities carried out by the CAB, the community wardens and the wider voluntary sector perform vital functions in the city in relation to social and pastoral care, conflict resolution and environmental management – to name just a few examples. Crucially, the flood also highlights problems of intermediation within existing governance systems – most notably the difficult positioning of the loss adjuster in relation to residents' insurance claims. Although added complexities are introduced by the number of claims involved, this is not just an issue after big events such as the June 2007 floods. Instead, the problems involved are familiar – it is just that the scale of these events makes them more visible.

Thirdly, what we learn about intermediaries from this case study has implications for the governance of the urban environment. As described earlier in the chapter, current policy initiatives place an emphasis on adaptation and building resilience for the future, which is particularly important for cities in the context of climate change (Berkes et al, 2003; Brooks, 2003). One of the key issues involved in developing resilience is learning how to build spare capacity within institutions and urban environments themselves, so that they have the ability to respond if a disaster occurs (see Wildavsky, 1988; Perrow, 1999). Essentially, the lesson seems to be one of developing enough requisite variety to respond to the uncertainties, not just of the disaster event, but the subsequent recovery process.

The kinds of intermediary roles performed by Hull Community Wardens and the voluntary sector are vital here as these organizations have the ability to offer a high level of flexibility in their roles, thus allowing them to adapt to the specific nature of the tasks required should a disaster occur. However, as we have demonstrated throughout the chapter, their ability to step into this role is, in large part, a function of the hidden intermediation work that they already perform within the urban environment, and the social networks that stem from this. Consequently, their post-disaster role cannot be separated from their business-as-usual role, which is not always well-recognized. In order for these organizations to be successful after disasters, their daily work of intermediation must also be acknowledged and resourced accordingly.

Unfortunately, economic pressures since the floods have had the opposite effect and funding cuts for Hull's warden service have resulted in a city-wide team of 110 wardens being reduced to just 38 (Goodwin Development Trust, 2009). Hull's CAB service was also threatened when the city council announced its intentions to withdraw its funding of the CAB and put a contract for a Community Legal Advice Centre out to tender (BBC, 2008). This raises questions, not only about who could step in to help if another disaster were to occur in the city, but also how the hidden kinds of intermediation that these organizations perform on a daily basis will be replaced.

To conclude, then, disasters may involve exceptional circumstances, but they can also tell us much about the everyday work of intermediation that goes on behind the scenes in managing the urban environment. This chapter shows how policy change at the local and national level has given rise to particular kinds of intermediation which translate these policies into practical change on the ground. Consequently, what seems to be the technical problem of managing flooding actually involves a reconfiguration of social relations and a renewed understanding of the roles that intermediaries play in urban governance on a daily basis.

Notes

1 Defined as those who may not have been flooded themselves, but who have been working with flood victims as part of their employment. The 18 frontline workers we have interviewed comprise two teachers, three caretakers/community centre managers, three community wardens, eight council/voluntary sector employees, one journalist and one district nurse.
2 All names are pseudonyms to protect the anonymity of the participants.
3 Other examples of cities with community warden schemes include Portsmouth and Bath.

References

Alaszewski, A. (2006) *Using Diaries for Social Research*, Sage, London
BBC (2008) 'Advice staff protest over closure', http://news.bbc.co.uk/1/hi/england/humber/7352161.stm, accessed 31 August 2010
Berkes, F., Colding, J. and Folke, C. (eds) (2003) *Navigating Social–Ecological Systems: Building Resilience for Complexity and Change*, Cambridge University Press, Cambridge
Brooks, N. (2003) 'Vulnerability, risk and adaptation: A conceptual framework', Working paper 38, Tyndall Centre for Climate Change, University of East Anglia
Cabinet Office (2008) *The Pitt Review: Lessons learned from the 2007 floods*, The Cabinet Office, London
Convery, I., Mort, M., Baxter, J. and Bailey, C. (2008) *Animal Disease and Human Trauma: Emotional Geographies of Disaster*, Palgrave Macmillan, London
Coote, A. and Lenaghan, J. (1997) *Citizens' Juries: Theory into Practice*, IPPR, London
Coulthard, T., Frostick, L., Hardcastle, H., Jones, K., Rogers, D., Scott, M. and Bankoff, G. (2007) 'The June 2007 floods in Hull: Final Report', UK Independent Review Body, Kingston-upon-Hull, UK

Coxon, A. (1996) *Between the Sheets: Sexual Diaries and Gay Men's Sex in the Era of AIDS*, Cassell, London

Daniels, R.J. et al (eds) (2006) *On Risk and Disaster: Lessons from Hurricane Katrina*, University of Pennsylvania, Philadephia

Defra (2005) *Making Space for Water: Developing A New Government Strategy for Flood and Coastal Erosion Risk Management in England: A Delivery Plan*, Defra, London

Defra (2008a) *Consultation on policy options for promoting property-level flood protection and resilience*, Defra, London

Defra (2008b) 'A National Flood Emergency Framework: Proposals for consultation', Defra, London

Defra (2009) 'Draft Flood and Water Management Bill', Defra, London

Elliot, H. (1997) 'The use of diaries in sociological research on health experience', *Sociological Research Online*, vol 2, no 2

Few, R., Ahern, M., Matthies, F. and Kovats, S. (2005) 'Health and flood risk: A strategic assessment of adaptation processes and policies, Tyndall Centre for Climate Change Research Technical Report 17

Goodwin Development Trust (2009) 'Wardens', 26 October 2009, http://www.goodwintrust.org/index.php?secid=06 , accessed 31 August 2010

Hayes, N. (2000) *Doing Psychological Research: Gathering and Analysing Data*, Open University Press, Oxford

Kashefi, E. (2006) 'Citizens' juries: From deliberation to intervention', PhD thesis, Lancaster University, Lancaster, UK

Kashefi, E. and Mort, M. (2000) 'I'll tell you what I want, what I really really want!', Report of the SW Burnley Citizens' Jury on Health and Social Care, commissioned by Burnley Primary Care Group 2000, Burnley, UK

Mort, M., Convery, I., Bailey, C. and Baxter, J. (2004) 'The health and social consequences of the 2001 foot and mouth disease epidemic in North Cumbria', www.lancs.ac.uk/shm/dhr/research/healthandplace/fmdfinalreport.pdf, accessed 31 August 2010

Moss, T., Medd, W., Guy, S. and Marvin, S. (2009) 'Organising water: The hidden role of intermediary work', *Water Alternatives*, vol 2, pp16–33

Perrow, C. (1999) *Normal Accidents: Living with high-risk technologies*, New Jersey, Princeton.

Tobin, G.A. (1999) 'Sustainability and community resilience: the holy grail of hazards planning?', *Environmental Hazards*, vol 1, no 1, pp13–25

Verbrugge, L.M. (1980) 'Health diaries', *Medical Care*, vol 18, pp73–95

Whittle, R., Medd, W., Deeming, H., Kashefi, E., Mort, M., Twigger Ross, C., Walker, G. and Watson, N. (2010) 'After the rain – learning the lessons from flood recovery in Hull', final project report for 'Flood, vulnerability and urban resilience: A real-time study of local recovery following the floods of June 2007 in Hull', Lancaster University, Lancaster, UK

Wildavsky, A. (1988) *Searching for Safety*, Transaction Publishers, New Jersey

Yohe, G. and Tolb, R.S.J. (2002) 'Indicators for social and economic coping capacity – moving toward a working definition of adaptive capacity', *Global Environmental Change*, vol 12, pp25–40

Zimmerman, D.H. and Wieder, D. (1977) 'The diary-interview method', *Urban Life*, vol 5, no 4, pp479–498

Conclusions: The Transformative Power of Intermediaries

Simon Marvin, Simon Guy, Will Medd and Timothy Moss

Introduction

The transformation of cities depends critically upon the reconfiguration of the networked infrastructures that underpin them, which, in turn, are constantly being reshaped by a range of competing concerns: economic, technological, ecological and social. Exploration of the role of production and consumption interests in the dynamics of urban change is not new and our previous work has aimed at contributing to an understanding of these processes (Guy et al, 2001). What we have tried to introduce to the debate through this book is a critical examination of the role of intermediaries, positioned between production and consumption, across network transitions, and in different urban and regional settings. In doing so, we have explored a wide variety of different socio-technical contexts – ranging from energy, waste, flooding, water, transport, specific technologies, smart meters, labelling and water saving to wastewater treatment – examined through a wide range of different sectoral contexts – public, private, voluntary and various partnerships – and explored through different professional interests, including, for instance, architects, public servants and consultants. What emerges is a complex and shifting patchwork of socio-technical relations with no simple organizational logic.

As a result, it is not easy to look back and identify overarching conclusions or policy prescriptions that can be readily summarized and offered as simple solutions. Intermediaries can take many different forms, emerge in very diverse contexts, operate in multiple ways and pursue their own agendas. Simplistic and idealistic notions of intermediaries as benign catalysts of change hamper rather than advance our understanding of their transformative potential. For this reason a more differentiated, critical approach is required when it comes to summarizing their value. To this end we return to the critical questions set out at the start of the book to frame the following synthesis of the key findings from across all the chapters, noting both the patterns and exceptions.

We conclude by exploring the wider implications for policy and for future research in this field.

Key findings

What did we try to achieve with the book? The overall aim was to investigate whether intermediaries are transformative in reshaping the socio-technical organization of infrastructure, or whether they actually sustain obduracy and the status quo. There were three subordinate objectives to this: firstly, revealing the often hidden and invisible role of intermediaries in making infrastructure work and transforming it; secondly, identifying their positioning between processes of production and consumption and their practices of social engagement; finally, assessing the wider consequences and implications of intermediary activities in local practices and the governance of infrastructure. Below we present some tentative responses to these objectives in the form of seven sets of critical findings.

Development of intermediaries as responses to privatization, fragmentation and pressures for change

The book has shown that the emergence of intermediaries as novel 'actors' – that is, both in the creation of new intermediaries and the transformation of existing intermediaries – is powerfully shaped by the reconfiguration of the social organization of infrastructure networks through privatization, fragmentation and a range of new pressures: economic, social, regulatory and environmental. Looking back over the chapters, we can identify a range of responses, loosely grouped into three styles.

Firstly, we note the development of new intermediaries, usually public or public–private partnerships, that are attempting to transform the practices of infrastructure management. From the case studies offered in this book, these would include 'systemic' intermediaries concerned with managing socio-technical change in the Californian energy systems, competing agencies with different visions of urban technology futures in London, the process of green electricity labelling promoting new environmental priorities in electricity markets, the role of the Centre of Competence for Water (KWB) in Berlin attempting to coordinate and capture wider economic, and ecological benefits of water privatization and the role of strategic intermediaries in the North West of England, coordinating across institutional scales to promote integrated water management. Each of these intermediaries is attempting, in very different ways, to reassert ecological and social priorities in what is often a vacuum within formal governance networks, and to apply new pressures to create systemic change in the socio-technical organization of infrastructure.

Secondly, we have identified important changes to the practices of existing intermediaries in response to the shifting contexts of infrastructure management, leading to the development of novel ways of dealing with perceived social and environmental deficits in socio-technical networks. Here the book has examined the role of consultants in attempting to insert innovative technologies into waste-water networks, the changing role of architects as interpretive intermediaries in ensuring new energy priorities and standards are met in new buildings, the potential transformation of the utility meter into a 'smart' interactive device acting as an 'obligatory' intermediary, thereby ensuring it plays a more active role in energy saving, and the roles that existing informal and community intermediaries play in making flood response work more effectively. In all these cases there were efforts by existing intermediaries, both market-based and public, to develop new roles and priorities in intermediating effectively between production and consumption interests.

Finally, a third type of intermediary revealed in the book was the emergence of new market intermediaries as a result of the 'disintermediation' of the travel sector. Here we saw how a combination of sectoral change and new technologies created a new set of market-based intermediaries that displaced existing intermediaries, to play a critical role in further accelerating demand for air travel. These types of 'dark' intermediaries are more problematic in shaping socio-technical change, effecting an acceleration in consumption by maximizing use of the network, despite social and environmental priorities to reduce aviation intensity.

The book provided some evidence that structural shifts in the organization of infrastructure – privatization, liberalization and fragmentation of the sector – have created a new context within which new and existing intermediaries have either emerged (as new intermediaries) or have reconfigured their activities (as existing intermediaries). In the wake of shifting contexts, these intermediaries are either reasserting or simply inserting ecological, social and/or territorial priorities marginalized in the current debate and practice, or – in the case of market intermediaries – exploiting new commercial opportunities offered by disintermediation.

Making visible the hidden work of intermediaries

A key objective of the book has been to make visible the largely hidden work of intermediaries in making socio-technical networks work effectively. The book has provided detailed case studies and empirical work across different infrastructures and local contexts, which illustrate the critical and contested roles that intermediaries play in attempting to ensure that privatized infrastructure systems are socially, economically and environmentally optimal in resolving the tensions between these goals. In uncovering these roles, we have been particularly concerned to make explicit and visible the wider social visions that inform intermediary activity in order to better understand whether or not intermediaries have an aspiration to develop a transformed socio-technical network, or whether they are more narrowly focused around the maintenance of the status quo. Here the critical issue is what vision of the future they are working towards. Is it a vision of systemic transformation, or more about making market-oriented infrastructure work effectively in economic terms within the limits and constraints of the existing social organization of infrastructure? This raises further questions about how intermediaries view themselves, either as broadly based and inclusive agents of societal change, or much more narrowly based mediators responding to specific pressures and opportunities in order to implement focused priorities developed elsewhere. From this arises the question of power, conflict and tensions between multiple visions of different socio-technical futures, and how contested visions of the future are understood and resolved. We will consider these issues in more detail below.

Transformative intermediaries

A particular group of intermediaries does indeed aspire to transform the socio-technical organization of infrastructure. What is distinctive about this group of intermediaries is that they develop a wider social vision of a transformed socio-technical network according to their own, rather than external, priorities, and that they develop a more broadly based and participative network of relations within both the production and consumption sphere, attempting to purposively shape these relations according to their wider visions.

Of particular relevance here are the strategic and systemic intermediaries constituted around managed socio-technical change in the energy sector in California and London, the electricity markets in Germany and Switzerland, the water sectors in Berlin and the North West of England, the potential of smart metering technologies, and, to some extent, the informal and community intermediaries developed to manage flood response over the longer term. In all these cases – with the possible exception of flooding, which re-emphasized a return to normal – the role of the intermediaries was constituted around longer-term and systemic change in the organization of infrastructure.

Within each of these cases, we found evidence of at least partial transformations. In the case of California, agreement was forged between a wide range of stakeholders on the technological options to pursue in fuel cells. Regarding London's energy infrastructure, there was an attempt to hold together a vision of progressive urban governance in contrast to a set of interests that viewed London largely as a test-bed for multinational companies. In the case of green electricity labelling, a new independent and trustworthy intermediary was able to develop new ecological criteria for complex and confusing markets that helped accelerate green consumption. In Berlin, a new intermediary network drew actors of water management together around an agenda for coordinated research and technology development for the region. In the North West of England, ecological priorities were translated into action by three intermediaries positioning themselves as partners, go-betweens and facilitators. The potential of smart meters mediating between electricity providers and users was identified by government as a route to more sustainable energy consumption. In the case of flood recovery, informal and community intermediaries made up for the shortcomings of market intermediaries, such as loss adjusters commissioned by insurance companies. In all these cases, we can read across the chapters the ways in which intermediaries were able to enable processes and outcomes that would not have happened without their interventions. However, we must be careful not to overestimate the transformative potential of intermediaries.

Limits to intermediaries

While we have been able through the book to emphasize the transformative potential of intermediaries, the detailed case studies have also shown important limits. Even with the transformational examples cited in the section above, all the authors are careful to set out the limits and constraints on transformative action. For instance, in the case of the California fuel cell experiment, although agreement was formed between diverse actors, the intermediation was not able to deliver transformative action without structural change at other levels. While the London case demonstrated the dual existence of progressive and market-based visions of a future London, there was little interaction between these perspectives. Although green labelling has helped expand the market for green electricity, the latter still represents only a small proportion of total electricity generated in Germany and Switzerland. In the case of Berlin, the wide-ranging priorities for the Centre of Competence for Water were gradually reduced to a much narrower focus on research and technology, at the expense of the employment and ecological priorities of the city. While the intermediaries in the North West of England work effectively across scales in promoting water protection, the same regulatory framework can make intermediation difficult in the case of the chemical sector. Although smart meters have the potential to reduce consumption, this requires that ecological priorities are asserted in the design, development and, most importantly, the configuration and implementation process. What we can clearly see across all these cases is how context can be both enabling and disabling for the work of intermediaries.

This contextual framing of intermediation is further emphasized in another set of case studies. In particular, the case study of the consultancy involved in the waste-water treatment sector graphically illustrates the potential of intermediaries to shape new innovative technologies and applications, but also highlights the critical role of social and cultural factors in preventing successful translation into action. Similarly, the case study of architects shows the sheer complexity and ambiguous nature of the construction of intermediary space. Although many architects desire a more transformative role, their ability to act in such a way is bounded by the complexity, volatility and ineffectiveness of building regulations.

The 'darker side' of intermediation

As well as limits to intermediaries, there is also a more worrying set of issues around what Sally Randles and Sarah Mander describe as the 'darker side' of intermediation. Critically, their case study shows how 'disintermediation' has created a new set of market-based intermediaries that play a critical role in accelerating use of aviation in contrast to wider environmental policy objectives. What this reveals is that hidden intermediaries can play very problematic roles in accelerating consumption. Likewise, the case study of flooding also revealed how some market-based intermediaries, such as the loss adjusters, were not always providing flood victims with the full information on insurance claims, siding rather with the insurance companies in attempting to minimize their costs. Here it was the voluntary sector and community wardens that intervened, taking on a new intermediary role to assist low-income households with their claims. They, however, proved vulnerable to budget cuts which limited further intermediation.

Societal learning about socio-technical transformation and obduracy

Despite the limits to the transformative potential of intermediaries and the darker side of some, especially market-based intermediaries in accelerating consumption, we remain convinced that the transformative experiences illustrated here demonstrate the value in exploring their potential, for three reasons. Firstly, in a context of privatized provision and new pressures on infrastructures, strategic and systemic intermediaries provide an important context for attempting to develop alternative social, ecological and territorial priorities into market-based systems of resource provision. Secondly, the more that intermediaries develop their own social visions, the more widely they engage with others, and the more effectively they work across consumption and production interests in forms of what Harald Rohracher's chapter described as 'hybrid governance', the more likely they are to produce transformative implications and consequences. Narrow social visions, minimal participation and a conduit-like way of working are not likely to produce such changes. This means that we can identify some of the conditions in which intermediaries are likely to be more effective than others. Finally, all these processes – whether partially successful, with limits or failures – also tell us a lot about the level of obduracy and limits to successful transitions in socio-technical infrastructure. We argue through the book that intermediaries and practices of intermediation provide a critical setting for wider societal learning about these limits, and where more deep-seated structural change is required to create a new context for intermediary activities.

The importance of place for intermediation

Looking across all the case studies, it is clear that intermediaries do not, or perhaps even cannot, work in a vacuum. Both opportunities for, and constraints to, intermediation depend critically on the setting or 'place' in which intermediaries operate. Previous work on the shaping of infrastructure has noted the obduracy of technical networks and built environments, and it is precisely this challenge of opening-up, making flexible and reconfiguring both networks and places that intermediaries take up. In doing so, intermediaries have to acknowledge, mediate and engage with the social, technical and spatial dimensions of urban environmental change.

This engagement with the socio-technical and spatial reordering of cities is particularly visible in some case studies. In the case of architects tackling the maze of environmental regulations as interpretive intermediaries, the remaking of buildings through carbon neutral design is a direct intervention into the reshaping of the urban fabric with implications for the look, feel and location of cities as well as the less visible flow of resources and release of carbon. Similarly, the struggle over the future vision of London that takes place between policies and plans necessitates intermediaries grounding their interventions in arguments over the materiality, shape and intensity of urban life in the metropolis, thereby taking a position on the organization and prioritization of political values, social interests and economic activities. Intermediaries cannot simply accept place as a container for their interventions. The case of integrated water management in the North West of England highlighted the fluidity of even supposedly natural boundaries of places, and how the work of intermediation can often be focused on the struggle to redraw these spatial scales to better enable productive collaborations and stimulate innovation.

What next for intermediaries?

In this section we look forward from the analysis developed in the book at the implications for future policy development, and a further research agenda on intermediaries and intermediation.

Future policy implications

Overall, the argument of the book is that there is considerable merit in thinking through further the wider policy implications and lessons of the analysis of intermediaries. This is particularly relevant for those policy-makers interested in the development and acceleration of systemic change in the socio-technical organization of infrastructure networks, and in making cities and regions and their infrastructure systems more resilient in the longer term. In particular, we have identified five sets of implications of our work for these interests in network and territorial transitions and their interdependence.

Firstly, the book has highlighted the critical importance of looking at complex and potentially interlinked 'chains' of intermediaries that link production and consumption together over socio-technical networks. Central to this is the need to effectively 'map' out these intermediaries. We note, for example, the different but interlinked intermediaries in the chapter by Randles and Mander on the role of virtual intermediaries in ratcheting up air travel. Alternatively, the challenge might lie in identifying the role of different styles of intermediation, as in the case of smart metering shaping the relationship between utilities and users in quite different ways, and with very different effects on resource use.

Secondly, the critical questions that need to be asked about these intermediaries once they are identified are what they do, how they work, and what implications and consequences they have for the reshaping of socio-technical systems. Do they, for instance, accelerate consumption, or do they seek to promote resource-saving behaviour or the development of renewable and green electricity? We have shown in the book that it is necessary to seek out the often hidden and invisible intermediaries, and make much more visible and explicit their multiple and sometimes contradictory roles in shaping resource use over socio-technical networks.

Thirdly, the issue for policy-makers is then not only mapping and understanding which intermediaries are concerned with the maintenance of obduracy in the organization of socio-technical systems, but also which ones are concerned with transformation. Here there are a number of critical issues for policy-makers concerning both the limits and potential of intermediaries for accelerating system change. Central to this is understanding the degree to which intermediaries are concerned with wider societal visions of transformation and change in the socio-technical organization of infrastructure, or with the maintenance of the status quo. Of particular interest here are the intermediaries concerned with attempting to reshape networks, while pushing forward new social and environmental agendas. This was the priority of the intermediaries involved in electricity labelling, water research, environmental buildings and implementing the Water Framework Directive. All these represented attempts to insert new social, environmental and place-based agendas into the management and development of urban infrastructures and social relations.

Fourthly, the issue then is how these practices of intermediation can be made more effective. How can alternative priorities work and, specifically, what could policy-makers do to support them? What has emerged from the chapters of this book is the need for clear social visions, a wider role for participants in the process, flexibility and innovative use of translation, and a supportive context that enables intermediaries to utilize resources and networks effectively. Across all the chapters, we could observe the fragility, uncertainty and contingency shaping an intermediary's ability to mediate effectively between different social interests and the limits of these processes. In almost all our cases of systemic and strategic intermediaries, there is an explicit commitment to reshape the ways that the market-based and often fragmented provision of infrastructure works in order to make it socially and environmentally more effective, yet without necessarily challenging the fundamental basis of its social organization. Herein lies the ambivalence and ambiguity of intermediaries: they can make some changes, but are not sufficient to effect fundamental change on their own.

Fifthly, what is clear is that practices of intermediation provide an excellent context for wider societal learning about both the level of obduracy in socio-technical networks and the potential to effect systemic change. What the case studies in this book illustrate is the transformative potential of effective intermediaries that have a well understood and supportive context, are driven by a wider vision of what they are trying to achieve, generate effective hybrid frameworks for working between production and consumption interests, and take a reflexive approach to learning about their effectiveness, reshaping their activities and priorities in response. Thus we saw that valuable lessons can be learnt from, for example, the ways in which smart meters can be designed to reduce resource consumption, despite the alternative priorities that can be asserted by the social interests shaping these systems. In the case of flood recovery, we observed how the most vulnerable depend upon informal intermediaries, such as citizens advice centres and neighbourhood wardens, but also how reduced funding and support for these intermediaries diminishes the effectiveness of further responses to future flooding. In the case of Berlin, the intermediary activity of the KWB became increasingly focused on research and technology rather than on employment and wider environmental benefits. All these are valuable lessons that can inform the development and constitution of policy responses to the development and management of intermediaries.

Further research agendas

In terms of further research agendas, there are three sets of priorities that would be helpful in taking forward an understanding of intermediaries and intermediation. Firstly, we need to expand our conceptualization of infrastructure networks from the current primary focus on production, consumption and regulation to include the role of intermediaries and intermediation between different sets of social interests. Critical here is the development of conceptual frameworks and empirical research to more clearly understand the role and significance of intermediaries in constituting and shaping the future development of infrastructure networks. The scope of enquiry needs broadening so that analysis and prescription includes the potentially critical role of intermediaries not only in maintaining obduracy and accelerating consumption, but in shaping transformative change. Secondly, there is a need to better understand the forces involved in adapting existing intermediaries and generating new intermediaries, so as to promote more strategic roles for intermediaries in shaping systemic change to socio-technical networks. Critical to this is developing further work on understanding how effectiveness can be enhanced, but also on understanding the limits to change that then requires more structural and fundamental shifts in the systems of production. Finally, there is clearly potential for researchers to contribute more widely to public and societal debates about the wider social visions of future socio-technical networks, in order to help construct frameworks in which intermediaries can help reshape infrastructure networks along more sustainable pathways.

Reference

Guy, S., Marvin, S. and Moss, T. (eds) (2001) *Urban Infrastructure in Transition. Networks, Buildings, Plans*, Earthscan, London

Index